Goldsmiths & Silversmiths

GREAT CRAFTSMEN

Goldsmiths & Silversmiths

HUGH HONOUR

G.P. PUTNAM'S SONS NEW YORK

Designed by Trevor Vincent
for George Weidenfeld and Nicolson Limited, London

Phototypeset in Great Britain by Keyspools Ltd, Golborne, Lancs.
and printed by Arnoldo Mondadori, Verona
Library of Congress Catalog Card Number: 77-142221
Printed in Italy

Contents

List of Plates

The author and publishers are grateful to the owners and trustees of the various private and public collections listed below for permission to reproduce photographs, and for their co-operation in allowing objects from their collections to be specially photographed for this book. They would also like to thank the photographers Derrick Witty, John R. Freeman & Co., and Gordon Robertson.

LIST OF ILLUSTRATIONS

LIST OF PLATES

LIST OF PLATES

Museum of Art, New York; Rogers Fund 1947)
Design of spoon handle inscribed by Antonio Faenza *(Metropolitan Museum of Art, New York; Rogers Fund 1947)*

HANS PETZOLT
(between pages 86 and 91)
Nautilus Cup *(Museum of Decorative Arts, Budapest: photo Corvina Press)*
The Diana Cup, 1610–20 *(Kunstgewerbemuseum, West Berlin)*
Traubenpokal, 1610–12 *(Kunstgewerbe-museum, West Berlin)*
Double cup *(Rijksmuseum, Amsterdam)*
Ostrich egg cup, 1594 *(Minneapolis Institute of Arts: Christina N. and Swan J. Turnblad Fund)*

GASPARE MOLA
(between pages 92 and 95)
Parade helmet and shield in silver, partly gilt *(Museo Nazionale, Florence: photo Bertoni Fotografie, Florence)*
Sword hilt *(Musée de l'Armée, Paris)*

PAULUS VAN VIANEN
(between pages 96 and 103)
Ewer and basin executed in 1613 *(Rijksmuseum, Amsterdam)*
Silver relief of the sleeping Argus *(Rijksmuseum, Amsterdam)*
Tazza of 1607 *(Rijksmuseum, Amsterdam)*
Silver relief depicting Pan and Syrinx, 1603 *(Rijksmuseum, Amsterdam)*
Bowl by Adam van Vianen, 1618 *(Rijksmuseum, Amsterdam)*
Ewer with scenes from ancient history by Adam van Vianen, 1621 *(Rijks-museum, Amsterdam)*

CLAUDE BALLIN
(between pages 104 and 109)
Detail from a tapestry of *Les Maisons Royales (Musée des Arts Décoratifs: photo Connaissance des Arts, R. Guillemot)*
Design for a silver chandelier *(National Museum, Stockholm)*
Design for a fire-dog *(National Museum, Stockholm)*
Design for a guéridon *(National Museum, Stockholm)*
Table-centre by Claude II Ballin *(Hermitage Museum, Leningrad)*

CLAES BAERDT
(between pages 110 and 113)
Silver dish *(Fries Museum, Leeuwarden: photo Frans Popken)*
Silver dish, 1681 *(Fries Museum, Leeuwarden: photo Frans Popken)*
Pair of salts, 1689 *(Rijksmuseum, Amsterdam)*

GIOVANNI GIARDINI
(between pages 114 and 121)
Papal mace, 1696 *(Victoria and Albert Museum, London; copyright reserved)*
Drawing of a teapot from *Promptuarium Artis Argentaria (photo John R. Freeman)*
Holy water stoup *(Minneapolis Institute of Arts)*
Drawing of shell-shaped stoup from *Promptuarium . . . (photo John R. Freeman)*
Drawing of a teapot from *Promptuarium . . . (photo John R. Freeman)*

ANTHONY NELME
(between pages 122 and 127)
Silver-gilt altar candlestick from St George's Windsor *(By kind permission of the Dean and Canons of Windsor: photo George Spearman)*
Tankard, 1683 *(Courtesy of the Masters of the Bench of the Inner Temple: photo Derrick Witty)*
Candlesticks supported by figures of slave boys *(photo Sotheby's)*
'Pilgrim' wine bottle, 1715 *(Devonshire Collection Chatsworth; courtesy of the Trustees of Chatsworth Settlement)*
Head of toaster *(Queen's College, Cambridge: photo James Austin)*
Inkstand made in 1717 *(Manchester City Art Gallery; Assheton Bennett Collection)*

JOHN CONEY
(between pages 128 and 131)
Chocolate pot *(Museum of Fine Arts, Boston, Massachusetts)*
Mascarene teapot *(Metropolitan Museum of Art, New York; Bequest of A.J. Clearwater)*
Stoughton cup made in the 1690s *(Harvard University)*
Sugar-box *(Currier Gallery of Art, Manchester, New Hampshire)*

LIST OF PLATES

LIST OF PLATES

13

LIST OF PLATES

ROBERT-JOSEPH AUGUSTE
(between pages 222 and 225)
Pot-à-oille engraved with the arms of
Otto Von Bloehme *(Private Collection:
photo Schnapp, Realités)*
The Empress's nef by Henri Auguste
(Château de Malmaison: photo Laverton)
Oil and vinegar stand 175–6 *(Musée du
Louvre, Paris: photo Archives Photo-
graphiques)*

PAUL REVERE
(between pages 226 and 231)
Portrait of Paul Revere by J.S. Copley
*(Museum of Fine Arts, Boston: Gift of
Joseph W., William B., and Edward H.
R. Revere)*
Porringer made by Apollos Rivoire
*(Metropolitan Museum of Art, New York;
Bequest of A. T. Clearwater)*
Tankard *(Metropolitan Museum of Art,
New York; Bequest of A. T. Clearwater)*
Tea-pot made by Moses Brown in 1789
*(Museum of Fine Arts, Boston; Pauline
Revere Thayer Collection)*
Tankard engraved with the coat of
arms of the Jackson family *(Museum of
Art, Rhode Island School of Design,
Providence)*

MARTIN-GUILLAUME BIENNAIS
(between pages 232 and 237)
Nécessaire de voyage made for
Napoleon's second empress, Marie
Louise *(Private collection; photo Ponchel,
Realités)*
Contents of the *nécessaire de voyage*
*(Private collection; photo Ponchel,
Realités)*
Tea-urn made in about 1800 *(Private
collection; photo R. Bonnefoy,
Connaissance des Arts)*
Crown made for the coronation of the
first King of Bavaria in 1806
(Schatzkammer der Residenz, Munich)
Ceremonial sword made in 1804
(Schatzkammer der Residenz, Munich)

PAUL STORR
(between pages 238 and 243)
The Nile Cup, made in 1799 *(National
Maritime Museum, Greenwich)*
The Theocritus Cup made in 1812

*(Reproduced by gracious permission of
H.M. the Queen)*
Two-handled cup made in 1806
*(Cleveland Museum of Art; Bequest of
John L. Severance)*
Centrepiece made for Sir Arthur
Wellesley *(Victoria and Albert Museum,
London; copyright reserved)*

ROBERT GARRARD
(between pages 244 and 249)
Tureen made in 1824–5 *(Campbell
Museum, Camden, New Jersey)*
Table-centre with the 1st Duke of
Marlborough *(Collection of the Duke of
Marlborough, Blenheim Palace,
Oxfordshire)*
Moorish table-centre *(Reproduced by
gracious permission of H.M. the Queen)*

GEORGE RICHARDS ELKINGTON
(between pages 250 and 255)
A page from Elkington's 1847
catalogue *(photo John R. Freeman)*
Teapot designed by Christopher
Dresser *(photo by courtesy of* The Studio*)*
Electrotype of an ewer by François
Briot *(Victoria and Albert Museum,
London: photo Derrick Witty)*
Enamelled vase *(Osterreichisches
Museum für angewandte Kunst, Vienna)*

FRANÇOIS-DÉSIRÉ FROMENT-MEURICE
(between pages 256 and 261)
Bracelet made in 1841 *(Musée des Arts
Décoratifs, Paris)*
Table-centre and a preliminary sketch,
made by Froment-Meurice for the
Duc de Luynes
Engraving of a dressing-table made for
the Duchess of Parma in 1849, from the
catalogue of the 1851 Exhibition
*(Library of the Royal Institute of British
Architects, London)*
Drawing of the cane handle made for
Balzac *(Victoria and Albert Museum,
London; photo Derrick Witty)*
Toilette de Venus, a statuette in gold and
ivory
Engraving of the gold inkstand
presented to Pius IX

LIST OF PLATES

CHARLES CHRISTOFLE
(between pages 262 and 269)
Coffee-set made in the 1830s *(Musée Christofle; photo Alain Bouret)*
Table-centre from the service made for Napoleon III *(Musée Christofle; photo Kollar)*
Plate from the electro-plated service of Napoleon III *(Musée des Arts Décoratifs, Paris; photo Giraudon)*
Jug in the Louis-Philippe style *(Musée Christofle; photo Kollar)*
Tea-set from *Modèles d'Orfèvrerie moderne de la Fabrique de Charles Christofle et Cie (Bibliothèque des Arts Décoratifs, Paris)*
Drawings of tea-urns made by the factory of Christofle
Plate *(Österreichisches Museum für angewandte Kunst, Vienna)*

HENRY GOODING REED
(between pages 270 and 273)
Britannia Metal tea-set *(Messrs Reed and Barton, Taunton, Massachusetts)*
Spoons made in the 1890s *(Messrs Reed and Barton, Taunton, Massachusetts)*
Electro-plated tea-set *(Messrs Reed and Barton, Taunton, Massachusetts)*
Display wagon in 1899 *(Messrs Reed and Barton, Taunton, Massachusetts)*

CHARLES LEWIS TIFFANY
(between pages 274 and 279)
Silver pitcher made for Colonel A. Duryee *(Museum of the City of New York; Bequest of Emily Frances Whitney)*
Candelabrum from a wedding present service made in 1890 *(Museum of the City of New York)*
Silver tureen made *c.* 1870 *(Museum of the City of New York)*
Gold tea-set made for Samuel Sloan *(Museum of the City of New York)*
Silver tray made for the completion of the New York Subway, 1904 *(Museum of the City of New York; Gift of August Belmont)*

LUCIEN FALIZE
(between pages 280 and 283)
Dish made by Bapst et Falize in 1889 *(Musée des Arts Décoratifs, Paris)*

Engraving of the toilette of Princess Laetitia Bonaparte *(Bibliothèque Nationale, Paris)*
Details of the enamelled gold cup made by Lucien Falize in 1889 *(Musée des Arts Décoratifs, Paris)*

PETER CARL FABERGÉ
(between pages 284 and 289)
Imperial Russian Easter Egg presented to the Dowager Empress Marie Feodorovna in 1897 *(Virginia Museum of Fine Arts: Lillian Thomas Pratt Collection)*
Imperial Russian Easter Egg presented to Czarina Alexandra Feodorovna in 1912 *(Virginia Museum of Fine Arts; Lillian Thomas Pratt Collection)*
Cigarette case by A. Fredrik Hollming, 1912–15 *(Musée des Arts Décoratifs, Paris)*
Russian jewelled Easter Eggs *(Virginia Museum of Fine Arts; Lillian Thomas Pratt Collection)*
Tea service in the Louis XVI style *(California Palace of the Legion of Honor, San Francisco: Spreckels Collection)*

CHARLES ROBERT ASHBEE
(between pages 290 and 293)
Design for an electric lamp for the Grand Duke of Hesse *(photo Derrick Witty)*
Salt cellar *(Victoria and Albert Museum, London: photo Derrick Witty)*
Pair of salts made in 1900 *(Collection of C. Jerdein)*
Dish with looped handle *(Victoria and Albert Museum, London; photo Derrick Witty)*
Tray *(Victoria and Albert Museum, London: photo Derrick Witty)*

GEORG JENSEN
(between pages 294 and 299)
Silver fruit cup, 1914 *(Musée des Arts Décoratifs: photo Hélène Adant)*
Cocktail shaker *(Georg Jensen, Sölvsmedie, Copenhagen)*
Fruit bowl made for the 1925 Paris Exhibition *(Busch-Reisinger Museum, Harvard University)*

15

LIST OF PLATES

Jug designed by Johan Rohde
(Kunstindustrimuseum, Copenhagen)
Knife, fork and spoon by George
Jenson *(Jenson & Co., Copenhagen)*

JOSEPH MARIA OLBRICH
(between pages 300 and 303)
Tea caddy made in 1901 *(Hessisches
Landesmuseum, Darmstadt; collection of
Marianne Klostermann-Olbrich)*
Fork and spoon *(Hessisches Landes-
museum, Darmstadt; collection of Lotte
Rauff)*
Knife and fork *(Hessisches Landes-
museum, Darmstadt)*

JEAN PUIFORÇAT
(between pages 304 and 307)
Coffee pot made in 1922 *(Musée des
Arts Décoratifs, Paris)*
Soup tureen *(Musée de Grenoble :
photopress)*
Sugar caster *(photo Bibliothèque Forney)*
Knife, fork and spoon made in 1943
*(Musée des Arts Décoratifs, Paris ; photo
Hélène Adant)*

WILHELM WAGENFELD
(between pages 308 and 311)
Ashtrays by Marianne Brandt *(Museum
of Modern Art, New York : Gift of John
McAndrew)*
Table-lamp by Wilhelm Wagenfeld
and K.J.Jucker *(Museum of Modern Art,
New York : Gift of Philip Johnson)*
Nickel-silver tea-set, made at the
Bauhaus, Weimar *(Schlossmuseum,
Weimar ; photo Klaus Beyer)*
Nickel-silver tea cannister made at the
Bauhaus, Weimar, 1924 *(Schloss-
museum, Weimar ; photo Klaus Beyer)*
Tea-pot by Marianne Brandt, 1924
*(Museum of Modern Art, New York ;
Phyllis B.Lambert Fund)*

Introduction

This book is a sequel to my *Cabinet Makers and Furniture Designers* (published in 1969) and is similarly the result of an enquiry into the role played by individuals in the history of the decorative arts. It was prompted partly by natural curiosity about the personalities behind the many beautiful works in gold, silver and other precious substances in churches, museums and private collections. I wanted to investigate how changes in artistic styles influenced and were influenced by goldsmiths and silversmiths. I was also anxious to discover how these craftsmen were affected by shifts in attitude to the arts in general, by fluctuations in the relative values of labour and materials, and by the growth of industrialization. The answers to my questions were often confused and sometimes contradictory. Goldsmiths and silversmiths seldom emerge into the light of history save when they leave their workshops – like Philip Syng or Paul Revere – to engage in some other activity, or when they are overtaken by financial disaster – like François-Thomas Germain or Henri Auguste. But each of them seemed to tell me something of their craft and its history.

Goldsmiths and silversmiths are traditionally surrounded by an aura of mystery. No other craftsmen are as prominent in ancient literature and legend. Bezaleel, the goldsmith who wrought the Ark of the Covenant, table, mercy seat, six-branch candlestick and liturgical vessels for the Israelites, is mentioned in the Book of Exodus. Demetrius, a silversmith who made shrines for Diana of the Ephesians, appears discreditably in the Acts of the Apostles. Vulcan's handiwork – the armour of Achilles – is described at length in the *Iliad* (and this description was to exert some influence on goldsmiths from the sixteenth to the nineteenth century). In the *Niebelungenlied* there are the makers of the Tarnhelm and the Ring itself. Then there are the saints. St Dunstan and St Æthelwold have both been called goldsmiths, though they probably commissioned rather than executed works in precious metals. But the French St Eloi, patron saint of the craft, appears to have made reliquaries (though none survives), and St Bilfrith, an English anchorite, is recorded as the maker of a gem-studded cover for a book of Gospels which still existed in the seventeenth century.

In more recent literature there is René Cardillac, the mad goldsmith in E. T. A. Hoffmann's story *Fräulein von Scuderi*. Assisted and driven on by infernal powers, Cardillac commits murders in order to retrieve the masterpieces he has made and sold. Hoffmann was clearly inspired by the autobiography of Benvenuto Cellini who described in chilling detail his own occult experiences. But no real goldsmiths – not even Cellini – seem to have wished to recover works for which they had already been paid. So far as one can judge from the scanty evidence available, goldsmiths tended to be fairly hard-headed businessmen. The fact that they worked in the very materials of wealth set them apart from all other artists and craftsmen.

But what is a goldsmith? Dr Johnson's definition, '1. One who manufactures gold ... 2. A banker', which has been followed by most later dictionaries, is not entirely satisfactory. Until the mid-eighteenth century goldsmiths were sometimes bankers as well as craftsmen, and bankers were occasionally described as goldsmiths. The two roles could be either inter-related or separate. And in practice, the term goldsmith – and its equivalent in other languages, *orfèvre*, *orefice*, *Goldschmied* – has seldom been limited to those who made objects only of gold. For financial and other reasons, most goldsmiths have been obliged to work in silver and sometimes even base metals. The members of the Worshipful Company of Goldsmiths in London, for example, worked mainly in silver – yet they were never designated silversmiths. A goldsmith should properly be defined as a worker in precious metals. He may also cut and set precious and semi-precious stones, execute work in bronze and paint with enamels. But he remains distinct from the jeweller (engaged only in setting stones), the bronze worker (whether sculptor or caster), and the artist who applies enamels to base metals. Like Bezaleel, the goldsmith may be able 'to devise cunning works, to work in gold, and in silver and in brass, and in cutting of stones to set them, and in carving of timber, to work in all manner of workmanship'. Many of the goldsmiths described in this book had as wide a range of activity as Bezaleel (it should be remembered that the words brass and bronze were interchangeable in the usage of the translators of the Authorized Version of the Bible, and that Bezaleel's work as a carver in wood seems to have been limited to the construction of carcases which were covered with metal plates).

Strictly, a silversmith is no more than a type of goldsmith. But I have included 'silversmiths' in my title both in deference to current usage and because it would be incongruous, not to say absurd, to call G.R.Elkington or Charles Christofle 'goldsmiths'. Such men revolutionized the industry in precious metals and transformed the lives of innumerable craftsmen.

In the Middle Ages the goldsmith was the most highly honoured of all artists, mainly because he worked in the most precious materials. But attitudes towards him began to change in the Renaissance period. In Italy, the financial depression of the late fifteenth century drove young artists who had been trained as goldsmiths to work in such less costly materials as paint and stone. Attention also began to shift from the material to the artistic skill with which it was wrought. For the first time since Antiquity, a masterpiece by a great artist was seen to be worth substantially more than its weight in gold. Soon, however, artists disdained to work in materials which would be broken up and converted into cash in time of need, preferring media which would secure more lasting fame.

INTRODUCTION

And the public began to regard objects made in gold and silver as artistic-ally inferior to those in intrinsically valueless materials.

This change created a breach between artists and craftsmen and also between artist-goldsmiths like Cellini, Antonio Gentili or Wenzel Jamnitzer, who could be regarded as sculptors in precious metals, and the humbler craftsmen who were engaged in making silver objects for every-day use. The great quantities of silver which flooded into Europe as a result of the exploitation of America by the Spaniards only served to widen the breach. But generalizations are dangerous. In early eighteenth-century Dresden, J.M.Dinglinger – essentially an artist-goldsmith – was clearly ranked as high as, if not above, painters and sculptors working at the court of Augustus the Strong. At the same time in Paris, J.-A. Meissonnier, Thomas Germain and others who wrought objects which were both highly ornamental and intended for use at table, exerted some influence on the development of architecture and the figurative arts. In England, however, the goldsmith came to be regarded not so much as a craftsman as a tradesman.

It is instructive to see how, as the artistic prestige of goldsmiths de-clined, they gradually slipped out of biographical dictionaries of artists. By the early nineteenth century they had come to be regarded as of no more artistic importance than makers of furniture, pottery or glass. Sig-nificantly, the British *Dictionary of National Biography* (compiled in the late nineteenth century) finds room for numerous minor painters and sculptors but includes no goldsmiths and silversmiths apart from St Bilfrith, Matthew Boulton (as an engineer), G.R.Elkington (as inventor of electro-plating) and such banker goldsmiths as Sir Robert and Sir Thomas Viner. Neither Paul de Lamerie nor Paul Storr is mentioned.

The names of a very large number of post-mediaeval goldsmiths are recorded. In most European and North American cities, goldsmiths and silversmiths were (and still are) required by law to stamp their products with distinctive marks, usually composed of their initials. Thanks to the patient labours of generations of students, a high proportion of these marks have been identified with members of the various guilds of gold-smiths. All too often, however, investigation has stopped at this point. Of the lives of European goldsmiths we are but poorly informed. And for those who seek to investigate the artistic personalities of goldsmiths, makers' marks are almost as misleading as they are helpful.

Makers' marks are not, of course, comparable to artists' signatures. They were applied for the protection of the public, in order to expose any craftsman who made wares of an alloy inferior to that permitted by the laws of the place. They are guarantees of metallurgical rather than artistic quality. A maker's mark need not indicate the name of the object's maker or of the proprietor of the workshop in which it was made. It may merely identify the man who had it assayed. All foreign gold and silver objects, even if hall-marked in their place of origin, were required to be assayed and re-marked when they were imported into England. Thus, some pieces of silver which bear Elizabethan marks may be the work of German goldsmiths. Though often ignored, this regulation was still in force in the early years of the present century when Carl Fabergé unsuccessfully fought a legal action to prevent his products from being assayed (and often damaged) on importation into England. Elsewhere, in eighteenth-century Sweden for example, craftsmen who were not members of the goldsmiths' guild were obliged to pass the silver wares they had made to members for assaying and marking. Even when a maker's mark identifies a craftsman or the head of a workshop responsible for making a piece of silver, it does not necessarily identify the artist who designed or decorated it. Goldsmiths, especially those making useful objects, copied each other or relied on a common stock of patterns. The finest engraved decorations on English eighteenth-century silver were executed by independent engravers. Sometimes two or more goldsmiths made use of the same moulds for cast ornaments.

Although the names of so many goldsmiths are recorded, relatively few stand out as independent artistic personalities. I was, nevertheless, confronted with an *embarras de richesse* when I began to select fifty for the present book. Wishing to reveal something of the variety of people engaged in goldsmiths' work, I have included some makers of useful wares and a few industrialists as well as artist-goldsmiths. But I was obliged to omit many of the craftsmen I should have liked to include, simply because their work is too close in style to that of others whom I discuss. The inclusion of Anthony Nelme and David Willaume, for example, meant that Francis and George Garthorne, excellent though their work is, had to be left out; the presence of Biennais implied the absence of Jean-Baptiste-Claude Odiot. For the personal nature of my choice I make no apology. But I hope that those who feel that I have erred will be provoked to assemble the available material on other goldsmiths. For if there are more than enough books about old silver, far too few studies of individual goldsmiths and silversmiths have as yet been published.

A book like this must inevitably be based to a large extent on the researches of others and I should like to express my gratitude to the authors of books and periodical articles mentioned in the brief and selective bibliographies on pp. 313–16.

Tofori, September 1970   Hugh Honour

Vuolvinus

(fl. 850)

The high altar of the church of San Ambrogio, Milan, is one of the most beautiful examples of the European goldsmith's art. When it is on show, the brilliant glitter of its gold, silver, enamels and gem-stones catches the eye from afar; and closer inspection reveals that the reliefs are among the early masterpieces of Italian sculpture. The front is composed of gold panels of repoussé work framed by bands of enamel – delicately coloured blue, white and turquoise with every here and there a touch of sealing-wax red – set with cabochons and antique cameos and pearls. On the sides and back the panels are of silver with the raised figures partly gilt. They are framed by enamel bands similar to those on front, set with gems and also with little enamel discs from which impassive human heads peer out. A Latin inscription, in fine Carolingian lettering, runs round the back and declares:

> The beneficent shrine shines forth, lovely with its glittering panoply of metal and dressed with gems. But more potent than all its gold is the treasure with which it is endowed by virtue of the holy bones within it. This work the noble Bishop, famed Angilbert, offered with joy in honour of the blessed Ambrose who lies in this temple and dedicated to the Lord in the time when he held the chief place of this brilliant See. Father on high, look upon and pity thy loving servant, and by thy intercession may God bestow his divine blessing.

In a roundel, also on the back of the altar, St Ambrose is shown placing a crown on the head of Angilbert who clasps a miniature version of the altar in his hands. This is balanced by a relief of St Ambrose crowning a shyly stooping figure, identified by an inscription as VUOLVINI MAGIST PHABER – Vuolvinus or Wolvinus Master Smith. It is the earliest known representation of a real – rather than a mythological or merely generalized – goldsmith.

St Ambrose, whose life story is told in the reliefs on the back of the altar and whose bones lie beneath it, is a figure of capital importance in the history of Milan. He was a Roman official elected Bishop of Milan in 374 by popular acclamation, even before he had been baptized as a Christian. The city was then the administrative centre of the Western Empire and the seat of the Emperor. St Ambrose thus held a position of greater power than the shadowy Popes who ruled in Rome.

In the four centuries which elapsed between the death of St Ambrose (4 April 397) and the election of Angilbert as Archbishop of Milan in 824, the city declined in importance. Though still very rich, it ceased to be a centre of power. The Milanese who had adopted St Ambrose as their patron, and called themselves *Ambrosiani*, saw in the years of his episcopate the moment of their glory. Thus, Angilbert devoted special attention to adorning the church and enshrining the relics of his illustrious predecessor.

The doors at the back of the gold and silver high altar of S. Ambrogio, Milan. The roundels depict the Archangels Michael and Gabriel, the Bishop Angilbertus presenting the altar to St Ambrose, and (lower right) St Ambrose blessing the goldsmith Vuolvinus.

But who was Vuolvinus? Nothing is known of him apart from the terse inscription on the altar. An attractive theory identifying him with Vussin, a pupil of Einhard – the biographer of Charlemagne – and director of the Imperial workshops at Aachen, has been discountenanced. Although he has been claimed as a German, a Frenchman and, more specifically, a Breton, there is no good reason to suppose that he was not a Lombard. His work has, it is true, some affinities with manuscript illuminations of the schools of Rheims and Tours, but he need not be supposed to have gone to France. He could have seen such works in Milan. And there he could also have found products of the Imperial workshops, antique carvings and metalwork, and Byzantine objects which appear to have exerted some influence on the altar.

The ninth-century date of the altar has, however, been seriously questioned. In 1196 the cupola of the church fell in, crushing the ciborium above the altar, and some writers have suggested that it destroyed the altar as well. According to this theory the enamel panels, which are clearly of ninth-century origin, and perhaps the gems, are all that survive of the original and the reliefs were executed in the early thirteenth century. But it is now generally agreed that, with the exception of three panels on the front, which were replaced in the sixteenth century, the

left The gold front of the altar in S. Ambrogio, Milan, with six scenes from the life of Christ on either side of the central panel, which shows Christ in Majesty surrounded by emblems of the Evangelists and figures of the Apostles.

left The silver, partly gilt, back of the altar in S. Ambrogio, Milan, with six scenes from the life of St Ambrose on either side of the two doors which give access to the relics of St Ambrose beneath the altar.

right Detail of enamel panels on the altar in S. Ambrogio, Milan.

whole altar dates, as the inscription records, from the episcopate of Angilbert and that Vuolvinus flourished in those years.

Yet it is hard to believe that the altar is the work of a single artist. Even a casual glance reveals a marked stylistic difference between the gold front and the silver sides and back. The panels on the front are richer in composition and softer in modelling, while their figures have an emotional expressiveness which makes a striking contrast with the staid solemnity of those on the back. This may partly be explained by the difference in medium – gold is much softer and more easily modelled than silver. Yet there can be little doubt that the altar is the work of two, if not more, artists.

The front is dominated by the figure of Christ seated in majesty in the centre and surrounded by emblems of the Evangelists and figures of the Apostles grouped by threes. On either side there are six reliefs of scenes from the life of Christ, beginning in the lower left corner with the Annunciation.

Whereas the New Testament scenes on the front derive from patterns which had become well established by the ninth century, those from the life of St Ambrose on the other side have no known predecessors. This is, indeed, one of the earliest cycles of illustrations of the life of a saint. In the centre there are two doors which give access to the Saint's relics: they are decorated with the reliefs of Angilbert and Vuolvinus and of angels. The narrative scenes begin in the lower left corner with the baby St Ambrose in his cradle and his parents standing by, watching the bees that swarm above him and predicting the honey-sweetness of his eloquence. In the next scene he appears as an Imperial official, on horseback, trotting towards the province of Liguria and Emilia, the towers of a city behind him. This relief is balanced on the other side of the doors by one which shows him after his acclamation as Bishop of Milan, fleeing on horseback but halted by the hand of God. The next two reliefs depict his baptism and consecration as Bishop. In the one following he is shown dozing at the altar, while an acolyte respectfully tries to wake him. This is, in fact, a miraculous occurrence, for while he appeared to sleep he was transported to Tours to assist at the funeral of St Martin, as is shown in the following scene. The source of his ability as a preacher is indicated by a relief in which an angel whispers in his ear while he addresses a group of three men. The story of how he healed a cripple by accidentally touching his foot while celebrating Mass is the subject of the relief in the upper left corner. He is then shown in bed – his shoes neatly placed on a footstool beneath it – while Christ appears to him in a vision. This relief is paired with a similar one representing Honoratius Bishop of Vercelli in bed, called by an angel to go and administer the last sacrament to St Ambrose. The final relief depicts the death of St Ambrose, his soul borne up to heaven by an angel.

Silver, partly gilt, reliefs of scenes from the life of St Ambrose on the altar of S. Ambrogio, Milan. Reading from left to right, and bottom to top, the scenes represent: St Ambrose fleeing from Milan but halted by the hand of God; his baptism; his miraculous appearance at the funeral of St Martin of Tours; St Ambrose preaching; the Bishop of Vercelli called by an angel to go and administer the last rites to St Ambrose; the death of St Ambrose.

The side of the altar in S. Ambrogio, Milan, with reliefs of saints and angels.

The earnest simplicity of these compositions, their freedom from any details irrelevant to the stories they tell, the magnificent solidity of the figures and the gravity of all gestures, suggests that their author was well acquainted with antique Roman carvings, and not only those of the early Christian period. For if he has lost some of the naturalism of antiquity, he reveals a truly classical appreciation of the values of restraint and decorum.

As the name and portrait of Vuolvinus appear on the back of the altar it is generally assumed that he was responsible for this part, which is also the most aesthetically satisfying to modern eyes. But if, as seems likely, Vuolvinus was the head of the workshop responsible for making the whole altar, he would have executed the front rather than the back, especially as the front was in the more valuable metal. It is, however, possible that he confined his work to the preparation of the general design and the cutting and setting of the precious stones, which would probably have been regarded in the ninth century as a more important function than the hammering of reliefs or the making of enamels, no matter how intricate and skilful.

29

Nicolas of Verdun

(*fl.* 1181–1205)

It is often assumed that goldsmiths, as practitioners of a 'minor' art, must inevitably follow in the wake of developments in the 'major' arts of painting, sculpture and architecture. But is this so? Nicolas of Verdun was undoubtedly one of the greatest and most adventurous artists of his period. As Erwin Panofsky remarked, he was 'in the van of the development' of the early Gothic style. Yet he is generally regarded as a minor artist simply because his paintings are in enamel instead of tempera and his sculptures in gold instead of bronze or marble. It is significant that the most prominent of the few named European artists of the twelfth and thirteenth centuries are Reinier de Huy who, in 1107–18, made the magnificent bronze font now in the church of St Barthélemy, Liège; Godefroid de Huy (*c.* 1100–73) author of a vast enamelled crucifix base for the abbey church of St Denis near Paris; and, rather later, Nicolas of Verdun. All three were metal workers and came from the region of the Moselle. Their works, and those of their compatriots, were widely diffused and could thus exert greater influence than large-scale sculptures and paintings.

The date of Nicolas of Verdun's birth is not known. He is first recorded in 1181 when he inscribed (presumably on finishing) his great series of enamels at Klosterneuburg near Vienna. As these are the work of a highly accomplished artist it is generally assumed that he must have been born before 1150. And if, as seems likely, he was called to Klosterneuburg specially to execute the commission, he must already have achieved some renown. There can be little doubt that he is identical with the 'Nicolaus' who signed the so-called reliquary of the Virgin in Tournai Cathedral in 1205. A certain Nicolaus of Verdun, described as a *vitrarius* (a worker in glass) obtained citizenship of Tournai in 1217 as the son of a citizen. He is thought to have been the son of the goldsmith, who had presumably died shortly before. Of the several unsigned works attributed to Nicolas of Verdun on stylistic grounds, the most readily acceptable is the gold reliquary of the Magi in Cologne Cathedral, begun in the early 1180s. Badly damaged reliquaries of St Annone at Sieburg and St Pantaleone at Cologne (finished in 1186) and a little enamelled plaque of Bishop Bruno of Cologne (Art Institute of Chicago) show affinities with his work, but may equally well be by a follower. On the other hand, the Trivulzio candlestick in Milan Cathedral, often ascribed to him, clearly derives from another tradition.

The enamels at Klosterneuburg are among the most impressive paintings of their period and, thanks to their medium, retain all their delicacy of line and brilliance of colour. Originally made to cover the exterior of a pulpit in the abbey church, they were converted into an altar-piece triptych after a fire in 1330 when six more enamel panels and ornamental details were added. They are executed in champlevé enamel on copper.

The Three Marys at the Sepulchre. Incised copper panel by Nicolas of Verdun, on the altar of Klosterneuburg. This indicates the way in which a panel was prepared for enamelling.

Enamel is a vitreous material which will fuse with various other metals when fired at a high temperature. By the early mediaeval cloisonné process, the design for the enamels was made by soldering little metal walls – or cloisons – of flattened wire to a metal (often gold) ground and filling the compartments with enamel frit. The enamels on Vuolvinus's altar are of this type. The champlevé process, though invented at a very early date in Egypt and known to the Romans, was little used in mediaeval Europe until it was developed in the Mosan region in the twelfth century. The general design was engraved on a copper plate in such a way that the areas to be filled with enamel were scooped out. The effect is similar to that of cloisonné, though the metallic lines dividing one patch of colour from another tend to be thicker. The first stage of the process may be illustrated by a panel at Klosterneuburg on which Nicolas engraved the Three Marys at the Sepulchre, and later used the other side for a different scene.

The Klosterneuburg enamels are arranged in the typological manner beloved by mediaeval theologians, the upper register representing the

Moses returning from Egypt, enamel panel by Nicolas of Verdun, Klosterneuburg, near Vienna, finished in 1181.

world *Ante Legem* (before the institution of Mosaic law), the lower register *Sub Lege* (under Mosaic law) and the central one *Sub Gratia* (from the time of the Annunciation of the Virgin). Each scene in the central register is related theologically to those above and below it: thus Christ's descent into Hell is paralleled by Aaron protecting the houses of the Israelites above, and Sampson and the lion below; Christ entering Jerusalem by Moses returning to Egypt and by the sacrifice of the Paschal lamb. This complicated programme derives from St Augustine, but the immediate source was probably a treatise by Honorius Augustodiniensis of which there was a copy in the Klosterneuburg library.

The execution of this vast work may have taken Nicolas as long as ten years – he can hardly have finished it in less than five. And during this period he gradually moved from the Romanesque to the Gothic style. Even in the earliest scenes he manifests a reaction against the hierarchical stiffness and flatness of Romanesque paintings. His figures are not only more expressive but they are linked with one another in groups emotionally and, one might almost say, psychologically. The way in which

Joseph thrown into the well, enamel panel by Nicolas of Verdun, Klosterneuburg. The figure of Joseph appears to have been derived from an antique statue.

Moses, for example, riding on an ass turns his head to look back at the woman walking behind him, can hardly be paralleled in earlier mediaeval art. It is perhaps significant that the scene which reveals Nicolas's Mosan background most clearly is one that includes no human figures – the ocean borne on the backs of twelve oxen, which is more or less a painting of Reinier de Huy's font. As he proceeded Nicolas gradually made a complete break with the past – the compositions become more animated, the figures more naturalistic, and he reveals a greater awareness of three-dimensional space.

These are, in fact, among the very first paintings in the Gothic style. And like so many early Gothic works of art, they were inspired, to a great extent, by classical antiquity. Nicolas's vital figures clad in flowing drapery, which accentuate rather than conceal well-proportioned bodies, could hardly have been painted without knowledge of antique sculpture. As Panofsky remarked, it was 'in the workshop of Nicolas of Verdun . . . that the rippling and clinging drapery style characteristic of so much classical sculpture from the Parthenon down to Imperial Rome was first transplanted to a two-dimensional medium'. But the nudes are no less remarkable. The figure of Joshua, who is thrown into a cistern (a surprising parallel for the Descent from the Cross), is clearly taken from an antique statue of Bacchus or Ganymede. Were the scene not so clearly inscribed, it might well be supposed to represent the throwing down or the hiding of a pagan idol. And there could hardly be a greater contrast in feeling between this figure and that of Christ on the Cross, where Nicolas was obliged to follow a mediaeval tradition. But where did Nicolas see antique statues of sufficiently high quality and in sufficient quantity? Constantinople possessed the largest and incomparably finest collection of publicly visible antiquities. So it is tempting to suggest that before going to Klosterneuburg he may have spent some time in Constantinople where, of course, he could also have learned much about the art of enamel painting.

Detail of the Prophet Abdias on the reliquary of the Magi in Cologne Cathedral.

Shrine made to contain relics of St
Nicaise and St Piate, though generally
called the reliquary of the Virgin, made
by Nicolas of Verdun in 1205, but
heavily restored in the nineteenth
century. Tournai Cathedral.

The reliquary of the Magi, attributed
to Nicolas of Verdun, Cologne
Cathedral, c. 1190.

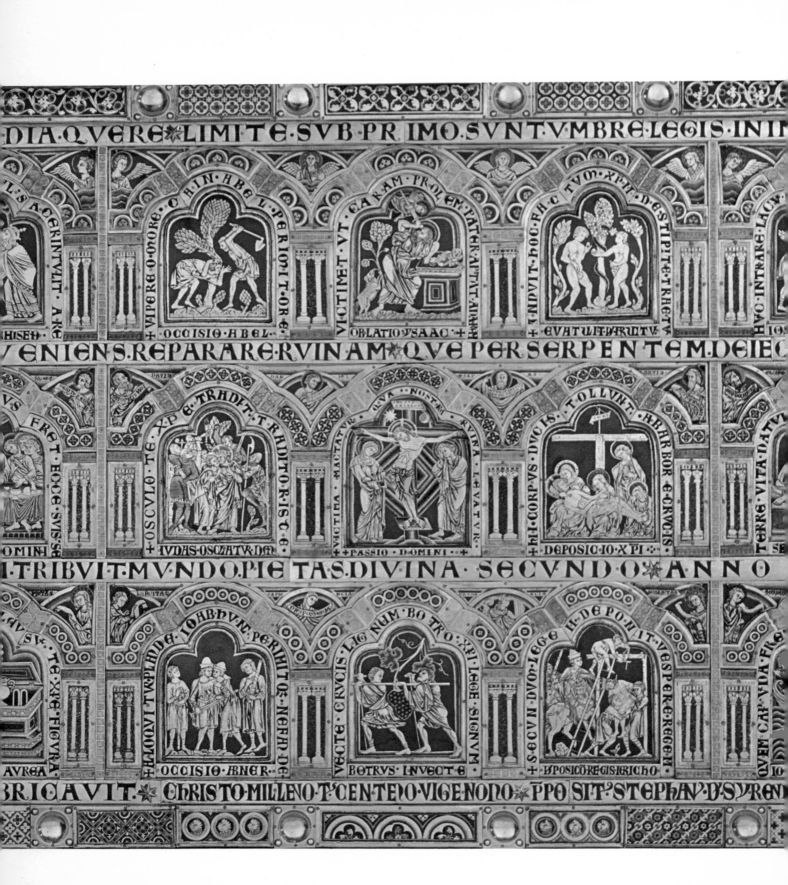

The central portion of the altarpiece – originally a pulpit – executed by Nicolas of Verdun for the Abbey Church of Klosterneuburg, near Vienna, and completed in 1181.

Nothing is known of Nicolas's activity between 1181 and 1205 when he signed the reliquary at Tournai. But he may well have executed the reliquary of the Magi in Cologne Cathedral in the interim. Here enamels are used only for decorations. The figures are in high relief and give an appearance of such solidity that it is difficult to appreciate that they are not modelled in the round. Though no more than 30 cm. (11·7 inches) high, they have the imposing presence of heroic-scale statues. Here again there are reminiscences of the antique, especially in draperies drawn tight over burly thighs. Made of silver-gilt and copper-gilt set with enamelled columns and panels, some very beautiful antique cameos and intaglios as well as many cabochons, it stands 170 cm. (66·3 inches) high and encloses relics of the Magi and Ss Nabor and Felix, brought from Milan to Cologne in 1164. Nicolas of Verdun was probably responsible for the general design and for making the robust figures of Prophets on the flanks and the enthroned Virgin and Child on the front. The sides appear to have been completed first, a little after 1190. On the upper part of the front Christ is seated in majesty between two angels while, on the lower register, the Virgin sits enthroned with the Child and the Magi present their offerings, watched by Emperor Otto IV who is traditionally said to have supplied the gold for this part of the work in 1198. The Baptism is represented on the right. With the exception of the Virgin these figures are much less monumental than the Prophets and are probably studio work: the figures on the other end seem to be later, probably made about 1220 to 1230. Unfortunately the reliquary was damaged by 'restoration' in 1807.

The reliquary of 1205 in Tournai Cathedral has been still more heavily restored and the inscription recording that 'Magister Nicolaus' was the maker is a late nineteenth-century copy of a destroyed panel. Though called the reliquary of the Virgin, it was made for relics of St Nicaise and St Piate. On the front Christ is shown in majesty between two angels, on the back there is an Adoration of the Magi, and on each side there are scenes from the life of Christ (some of which are entirely nineteenth century). Made of gilded silver, and other metals with decorations in enamel, it is 90 cm. (35·1 inches) high and 106 cm. (41·3 inches) long. The figures recall not only the Prophets on the Cologne reliquary but also the enamels at Klosterneuburg – the similarity of The Flight into Egypt with the enamel of Moses returning to Egypt is particularly striking. But antique influences have been more perfectly assimilated and, indeed, transmuted. Looking at these figures, one is reminded less of the antique sculptures which had enabled Nicolas to break with his immediate artistic past, than of the portal of St Sixtus at Rheims and of the north and south transept portals at Chartres which date from a decade later, and are among the major masterpieces of Gothic sculpture.

Ugolino di Vieri

(*fl.* 1329–80)

Ugolino di Vieri's masterpiece, the reliquary of the Sacro Corporale in Orvieto Cathedral, is one of the least accessible of all major works of art in Italy. It may, in fact, be seen by the public only twice a year – on Easter Day and on the feast of Corpus Domini – and then only fleetingly.

The story goes that in 1263 or 1264 a German priest was travelling to Rome in order to resolve his doubts about the dogma of transubstantiation. On his way he stopped at Bolsena, near Orvieto, and when he said his Mass the wafer which he had consecrated was miraculously transformed into a piece of flesh dripping with blood which stained the linen cloth or corporal. His doubts resolved, the priest hurried to Rome and told the Pope, Urban IV, who ordered the Bishop of Orvieto to take the host and blood-stained corporal into safe-keeping and went to inspect them himself. It is said that the miracle prompted Urban to institute the feast of Corpus Domini, for which Thomas Aquinas was commanded to compose the office. (The most famous depiction of the story is, of course, the fresco painted by Raphael in 1512 only five years before another German priest, Martin Luther, shook the Catholic world by his denial of transubstantiation.)

The relics were placed in the Cathedral of Orvieto, then a relatively small and insignificant church. And it was partly in order to provide them with a worthier setting that the present Cathedral was begun in 1290. The soaring façade, which still dominates the country for miles around, was begun in 1310 to the design of the sculptor and architect Lorenzo Maitani. Work was far enough advanced for the Bishop and canons to turn their attention to the interior by 1337. In April 1337 the treasurer of the Cathedral went to Siena 'to see about the making of the tabernacle' – presumably the reliquary. On the 8 May the first of a series of payments was made to the Sienese goldsmith Ugolino di Vieri. This great reliquary, standing 139 cm. (66·3 inches) high, was completed in time to be carried in the Corpus Domini procession in 1338, though the final payment for it was not made until December 1339. It cost 1,374½ golden florins, a sum which, as an eighteenth-century chronicler remarked, 'would appear exaggerated to those who have not seen the marvellous work'. An inscription on the base declares that it was commissioned by the Bishop, Tramo Monaldeschi, and canons of Orvieto and made by 'Master Ugolino and associated goldsmiths of Siena, A.D. 1338'.

As the form of the reliquary corresponds with the façade of the Cathedral, writers have suggested that it was designed by Lorenzo Maitani. But he died seven years before the work was begun. And as the whole Cathedral was conceived partly as a shrine for the relics of the Mass of Bolsena, it is hardly surprising that the reliquary should echo its façade. The beautifully-wrought statuettes of saints and angels surrounding the base and standing atop the pinnacles have been attributed to

The reliquary of the Sacro Corporale in Orvieto Cathedral, made by the Sienese goldsmith, Ugolino di Vieri, and completed in 1338. It enshrines the linen cloth – 'corporal' – used at the Mass of Bolsena.

Christat entering Jerusalem and *The Last Supper*, two enamel panels on the reliquary of the Sacro Corporale in Orvieto Cathedral.

Bartolomeo di Tomè, called Pizzino, a sculptor and goldsmith who later carved three statues for the Cappella di Piazza in Siena. There has been still more discussion about the authorship of the enamels, which have been assigned to as many as four different masters. But as none of Ugolino di Vieri's 'associates' is named in the inscription or the documents, one is bound to accept the implication that his was the guiding hand – however much or little of the work he did himself.

The enamels, unlike those of Nicolas of Verdun, are translucent and executed by a process which began to supersede champlevé in the late thirteenth century. Each silver plaque was modelled in very low relief, the enamel colours applied one at a time and fired after each application. Thus the enamel is darkest, almost opaque, where it covers deeply incised areas of the background and lightest on the foreground figures – the film of enamel over the faces is so thin that it barely colours them. The process is similar to, though not identical with, that of French and Rhenish *basse taille* enamel. And the question as to whether the French or Italian technique was invented first is of little importance as both were developed independently, though with the same aims – to exploit the translucency of the medium and to give greater realism to figurative work by abolishing the hard lines separating different colour areas. A chalice signed by Guccio di Mannaia and made between 1288 and 1292 for Pope Nicholas IV, who presented it to the church of San Francesco at Assisi, is the earliest dated example of Italian translucent enamel, called *lavoro di basso rilievo*.

The Passion scenes on the back and the lower register of the front of the reliquary derive from Duccio's *Maestà* painted for Siena Cathedral

Miracle of the Mass at Bolsena. On the left, the miracle taking place, and on the right, the German priest tells the Pope of the miracle. Enamel panels from the reliquary of the Sacro Corporale, Orvieto Cathedral.

between 1308 and 1311. But the enameller tended to increase the number of figures in each scene, sometimes to the point of overcrowding. He also added up-to-date architectural ornaments (like the Gothic windows above the Last Supper) and realistic details. In the scenes depicting the story of the Sacro Corporale – filling the upper two registers on the front of the reliquary – the enameller comes closer to the paintings of his contemporaries, Simone Martini and Ambrogio Lorenzetti. This is not, however, to suggest that he was a mere imitator, or that he relied on designs provided by either of these painters.

Like Simone, the enameller exploited Duccio's linear rhythms and subtle colour harmonies to which his medium enabled him to add still greater richness. And like Ambrogio Lorenzetti – in so many ways opposed to Simone – he sought after effects of greater emotion and psychological depth. A comparison between Simone's famous painting of St Louis of Toulouse (1317) and the enamel in which the Pope commands Thomas Aquinas to write the Corpus Domini office is revealing. Here, as in many of the other panels, the enameller shows himself a master of realistic, if sometimes inconsequential, detail.

It would be interesting to know something of Ugolino's work before he was commissioned to execute the reliquary. But he is a very shadowy figure. He was the son of a Sienese goldsmith, also called Ugolino, and is recorded for the first time in 1329 when he was living with his father and a brother named Giovanni in the Popolo di San Giorgio, Siena. The Biccherna register reveals that Ugolino and assistants – *orafo e chompagni* – were paid for the restoration of a cup on 31 December 1332. But it is reasonable to suppose that he had accomplished more important works

Silver paten with an enamel of the
Annunciation, attributed to Ugolino di
Vieri. Galleria Nazionale dell'Umbria,
Perugia.

before the authorities of Orvieto Cathedral called on him to make the
reliquary in 1337. In 1343 he and Viva di Lando were paid for restoring a
cup for the Consoli della Mercanzia in Siena, and a document of 27
November 1356 records a payment to *Ugolino et Viva orafi* for another
minor work. This suggests that he had entered into some form of
partnership with Viva di Lando.

The reliquary of San Savino in the Museo dell' Opera del Duomo,
Orvieto, is inscribed: UGOLINUS ET VIVA DE SENIS FECIERUNT ISTUM
TABERNACULUM. It is made of gilt brass set with translucent enamel
plaques. Whether it is earlier or later than the reliquary of the Sacro
Corporale is difficult to say. Its form is much more intricate, revealing a
nice appreciation of the linear and spatial effects of Gothic architecture.
There is no greater certainty about the dating of an enamelled chalice
recorded in a fifteenth-century inventory of the church of San Domenico,
Perugia and inscribed with the names of Ugolino and Viva. The chalice
has vanished, but a paten, enamelled with an Annunciation, has recently
been discovered and very plausibly associated with it.

On 20 April 1357 Ugolino was called to Pistoia to arbitrate in a dispute
between a Florentine silversmith, Pietro di Leonardo, and local authorities over work on the magnificent silver altar of St James. Then he
vanished from the scene and was not heard of again until 1380 when his
son married. He died before 1385 when his daughter was described as
del fu Ugolino (of the late Ugolino).

The reliquary of S. Savino, gilt brass set with enamel plaques, by Ugolino di Vieri and Viva di Lando. Museo dell'Opera del Duomo, Orvieto.

Leonardo di Ser Giovanni (fl. 1358–71)

Only the front of the altar of St James in Pistoia Cathedral had been completed when Ugolino di Vieri inspected it in 1357. This great corporative work of Italian silversmiths was gradually built up over a long period, like a Gothic cathedral. The flanks were begun soon after Ugolino's visit. Leonardo di Ser Giovanni was in charge of the chasing and gilding of the Epistle (or right-hand) side and, apparently, the design of the Gospel side.

The cult of St James is said to have been established at an early date in Pistoia and his intercession was thought to have protected the town from a Saracen invasion in 866. An 'Opera' or special magistracy was established in 1174 to maintain the chapel of St James and in 1265 commissioned a gold chalice and a silver cover for the Gospels from a Sienese craftsman, Pacino di Valentino, and in 1287 a small silver retable with high relief statuettes of the Madonna and Child and the Apostles. Though not recorded in any document, the reliefs on the altar frontal, or antependium, appear to have been made at about the same time.

Repairs to the altar were carried out in 1314 by Andrea and Jacopo di Struffaldo. An inscription records that the frontal was completed two years later by Andrea and Jacopo d'Ognabene, who seem to have been responsible for the six figures of prophets. In 1349, Maestro Gilio of Pisa was commissioned to execute the very beautiful seated figure of St James which was placed in the centre of the retable in 1353.

In 1357 Pietro di Leonardo of Florence was commissioned to execute the sides of the altar. It was at this moment that the 'Operaij' called on Ugolino di Vieri for advice. Pietro di Leonardo's design for the Epistle side seems to have been accepted, but when work began in 1361 Leonardo di Ser Giovanni was put in charge of the work of chasing and gilding the nine reliefs of Old Testament scenes, completed in 1364. Three years later Leonardo di Ser Giovanni was entrusted with the execution of nine scenes from the life of St James for the Gospel side of the altar.

Nothing is known of Leonardo di Ser Giovanni before 1358, when he became a member of the Florentine Arte della Seta and was said to be *del popolo di Santa Lucia d'Ognissanti di Firenze*. He must have proved his ability as a goldsmith before 1361 when he began work on the Pistoia altar. In 1366 he and Betto di Geri were commissioned to execute a dorsal, later incorporated in the altar of St John the Baptist for the Baptistery in Florence, and in the following year began the Gospel side of the Pistoia altar. A comparison between these two works shows, as Professor Steingräber has remarked, 'that Leonardo was in both the guiding artistic force, in spite of the necessary differences resulting from the employment of different collaborators in each work'. He must surely have been the leading Florentine goldsmith of the day, employing a fairly large staff of assistants.

Silver relief of Biblical scenes on the Epistle side of the altar of St James in Pistoia Cathedral, representing (reading from the upper left corner) the creation of Adam and Eve; the expulsion from Paradise; Cain and Abel; Noah building the Ark; the sacrifice of Isaac; Moses on Mount Sinai; the coronation of Solomon; the birth of the Virgin; the marriage of the Virgin. The reliefs were probably designed by Pietro di Leonardo and executed under the direction of Leonardo di Ser Giovanni.

The Gospel side of the silver altar of St James in Pistoia Cathedral.
The nine reliefs on this side of the altar represent
scenes from the story of St James and are by Leonardo di Ser Giovanni.
The superstructure, which was added shortly after 1400,
incorporates half-length figures attributed to Brunelleschi.

Leonardo's work on the Pistoia altar is well documented. The contract, dated 22 December 1367, stipulated that the subjects of the reliefs were to be specified by Jacopo Franchi on behalf of the Opera. As soon as each relief had been completed, it was to be taken, at the expense of the Opera, from Florence to Pistoia for inspection. The whole work, including friezes and ornaments, was to weigh no more than 32 lb and Leonardo was to receive 5 lire for each ounce of silver worked. It was to be completed by January 1371. Before the end of February 1368 Leonardo and an assistant took the first 'quadro' – or relief – to Pistoia. There are references to others being taken to Pistoia before 8 April 1371 when a group, probably the final panels, were presented. The whole work was finished by June 1371 when it was assayed in Florence and the authorities regaled with *cialdoni* (a kind of biscuit) and *malvagia* (Malmsey wine). It was accompanied as far as the gate of Florence by the mace-bearer of the Priori; and although it was free of customs duties, the documents record tips given to the *gabellieri* (excise officers) as well as the mace-bearer and Leonardo's assistants. When it reached Pistoia the bells of the Cathedral were rung in welcome. On 26 July, the feast of St James, the final payment was made to Leonardo.

The scenes represent, reading from left to right and top to bottom: the calling of St Peter and St Andrew; Mary, mother of James and John, presenting her sons to Christ; the calling of St James; St James preaching; the arrest of St James; St James before the judge; the baptism of a convert; the beheading of St James; the translation of St James's body to Compostella. Somewhat surprisingly the stories about St James and Hermogenes, illustrated on the walls of the Santo in Padua in 1376 and immensely popular in Spain, are omitted from this cycle. The rather overcrowded scenes demonstrate a grasp of late Gothic composition, while the figures, whether clad in sweeping garments or stiffly encased in armour, reveal a surprising mastery of form. The 'Operaij' of Pistoia had reason to be pleased with the work on which they had lavished their funds.

The scenes on the front of the altar of St John, now in the Museo dell' Opera del Duomo, Florence, seem slightly more mature. That showing St John before Herod is very similar to St James before the judge at Pistoia. But the Florentine figures are in higher relief and still more firmly modelled. And each one is more of an individual. Here Leonardo was assisted by Betto di Geri, Cristofano di Paolo and Michele Monti, of whom little is known. But the front of the altar is dominated by the statue of St John, the work of a far greater artist – Michelozzo di Bartolomeo.

Leonardo di Ser Giovanni belongs to a group of artists working at a somewhat inauspicious moment, between two periods of great artistic

The arrest of St James,
panel from the
silver altar of St James
in Pistoia
Cathedral.

St John before Herod, silver relief by Leonardo di Ser Giovanni on the altar of St John in the Museo dell'Opera del Duomo, Florence.

vitality and expansion. The achievements of Giotto, Duccio, Pisano and their immediate followers lay behind him. If his works are compared with the frescoes of such Florentine contemporaries as Lippo Vanni, Agnolo Gaddi or Spinello Aretino, it will be seen that he was by no means inferior. He was, indeed, one of the most distinguished artists of his day, as well as the leading goldsmith. But it is difficult to see him as an independent personality. At Pistoia he contributed to a work begun long before and finished later. He began the Florentine altar but his work on it is overshadowed by the contributions of early Renaissance artists.

The retable of the Pistoia altar was rearranged and augmented in 1386

Two scenes of the Life of St John from the altar of St John in the Museo dell'Opera del Duomo, Florence.

by Pietro d'Arrigo. In 1399 the relief of Christ, which crowns it, was added by Nofri di Buto of Florence and Atto di Piero Braccini of Pistoia. Work was begun on the sides of the retable in the same year. Documents name Atto di Piero Braccini, Nicolo di Guglielmo, Domenico da Imola and, most interestingly, 'Pippo da Firenze' who has been identified as the twenty-three year old Filippo Brunelleschi, who is known to have begun his momentous career as a goldsmith. Two half-length figures of prophets bursting out of quatrefoils are so similar to the competition relief which Brunelleschi submitted for the Baptistery doors in Florence that they are generally attributed to him.

49

Antonio del Pollajuolo

(*c.* 1431–98)

Antonio del Pollajuolo is much better known than any of the gold-smiths previously mentioned in this book. He is known, of course, as a painter – one of the greatest Florentine early Renaissance artists. But he won contemporary renown for his work in silver (later in bronze), and it was not until after his death that interest shifted to his paintings. Born in about 1431, he was the son of Jacopo d'Antonio, a fairly prosperous poultry dealer (hence the nickname 'del Pollajuolo') who had him apprenticed to a goldsmith. Vasari was later to state that the goldsmith under whom Antonio studied was 'Bortoluccio Ghiberti' – presumably Bartolommeo di Michele, the step-father of Lorenzo Ghiberti. But it seems more likely that he was apprenticed to Lorenzo Ghiberti or to his son, Vittorio, who began to assist Lorenzo on the last of the Baptistery doors in Florence in 1439 and continued to work on its frieze until 1466–7. Both Lorenzo and Vittorio Ghiberti were goldsmiths as well as bronze sculptors, though none of their works in precious metals survives. It is perhaps significant that Antonio del Pollajuolo first emerged as an inde-pendent craftsman in 1456 – the year after Lorenzo Ghiberti's death – when he and two other goldsmiths were commissioned to execute a massive silver crucifix for the Florentine Baptistery.

On 22 February 1457 the *Consoli* of the wealthy guild of Mercatanti commissioned Miliano di Domenico Dei, Antonio del Pollajuolo and Betto di Francesco di Betto – known as Betto Betti – to make a reliquary for a relic of the True Cross, supposed to have been given to Florence by Charlemagne. (It is not known why the two parts of the cross were com-missioned from different goldsmiths.) A document of the following year reveals that Betto Betti was responsible for the upper part. The cross was finished in 1459 when Betto Betti was paid 1,030 florins and Pollajuolo 2,006 florins. (Dei's name is not mentioned in the receipt and he had probably died in the interim.) It is a masterpiece of early Renaissance art with a tabernacle reminiscent of the lantern on Brunelleschi's cupola of Florence Cathedral, exquisitely modelled statuettes and several silver reliefs wrought with an athletic sparseness of line, that rare combination of grace and strength, characteristic of Pollajuolo's later paintings, draw-ings and engravings. Originally it glittered with translucent enamels, most of which have now flaked off. Greatly prized by the Florentines, it was pawned in 1529, when the city was in urgent need of money and many works in precious metals were destroyed, but soon redeemed and may still be seen in the Museo dell' Opera del Duomo in Florence. Unfortu-nately some alterations were made when the relic was removed and placed in another shrine in the late seventeenth or early eighteenth century.

In 1465 Pollajuolo made a pair of silver candlesticks to stand on either side of the cross in the Baptistery but they seem to have been melted down in 1529. His third commission for the Baptistery was given him in 1477,

Detail of the tabernacle by Antonio del Pollajuolo on the cross made for the altar of the Baptistery in Florence, Museo dell'Opera del Duomo, Florence.

above The baptism of Christ by Antonio del Pollajuolo, engraved silver panel on the Baptistery Cross.

left The Angel of the Annunciation by Antonio del Pollajuolo, engraved silver panel on the Baptistery Cross. Museo dell'Opera del Duomo, Florence.

when he and four other artist-goldsmiths were called on to execute reliefs to flank the work, which Leonardo di Ser Giovanni had begun, and convert it from a dorsal into an altar. Models were completed in July, work on the silver panels began in the following January, the reliefs were finished in 1480 and the rich framework surrounding them three years later. Verrocchio executed the relief of the *Beheading of St John the Baptist*, Antonio Salvi and Francesco di Giovanni *The Dance of Salome*, Bernardo Cennini *The Visitation*, and Pollajuolo *The Birth of St John the Baptist*. The contract stipulated that the figures should be the same size as those on the earlier reliefs, and the framework exactly the same – that is to say in the high Gothic style which was now outmoded. But Pollajuolo and his colleagues could hardly fail to modernize details of decoration and costume. He provided the room in which St John is born with windows like those in Alberti's Palazzo Rucellai.

A reliquary bust of St Octavian in the Museo Diocesano, Volterra, is generally attributed to Pollajuolo. But apart from the Baptistery cross and altar relief none of his many documented works survives. He is known to have made, for instance, a reliquary for the arm of St Pancras (1460–3), a silver girdle and chain for Filippo di Cino Rinuccini (1461–2), a silver helmet given by Lorenzo il Magnifico to Federigo da Montefeltro (1472), a large basin for the Signoria of Florence (1473), a crucifix for the Carmine (1473), a reliquary for a finger of St John the Baptist and a silver book-binding (1478). In 1466 he designed the splendid set of gold and silk embroidered vestments which still survive in the Museo dell' Opera del Duomo in Florence. He also began to work as a painter – both independently and in collaboration with his brother Piero – in the 1460s and in 1467 began work on the decorations of the chapel of the Cardinal of Portugal in the church of San Miniato al Monte. There can be no doubt that he prospered. By 1469 he had enough money to buy a farm near Pistoia, to which he gradually added fields until it became quite a large estate yielding an annual income from the sale of wine, oil and grain. He visited Rome for the first time in 1469. In 1484 he returned there and spent most of his remaining years working on the bronze tombs for Popes Innocent VIII and Sixtus IV in St Peter's.

Some fifty years after Pollajuolo's death Giorgio Vasari wrote a biographical account of him which, though inaccurate in detail, is of great interest for the light it throws on changing attitudes to goldsmiths. After describing, inaccurately, his work as a goldsmith he continued: 'Thence, realising that that art would not give much fame to his labours and desiring a more lasting reputation, he resolved to abandon it. As his brother was working as a painter, he went to him to learn the technique of handling colours. Finding this art so different from that of a goldsmith he would probably have reverted to his original occupation had he not entirely resolved to give it up. But impelled by a sense of shame he learned the technique of painting in a few months and became an excellent master.' In fact, as we have seen, Pollajuolo worked as a goldsmith until he went to Rome in 1484 and was mainly engaged in the closely allied art of bronze sculpture. In legal documents he normally called himself a goldsmith – *horafo* as he spelt the word – and in his signatory inscription on the tomb of Pope Sixtus IV he described himself as 'famous in silver, gold, painting and bronze'. At this date the goldsmith was still the most highly respected of artists.

Vasari also remarked on some paxes which Pollajuolo executed in enamel and could hardly have been better if painted with a brush. These have vanished but probably resembled the plaques on the Baptistery

Silver cross made for the altar of the Baptistery in Florence by Antonio del Pollajuolo and Betto Betti, 1457–9, Museo dell'Opera del Duomo, Florence.

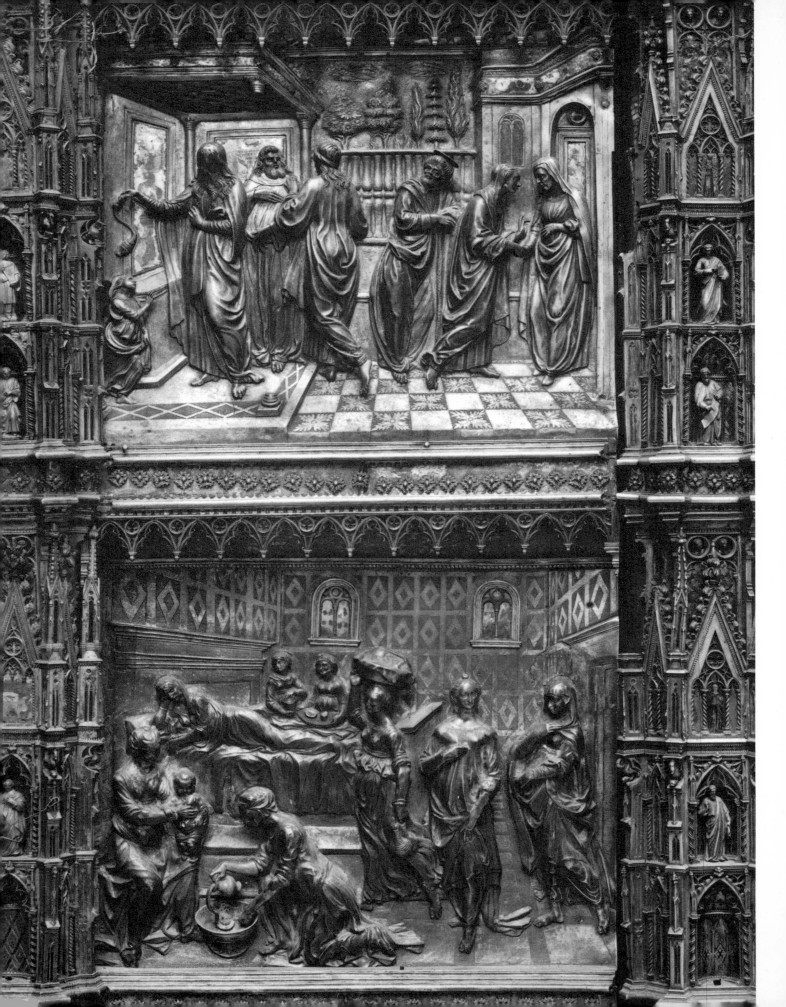

Two scenes from the story of St John the Baptist: (*above*) the Visitation by Bernardo Cennini; (*below*) the Birth of St John by Antonio del Pollajuolo. From the silver altar made for the Baptistery in Florence 1477–80.

cross. He clearly had a considerable reputation for work of this type. According to Cellini, Maso Finiguerra's *nielli* (engraved silver plaques filled with a black enamel-like substance) were all executed after Pollajuolo's designs. Prints could be taken from these *nielli* and many have survived though the original plaques have been lost. Indeed, the highly skilled art of engraving such plaques contributed greatly to the development of print making. And Pollajuolo was responsible for one of the finest and earliest of all prints made from an engraved copper plate – the famous *Battle of Naked Men*. At that time prints were regarded in Florence as no more than by-products of the silversmith's art.

The remarks of Vasari and even Cellini serve to remind one that a sharp distinction was first drawn between the arts and crafts, or the major and minor arts, in the early sixteenth century. Many factors contributed to this – the revival of ancient myths about painters and sculptors, derived from Pliny; a heightened appreciation of the figurative arts; and, of course, the emergence of such heroic figures as Leonardo da Vinci and, especially, Michelangelo. The quantities of gold and silver objects destroyed to replenish the exchequer in early sixteenth-century Florence showed all too clearly that artists could derive no lasting fame from works in precious metals – at a time when fame was indeed the spur of artistic enterprise. Moreover, the economic depression which resulted in a dearth of large scale commissions for work in precious metals drove young artists from the goldsmiths' shops to the studios of painters and sculptors. Verrocchio, for instance, is said to have turned to painting and sculpture for want of occupation as a goldsmith. Ironically, the great influx of silver into Europe in the mid-sixteenth century served to widen rather than narrow the breach between the artist and the silversmith, who was now handling a material that was much less valuable than it had been in the Middle Ages, and had consequently lost much of its mystery.

Sebastian Lindenast

(*c.* 1460–1526)

In the Victoria and Albert Museum in London there is a covered cup in the form of a mediaeval castle – its body is embossed to simulate rusticated masonry; its feet are fashioned like three tiny gate-houses apparently containing flights of steps which lead up to the ring of fortifications round the base; its top consists of buildings huddled round a spired church. At first sight it may seem a realisation of some Romantic's dream of the Middle Ages. But it was, in fact, made in Nuremberg in the late fifteenth or early sixteenth century and may thus be called late mediaeval. Yet it dates from a period when gunpowder was making fortresses less impregnable, and the Holy Roman Emperor, Maximilian was leading a revival of chivalry. We may not, therefore, be entirely wrong in detecting in this piece a note of yearning for a more colourful and picturesque past.

The cup is made of copper, gilt and partly enamelled. Although it bears a mark that has not been identified with any certainty, it is generally believed to have been made in Nuremberg by Sebastian Lindenast the Elder, the most prominent member of a family of craftsmen who had the monopoly of gilded and silvered copper wares made in the city from the mid-fifteenth to the mid-sixteenth century.

The first member of the Lindenast family recorded in Nuremberg was Peter, a locksmith, who became a Bürger in 1430. Kunz Lindenast, the father of Sebastian (and possibly the son of Peter) became a Bürger in 1455, obtained the privilege of making silvered and gilded copper objects and died in 1494. Sebastian appears to have been born in about 1460. The fact that one Lienhard Weh was apprenticed to him in 1490 reveals that he was then a master-craftsman and married. In 1494 he is recorded in the service of Bishop Windler at Brixen, but he was back in Nuremberg by 1499, living in Spittlertor.

Johann Neudörfer, the chronicler of Nuremberg, says that Sebastian Lindenast 'and Peter Vischer the elder, bronze-caster, also Master Adam Kraft, grew up together like brothers and went about together even as old men and always behaved together as though they were still apprentices'. They seem to have shared a common desire for naturalism. Lindenast's most famous work, the Männleinlaufen, a clock on the exterior of the Liebfrauenkirche in Nuremberg, has large figures of the Emperor Karl IV, the seven Electors, trumpeters, drummers and fifers who spring into action at noon each day. It was made, or rather reconstructed, between 1506 and 1509. The figures have suffered much in the centuries and those that survive have been called copies of copies of the originals. But when examined and restored after World War II several seemed to date from the early sixteenth century.

A statuette of St James the Greater (Germanisches Nationalmuseum, Nuremberg), clearly deriving from the same period and circle of artists,

Castle cup, copper gilt and enamelled, attributed to Sebastian Lindenast of Nuremberg. Victoria & Albert Museum, London.

right Bowl, with the statuette of a hart in the centre, made of silvered copper and attributed to Sebastian Lindenast. Germanisches Nationalmuseum, Nuremberg.

above Book-binding with gilt copper ornaments by Sebastian Lindenast, 1519. Bayerisches Staatsarchiv, Nuremberg.

is generally attributed to Lindenast. Though of gilt and silvered copper, it is executed with as much delicacy as any contemporary work in silver. A bowl made of the same materials and of the same high quality is also assigned to him. In 1519 Lindenast executed gilt copper ornaments for the binding of a civic register, incorporating such motifs as putti and harpies which reveal that he had begun to adopt the vocabulary of the Italian Renaissance style. It appears that he also worked in silver.

Sebastian Lindenast died in 1526. The inventory of his estate reveals that he must have been prosperous and also gives some indication of the range of his work. In addition to tankards, sweet-meat bowls, silvered beakers and plates, gilded cups, patens, monstrances and altar candlesticks, several more elaborate pieces are listed. Four silvered 'Brustbilder' were probably bust-shaped reliquaries. There were reliefs of the Madonna, the Crucifixion and, on one panel, the fourteen *Nothelfern* (Saints whose aid was invoked against diseases and other evils). He had three sons, Sebastian the younger, Sebald and Joseph, all of whom followed his trade.

Statuette of St James the Greater,
copper silvered and gilt, attributed to
Sebastian Lindenast, who had the
monopoly of making silvered copper
objects in late fifteenth-century
Nuremberg. Germanisches Nationalmuseum, Nuremberg.

Enrique de Arfe

(c. 1470–c. 1545)

Enrique de Arfe takes his Spanish name from the village of Harff in the Rhineland where he was born in about 1470. He was probably trained in Cologne and must have set off for Spain before the end of the century. His earliest known work is a *custodia* – a Spanish type of very large but portable tabernacle – made for the Abbey of San Benito at Sahagún, a small town half-way between León and Palencia. This very delicate fabrication of interlacing ogee arches and pinnacles, hung about with little bells, provided an impressive demonstration of his ability. It may well have encouraged the chapter of León Cathedral to commission him – Enrique de Colonia as he is called in the document – to execute a still larger and more elaborate *custodia*, some ten feet high. Unfortunately it was destroyed in 1809 to help pay for the war against Napoleon, but a description by the eighteenth-century writer Antonio Ponz gives an impression of its richness. Before it was finished, in 1522, Enrique had begun *custodias* for the cathedrals of Toledo and, still further afield, Cordova.

Enrique was chosen to execute the *custodia* for Toledo in preference to two other foreigners who had submitted designs, the sculptor Diego Copin de Holanda and the painter Juan de Borgoña. This vast work, three metres (10 feet) high and weighing 172 kg. (more than three hundredweight) is adorned with two hundred and sixty statuettes and has justly been called 'the last word in Gothic ecclesiastical silver'. It is a mesh of Gothic archways, crocketted and pinnacled, set with pearls and precious stones and crowned by a cross which is said to have been made with the first gold brought from America by Columbus. Every year, on the feast of Corpus Domini, it is carried through the dark winding streets of Toledo. The Cordova *custodia*, completed in 1518, is less weighty but hardly simpler in style. He made another, now in the treasury of Cadiz Cathedral, on a much smaller scale but with similar delicately interlaced ogee arches.

Though patronised by cities in the south of Spain, Enrique appears to have lived and kept his workshop in León. To produce his vast *custodias* and the many smaller objects to which his grandson, Juan, alludes (processional crosses in Cordova and León have plausibly been attributed to him) he must have employed a staff of assistants, some of whom were probably foreigners like himself. No document refers to commissions given him after 1524; but he may well have continued to direct his workshop, perhaps producing only small-scale objects, until his son Antonio (born in about 1510) was old enough to take it over. He is last heard of in 1545 and probably died soon after. By this time, of course, his intricate late Gothic style would have seemed very old fashioned.

The earliest recorded work by Antonio de Arfe is the *custodia* in the Cathedral of Santiago di Compostella, begun in 1539 and finished six

left Custodia made by Enrique de Arfe for Toledo Cathedral between 1515 and 1523.

right Custodia made by Enrique de Arfe for Cordoba Cathedral, begun in 1518.

left Custodia in the Cathedral of Santiago di Compostella, the earliest recorded work of Antonio de Arfe (son of Enrique), begun in 1539 and finished in 1545.

right Custodia made for Seville Cathedral by Juan de Arfe, who was the grandson of Enrique, but regarded himself as a theorist and 'architect in silver,' rather than a craftsman.

years later. This is in the Renaissance style and his son, Juan, was to boast that it was the first piece of Spanish silver on which antique ornaments were correctly used. In fact, classical motifs had been adopted no less (or perhaps one should say no more) correctly by other silversmiths a decade earlier. He achieved an effect of greater simplicity in the *custodia* he made for the Church of Santa Maria at Medina di Rioseco (1552–4) enclosing a central group of statuettes of David, playing the harp, and four men carrying the ark of the Covenant. He has also been credited with a *custodia* made for Burgos Cathedral but destroyed in the Napoleonic Wars.

In 1552 Antonio de Arfe settled at Valladolid though he maintained a workshop in León. He is last recorded in 1566 (the date of his death is unknown), two years after his son, Juan, had signed the contract for his first major work – a *custodia* for the Cathedral of Avila. This work, which was completed in 1571, is more correctly classical than Antonio's productions, with nicely proportioned Ionic and Corinthian columns. It is, in fact, distinctly chaste. Juan also executed a *custodia* in the form of a four-storey circular temple more than three metres (10 feet) high for Seville Cathedral.

Enrique and Antonio de Arfe appear to have seen themselves simply as expert silversmiths. But Juan, who represents the third generation, was determined to be more than a craftsman. In 1572 he published a technical book on the working and assaying of plate: *Quilatador de la plata, oro y piedras*. But his more important and revealing publication is *De varia Commensuraçion para la esculptura y architectura* which appeared in Seville in 1585–7 and was several times reprinted in the seventeenth and eighteenth centuries. As if to demonstrate how high he stood above the workaday world of craftsmen, he wrote this somewhat tedious treatise in verse. Its professed aim was to lead silversmiths back to a true (that is to say classical) style. But it is also a piece of self-advertisement. Not content with puffing up his forebears, he sought to represent their works as architecture. He described himself as both a silversmith-architect *plater de maçoneria* and a sculptor in gold and silver *escultor de oro y plata*.

Ludwig Krug

(c. 1488/90–1532)

above Drawing of a cup by Ludwig Krug, from the inventory at the treasury at Halle. Hofbibliothek, Aschaffenburg.

opposite Silver-gilt cup set with shell cameos, attributed to Ludwig Krug. Museum of Decorative Arts, Budapest.

A drawing of five elaborate covered cups in one of Albrecht Dürer's sketchbooks is inscribed: 'Tomorrow I shall do more'. It has been suggested – and it is pleasant to imagine – that this note was addressed to the goldsmith Ludwig Krug. For there are close affinities between several of Dürer's drawings of pieces of silver and cups which are ascribed to Krug. And there can be little doubt that the two men were acquainted in the small artistic world of early sixteenth-century Nuremberg. Their fathers were both goldsmiths and, indeed, worked together on a silver vessel for the Holy Roman Emperor, Frederick III in 1489.

Hans Krug became a master craftsman in 1484, married Ursula Fugger (of the Nuremberg branch of the great banking family) and was master of the city mint from 1494 to 1509. His first son, Hans the younger, followed him as a goldsmith and engraver of dies for coins. Ludwig, the second son, engaged in a wider range of activities. Johann Neudörfer remarked on his skill in working silver, stone and other materials, and in portraiture (presumably for medals). More than a century later, J. von Sandrart included an account of him in the *Teutsche Akademie* (German Academy), an honour accorded to few goldsmiths. But unfortunately Krug worked at a time when Nuremberg goldsmiths were not bound to stamp their products with makers' marks, and only two signed works by him are known – a stone relief of *Adam and Eve* dated 1514 in the State Museum, West Berlin, and a drawing of a very elaborate cup. These have, however, enabled German scholars to construct a corpus of inter-related pieces of silver now generally ascribed to him or to the Krug family workshop. Several medals and prints have also been attributed to him.

The drawing of a cup inscribed with Ludwig Krug's name is in the *Hallesches Heiltumbuch* – an illustrated inventory of the treasury at Halle made in 1526. The cup, probably intended as a ciborium, has a stem fashioned like a tree-trunk attacked by a man with an axe; there are reliefs of Passion scenes on the bowl and a statuette of the Virgin crowns the cover. A silver-gilt cup formerly in the Moscow Kremlin (but now known only from photographs) had a strikingly similar base with a naked instead of a clothed man at the foot of the tree, a lobed bowl and a statuette of a youth holding a pomegranate on the cover. Several other cups bearing the Nuremberg city mark, and all of high quality, have been ascribed to Ludwig Krug by analogy with the drawing and the Kremlin cup, notably a covered cup from the Esterhazy collection (now in the Museum of Decorative Arts, Budapest) and another cup in the same museum with a similar base.

The bowl of one of the cups in Budapest is decorated with shell cameos. There are similar cameos on another in the treasury of the Basilica of Sant' Antonio in Padua which has likewise been ascribed to the Krug

Drawing of five cups by Albrecht Dürer, inscribed 'tomorrow I shall do more'. Landesmuseum, Dresden.

workshop. In form these pieces are similar to two cups, in the collection of Baron Schröder in London and in the Schatzkammer of the Munich Residenz, which are decorated not with cameos but coin-like reliefs of Roman Emperors (though it has been suggested that these cups were not made by Krug or even in Nuremberg). Both are crowned by little figures of soldiers in early sixteenth-century costume, connected stylistically both with the youth on the top of the Kremlin cup and two figures of peasant women as lively and well observed as those in drawings by Dürer, one on an egg-shaped cup in the Kunstgewerbemuseum, Berlin, the other in the Kunsthistorisches Museum, Vienna. Two handsome nefs or ship models which combine Gothic and Renaissance decorations have also been ascribed to Ludwig Krug, one in the treasury of Sant' Antonio, Padua, the other in the Germanisches Nationalmuseum, Nuremberg.

Ludwig Krug's stone relief of *Adam and Eve* in Berlin is a subtle variation on Dürer's famous print of 1504. Though no other works of comparable quality can be assigned to him, it suggests that he was one of the most gifted German sculptors of his generation. Yet it seems probable that he worked mainly as a silversmith. Neudörfer and Joachim von Sandrart suggest that he was, indeed, the leading Nuremberg silversmith of his day. And as Nuremberg metalwork was not only diffused but also imitated throughout northern Europe, this was a position of more than local importance. But he always seems to stand in the shadow of his much greater contemporary, Albrecht Dürer.

Covered cup attributed to Ludwig
Krug of Nuremberg. Kunsthistorisches
Museum, Vienna.

Benvenuto Cellini

(1500–71)

Benvenuto Cellini is the most famous of all goldsmiths. Whether or not he is the greatest is debatable. The only evidence is the famous salt-cellar made for François I of France and now in the Kunsthistorisches Museum, Vienna, three early eighteenth-century drawings of a morse made for Pope Clement VII but destroyed in 1797, and frequent statements in his own writings. The salt-cellar is certainly one of the finest surviving examples of sixteenth-century goldsmiths' work. But the drawings give no more than a faint idea of the brilliant glitter of the morse. And one is bound to take Cellini's statements about his prowess – whether amorous, pugnacious or artistic – with a grain of salt.

Cellini represented himself as an outstanding figure, unequalled for valour and ingenuity, the most highly praised and the most deeply wronged artist of his time, one who had not merely rivalled but surpassed the masterpieces of antiquity. The truly great of the world, he tells us – Popes, the King of France and the Grand Duke of Tuscany – responded to his genius by a type of kindred affinity and were restrained from rewarding him as he deserved only because of the machinations of lesser, more earthbound spirits – a minister, a mistress or a wife. Except for the 'divine Michelangelo', all contemporary artists were as jealous of him as he was scornful of them.

But Cellini was not, of course, quite so outstanding as he would have us believe. It is unlikely that the famous salt-cellar would occupy its position of splendid isolation if more of the many equally elaborate pieces by other sixteenth-century goldsmiths had survived. Most of those that have were assigned to Cellini in the eighteenth and nineteenth centuries, even though some (like Antonio Gentili's cross and candlesticks in St Peter's) were signed. One work – the Rospigliosi Cup in the Metropolitan Museum, New York – is still widely (though probably mistakenly) ascribed to him simply because it is of outstandingly high quality.

The tempestuous life that Cellini himself recorded is so full of incident that no brief summary can do it justice. By a literary convention of the time it is, indeed, composed of a series of linked but strikingly contrasted incidents. He was born in Florence on 3 November 1500. His father wanted him to be a musician but his own inclination was for *disegno* – the figurative arts – and he began to study under a goldsmith. In 1519 he went to Rome where he was to spend the greater part of the next two decades, as a goldsmith and medallist. The most notable object dating from these years appears to have been the diamond-set morse made in 1530–1 to fasten the cope of Clement VII. He made cap-badges and other small objects which goldsmiths of the time referred to as *minuteria*, also large silver vases classified as *grosseria*. He made medals and engraved dies for coins and seals.

Gold salt-cellar by Benvenuto Cellini, begun in Rome in 1540 and completed in France for François I before 1544. Kunsthistorisches Museum, Vienna.

Cellini went to France for the first time in 1537. Three years later he returned there, taking with him the model for a salt-cellar which he had begun for Cardinal Ippolito d'Este. François I commissioned him to execute this work in solid gold, also the bronze relief of the elegantly elongated *Nymph of Fontainebleau* (now in the Louvre) and many works in silver which have since vanished. Petted by the King and apparently patronised by the court, he took on a large international staff of craftsmen – probably as many as thirty. He wrote:

I took the best I could find and changed them often, retaining only those who knew their business well. These select craftsmen I worked to the bone with perpetual labour. They wanted to rival me; but I had a better constitution. Consequently, in their inability to bear up against such a continuous strain, they

Front of the morse or pectoral made by Benvenuto Cellini for Pope Clement VII in 1530–1, from an early eighteenth-century drawing in the British Museum by Francesco Bartoli. The morse was dismembered and melted down in 1797.

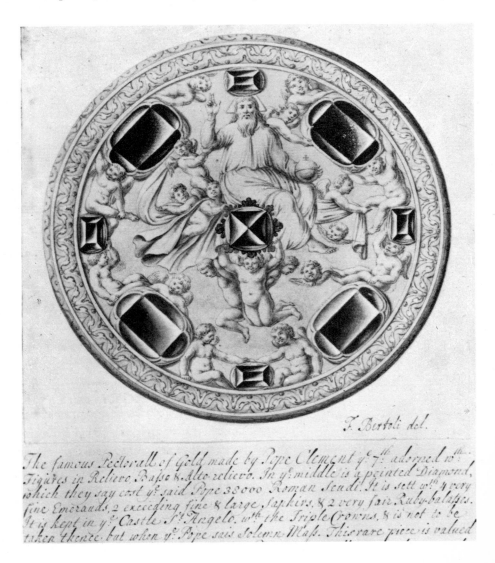

F. Bartoli del.

The famous Pectorall of Gold made by Pope Clement y^e 7th adorned wth Figures in Relievo Basso & Alto relievo. In y^e middle is a pointed Diamond, which they say cost y^e said Pope 38000 Roman Scudi. It is sett wth 4 very fine Emerauds, 2 exceeding fine & large Saphirs, & 2 very fair Ruby-balasses. It is kept in ye Castle St Angelo, wth the Triple Crowns, & is not to be taken thence but when ye Pope sais Solemn Mass. This rare piece is valued

took to eating and drinking copiously; some of the Germans in particular, who were more skilled than their comrades, and wanted to march apace with me, sank under these excesses and perished.

In 1545 Cellini returned to Florence where he passed the rest of his life, working mainly in bronze and marble. His works included the *Perseus, Apollo and Hyacinth* and *Narcissus*, a *Ganymede* incorporating an antique torso, busts of Cosimo I and Bindo Altoviti and finally a marble crucifix now in the Escorial in Spain. He began his autobiography in 1558, taking the story of his life up to 1562, though continuing to work on it until 1566. In 1568 he published his treatises. He died on 13 February 1571. The inventory of his effects reveals that he lived comfortably in his last years with a country place as well as a town house which had been given

Back of the morse made by Cellini for Clement VII.

The back part of the said Pectoral shewing ye Arms & Impresses of Pope Clement, finely embossed on gold.

Fr: Bertoli. del:

him by the Grand Duke. It records a fair quantity of furniture, pictures and a drawing by Michelangelo.

Cellini seems to have thought, in his last years, that he would attain immortality by his works on a large scale. But he continued to regard the salt-cellar as one of his masterpieces and described it in his treatises and, more than once, in his autobiography. In form it combines two types of object made to decorate the tables of the great – the ceremonial salt and the nef, or ship-model, which marked the place of the host and sometimes served as a container for his personal utensils. But Cellini conceived it as a piece of sculpture no less rich in imagery than in workmanship. Of his first sketch he wrote:

Wishing to suggest the intermingling of land and ocean, I modelled two figures considerably taller than a palm in height, which were seated with their legs interlaced, suggesting those lengthier branches of the sea which run up into the continents. The sea was a man, and in his hand I placed a ship, elaborately wrought in all its details, and well adapted to hold a quantity of salt. Beneath him I grouped the four sea horses, and in his right hand he held his trident. The earth I fashioned like a woman, with all the beauty of form, the grace, and charm of which my art was capable. She had a richly decorated temple firmly based upon the ground at one side; and here her hand rested. This I intended to receive the pepper. In her other hand I put a cornucopia, overflowing with all the natural treasures I could think of. Below this goddess, in the part which represented the earth, I collected the fairest animals that haunt our globe. In the quarter presided over by the deity of ocean, I fashioned such choice kinds of fishes and shells as could be properly displayed in that small space. What remained of the oval I filled in with luxuriant ornamentation.

Elsewhere he described the reliefs of night, day, twilight and dawn (after Michelangelo, though he does not say so) and the winds or seasons, on the base. He also records that François I greeted the completed work with the words: 'God be praised that here in our own day there be yet man born who can turn out so much more beautiful things than the ancients'.

Few objects could be more ornate than Cellini's salt-cellar. But his desire for variety was held in check by respect for overall uniformity. The two main figures, the female nude on top of the 'temple' (which looks more like a triumphal arch) and the four reliefs of the times of day on the plinth are in recumbent attitudes, all posed according to antique rules of *contrapposto*, subtly varied yet complementary. Earth and Sea are placed in poses which are similar, but not identical, so that they form a balanced group when seen from either side. The way in which arms and legs answer each other's movements suggests closer integration and gives the group a strongly erotic appearance by no means inappropriate to a composition which depicts the fecundity of the terrestrial elements.

Charles IX, the grandson of François I, gave the salt-cellar to the Archduke Ferdinand of Austria in 1570. It then entered the treasury of Schloss Ambras where it remained until the early nineteenth century when it was put on public view in Vienna. During this long period it was seen by few and could exert no direct influence. But, as we shall see, descriptions of this and other works by Cellini and his contemporaries seem to have inspired many later craftsmen who sought after richness and variety in metalwork. Cellini had, indeed, played a leading part in establishing the aesthetic and technical standards which leading goldsmiths were to strive to maintain in subsequent centuries.

Detail of the salt made by Benvenuto Cellini for François I. By the side of the female figure, Cellini wrote, 'I put a little Ionic temple, most richly wrought, and this was to hold the pepper'. Kunsthistorisches Museum, Vienna.

Wenzel Jamnitzer

(1508–85)

Portrait of Wenzel Jamnitzer by
Nicolas Neufchâtel. Musée d'art et
d'histoire, Geneva.

Wish me joy [wrote Horace Walpole in 1772], I have changed all my Roman
medals of great brass ... for the <u>uniquest</u> thing in the world, a silver bell for an
inkstand made by Benvenuto Cellini. It makes one believe all the extravagant
encomiums he bestows on himself: indeed so does his Perseus. Well, <u>my</u> bell is in
the finest taste, and is swarmed by caterpillars, lizards, grasshoppers, flies, and
masques, that you would take it for one of the plagues of Egypt. They are all in
altissimo, nay, *in outissimo relievo*, and yet almost invisible but with a glass. Such
foliage, such fruitage.

This object, now in the British Museum, is neither unique nor the
work of Cellini, but one of a group of bells decorated in the 'rustic' style
developed in mid-sixteenth-century Nuremberg by Wenzel Jamnitzer.
Jamnitzer is one of the several outstanding sixteenth-century goldsmiths
thrown into the shade by Cellini's autobiography. His life, in the
Nuremberg of Hans Sachs and the Meistersinger, was inevitably more
bourgeois and less exciting than Cellini's in Renaissance Florence, Rome
or Paris. But he was a man of some intellectual distinction sharing the
highly-sophisticated tastes and interests of his patrons. He was by no
means inferior to Cellini as a craftsman. And his astonishing abilities were
fully appreciated by contemporaries. As early as 1547 Neudörfer remarked that readers might think that he had been too generous in his
praise of Wenzel Jamnitzer and his brother Alberich because they were
his friends but all other connoisseurs who saw their work concurred in
his opinion. 'They wrought both silver and gold, had a great understanding of perspective and proportion, cut coats of arms and seals in silver,
stone and steel, enamelled in the most beautiful colours and brought the
art of engraving on silver to its highest pitch'. Alberich died in 1555 but
Wenzel's fame continued to spread far beyond Nuremberg. As *Kaiser-
licher Hofgoldschmied,* he served four Hapsburg Emperors. His works
seem to have been transmitted throughout Europe, even to England.

He was born in Vienna in 1508, the son of Hans Jamnitzer a goldsmith.
Together with his brother Alberich and their parents he went to Nuremberg sometime before 1534 when he was accepted as a Bürger and
married Anna Braunreuchen, who bore him eleven children. At about
this time he acquired a house in the Zistelgasse, the street in which
Dürer had lived. When he was appointed coin and seal die-cutter to the
city in 1543 he was described as *kunstreich*, a word implying artistic as well
as technical proficiency. Nine years later he was made master of the city
mint and thus official leader of the goldsmiths. In 1556 he became a
member of the *Grosse Rat* or great council of the city, in 1564 he was
designated a Hauptmann and in 1573 elected to the smaller council, described as the 'supreme political body' of Nuremberg. He died on 15
December 1585 and was buried in the Johannis-Kirchhof, near the graves
of Dürer, Veit Stoss and the Sachs family. The tombstone was adorned

76

Table-centre by Wenzel Jamnitzer, completed before 1549, when it was bought by the Nuremberg City Council. Rijksmuseum, Amsterdam.

Gilt bronze caryatid by Wenzel Jamnitzer, one of the only remaining fragments from the grandiose table-centre he began for the Emperor Maximilian II in 1556. Kunsthistorisches Museum, Vienna.

Nautilus shell, set in silver gilt by Wenzel Jamnitzer, c. 1570. Schatzkammer der Residenz, Munich.

with a bronze epitaph, portrait, coat of arms, symbols of the elements and the figure of Mother Earth derived from his 'Merckelsche' table-centre.

The 'Merckelsche' table-centre in the Rijksmuseum in Amsterdam (named after a Nuremberg merchant who saved it from the melting-pot in 1806) is Wenzel Jamnitzer's earliest surviving work and one of his best, completed before 1549 when it was bought by the City Council of Nuremberg. Almost a compendium of the goldsmith's art, it reveals his consummate mastery in modelling, embossing, engraving and enamelling, besides his peculiar talent for making casts of insects, reptiles and grasses. A metre (39 ins) in height, the piece consists of a female figure standing on a base, covered with plants and populated by small creatures, and holding above her head a bowl from the centre of which an enamelled vase of flowers rises. Plaques on the plinth and underside of the bowl are inscribed with Latin verses stressing the iconographical programme. For this is no mere decorative trifle, but an allegory of a type dear to all European humanists of the day: the main figure represents Mother Earth rising from a mound rich in the lower elements of creation and supporting fruits and flowers which are of service to men.

A table-centre-cum-fountain which Jamnitzer began for the Emperor Maximilian II of Austria in 1556 was larger in size (3 metres [118 ins] high and nearly 2 metres [78 ins] across) and still more complex in its programme. It was completed for the Hapsburg Emperor Rudolf II, but destroyed in the eighteenth century save for four magnificent gilt bronze caryatids representing the seasons.

Also in 1556 Jamnitzer began for the Archduke Ferdinand of Tirol a table-centre, which was to represent Adam and Eve in the Garden of Eden, but was never completed for lack of funds. Several letters which passed between the Archduke and the goldsmith have, however, survived and not only reveal how carefully the details of such a composition were discussed but throw some light on Jamnitzer's workshop. It appears that he employed two assistants who were artists of some ability – Jacopo da Strada, later to become Court Antiquary to the Duke of Bavaria, and Matthias Zundt, author of an influential book of goldsmiths' designs. He also employed his son Wenzel II who was to die young in Paris in 1572. But the City rules prevented him from expanding his workshop and he never had as many assistants as Cellini employed in Paris.

The *Kaiserpokal* – or Imperial cup – which Jamnitzer made in 1564 happily survives intact in the Kunstgewerbemuseum, West Berlin. Smaller in scale and far less complex than the table-centres, it is made to a standard sixteenth-century pattern. But the finial on the cover is a notable work of small-scale sculpture, with a statuette of the Emperor Maximilian II standing, sword in one hand, enamelled shield in the other, on a plinth above figures of Philip Ludwig, Count Palatine of Nurem-

The Kaiserpokal, a covered cup made by Wenzel Jamnitzer in 1564, probably for presentation to the Emperor Maximilian II, who is represented on the top. Kunstgewerbemuseum, West Berlin.

berg, and the bishops of Würzburg, Bamberg and Salzburg.

In 1568 Jamnitzer published his book on perspective with a frontispiece incorporating allegories of arithmetic, geometry, perspective and architecture – each a sinuous female figure with appropriate emblems – linked together by bands of strapwork (he used a similar design for a mirror frame now in the Metropolitan Museum, New York). It consists of a series of plates of three-dimensional forms rendered according to the rules of scientific perspective, which appeal to us now as examples of non-representational art. But in their own time they occupied a position on the borderline of art, philosophy and science. The book's sub-title refers to the 'five regular bodies of which Plato wrote in the Timaeo and Euclid in his Elements'.

How much Jamnitzer knew directly of Plato and Euclid it is difficult to say. But he must have been familiar with the work of Italian neo-Platonists who interested themselves in geometry, notably Luca Pacioli. And, of course, he had a closer forerunner in Albrecht Dürer who had been obsessed by geometrical and perspectival problems though he never learned to render the more complex forms satisfactorily. This was not the only way in which Jamnitzer may have been influenced by Dürer. The lobed forms which occur in many of his silver cups seem to derive from the designs of Dürer which achieved a kind of classic status in Nuremberg.

Jamnitzer incorporated representations of lizards, frogs and snakes on the base of a cup made for the abbess of a convent at Ratisbon in 1545–6 but now lost. A few years later Neudörfer remarked that the skill of the Jamnitzer brothers in 'casting little animals, worms, weeds and snails in silver and decorating silver vessels with them has never been heard of before. They have given me a solid silver snail cast with all kinds of little flowers and grasses which are so delicate and thin that they move when one blows on them'. But, he concluded, 'the praise for these works belongs to God alone'. In fact, bronze casts of reptiles and insects had been made by the great Paduan bronze sculptor Riccio and others in the Veneto in the previous century. And they belong to a phenomenon known macaronically, but not inappropriately, as the *Stil rustique*. While Jamnitzer was making his casts in silver, Bernard Palissy in France was doing the same in pottery. There was a widespread fashion for such things, which appealed not only to sophisticates who enjoyed a *frisson* given by reptiles, even when safely immobilized, but also to students of natural history.

Jamnitzer seems to have shared his patrons' interest not only in natural curiosities but also in that great sixteenth-century obsession, allegory. The revival of classical scholarship had made possible the creation of allegories still more intricately complex and obscurantist than those of

The lid of a silver box decorated with casts of shells and insects, by Wenzel Jamnitzer. Kunsthistorisches Museum, Vienna.

Silver-gilt casket set with diamonds, rubies, emeralds and heliotropes and decorated with allegorical figures and reliefs of the Labours of Hercules, made by Wenzel Jamnitzer, *c.* 1560. Schatzkammer der Residenz, Munich.

the Middle Ages. Complexity and obscurity had, indeed, come to be seen as positive virtues. With his highly developed interest in the relationship between the Platonic bodies and the elements, Jamnitzer had a mind well equipped to think out allegorical confections as involved as the table-centre for Rudolf II. And like all the best, and some of the least readable, sixteenth-century allegorical poems, this piece rested on antique authority: the description of the shield of Achilles in the eighteenth book of the *Iliad*. It is remarkable how many of the elements on Achilles' shield were incorporated in the table-centre, even the dancing peasants, for instance. But Jamnitzer had outdone Vulcan by representing the figures not only in the round but also in motion. As we have seen, sixteenth-century artists were bent on outdoing antiquity.

After Wenzel Jamnitzer's death in 1585, his sons Hans and Abraham continued to work in his manner. Hans took over many of Wenzel's motifs, both naturalistic and antique, and was probably responsible for the bell which Horace Walpole cherished. Christoph (1563–1618), the son of Hans, was a highly talented goldsmith. Several of his works survive, including a table-fountain in the form of one of Hannibal's elephants, now in the Museum of Decorative Arts, West Berlin. But they lack the many layers of meaning implicit in the work of Wenzel.

81

Antonio Gentili

(1519–1609)

Antonio Gentili is one of the several Italian goldsmiths overshadowed by the more colourful Cellini. His masterpiece, a large cross and pair of candlesticks placed on the high altar of St Peter's on great occasions, though signed with his name and fully documented, has often been attributed either to Cellini or to an anonymous craftsman working to designs by Michelangelo. This cross and pair of candlesticks are perhaps the finest surviving examples of work described in the sixteenth century as *grosseria*. And, as if to account for the grandeur of their conception, Gentili's first biographer, Giovanni Baglione, described him not as a goldsmith but as a sculptor.

The son of a goldsmith, Antonio Gentili was born at Faenza in 1519, probably trained under his father and settled in Rome about 1550. In 1551 he paid tax as a goldsmith who was not a member of the guild, but appears to have been accepted as a master craftsman next year. On the death of his father in 1558 he returned briefly to Faenza to put his affairs in order. But he was back in Rome by June 1561 when he married Costanza Guidi. Two years later he was elected one of the consuls of the goldsmiths' guild of which he was to be chamberlain (*camerlengo*) in 1569–70 and again in 1579–80. He began with a shop and house in via Pellegrino but in 1586 moved to a house in via Giulia which was to be his home until his death. Documents published by C. G. Bulgari reveal that Gentili often worked in partnership with other goldsmiths. He was appointed assayer to the Papal Mint in 1584, confirmed in this post in 1600 and passed it on to his son, Pietro, in 1602.

His first recorded commission was for twelve reliquaries ordered by Pope Pius V in 1570 to be executed to designs by Guglielmo della Porta in collaboration with a Florentine goldsmith named Pierantonio di Benvenuto Tati. Ten were to be in the form of busts, one a leg, another an arm, but all have been lost. He was paid for a silver reliquary made for the Society of Jesus in 1578. His next recorded work is the cross and candlesticks made to the order of Cardinal Alessandro Farnese, who paid him 13,000 scudi and presented them to St Peter's in June 1582. There is no mention of other works until 1593 when he and his son Pietro agreed to make, for 1,700 scudi, an elaborate base of a cross for the monastery of San Martino, Naples. This was still extant in the mid-eighteenth century but subsequently destroyed. Baglione remarks that he worked for 'great princes', without naming them, and that he made a fountain for Cardinal Farnese at Ronciglione besides providing designs for other fountains. Two reliquaries signed by him, dated 1589 and 1600, are recorded in Vatican inventories but seem to have disappeared.

Antonio Gentili died on 29 October 1609, and was buried in the church of San Biagio in via Giulia. His last months may well have been darkened by a lawsuit instigated against him by Teodoro, son of Guglielmo della

Detail of one of the figures of youths, strongly influenced by the work of Michelangelo, on the base of the altar cross made by Antonio Gentili for St Peter's, Rome.

Porta. The report of this affair is long, tedious and inconclusive. But in the course of his evidence Gentili revealed that he had many casts of sculptures by Michelangelo and other artists in his collection, and that he had been closely connected with Guglielmo della Porta and later with Bastiano Torrigiani, who is best known for his colossal bronze figures crowning the columns of Trajan and Marcus Aurelius.

Gentili derived his style from the generation of artists who had come under the immediate influence of Michelangelo. The cross and candlesticks in St Peter's are composed on Michelangelesque architectural and figurative elements – especially tabernacles with broken pediments and sinuous *ignudi*. The individual figures, as fine as any bronze statuettes of the period, are posed in a variety of ways permitted by the laws of *contrapposto*. Baglione said that they were the most beautiful works ever made in this manner.

The cross is set with eight, and each of the candlesticks with three, panels of rock crystal beautifully engraved with scenes from the life of Christ. They are of somewhat earlier date, having been carved by Giovanni dei Bernardi who died in 1553. The cross and candlesticks suffered some minor alterations when Cardinal Francesco Barberini added four more candlesticks, made to match by Carlo Spagna in 1670 and 1672, but of distinctly inferior quality.

The only other surviving works which can be attributed to Gentili – if only tentatively – are a knife, fork and spoon in the Metropolitan Museum, New York. The spoon corresponds closely with a drawing inscribed with his name. Every detail of each piece is wrought with a jeweller's delicacy and precision. Such a set including a fork (still a rarity in Italy and hardly known north of the Alps until the seventeenth century) must have been made for a person of some consequence. The prongs of the fork, like long-beaked birds, recall one of Giulio Romano's silver designs which exerted considerable influence in both Italy and France. But the handles are more elaborate, composed of a profusion of classical motifs which answer Baglione's description of Gentili's works – 'with many adornments and *bizzarie* as graceful as possible; where there are little figures, animals and diverse ornaments extraordinarily noble and charming to the eye'.

Candlestick, from the set of a cross and two candlesticks of silver-gilt set with crystal engraved plaques, made by Antonio Gentili for Cardinal Alessandro Farnese, who presented it to St Peter's in 1682.

Silver knife, spoon and fork probably
made in late sixteenth-century Rome
and attributed to Antonio Gentili.
Metropolitan Museum, New York.

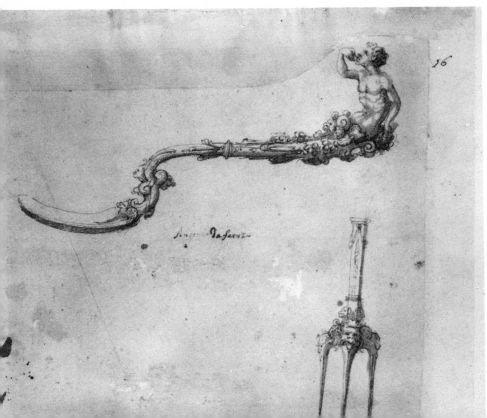

Designs for a spoon and fork inscribed
with the name of Antonio Faenza and
attributed to Antonio Gentili.
Metropolitan Museum, New York.

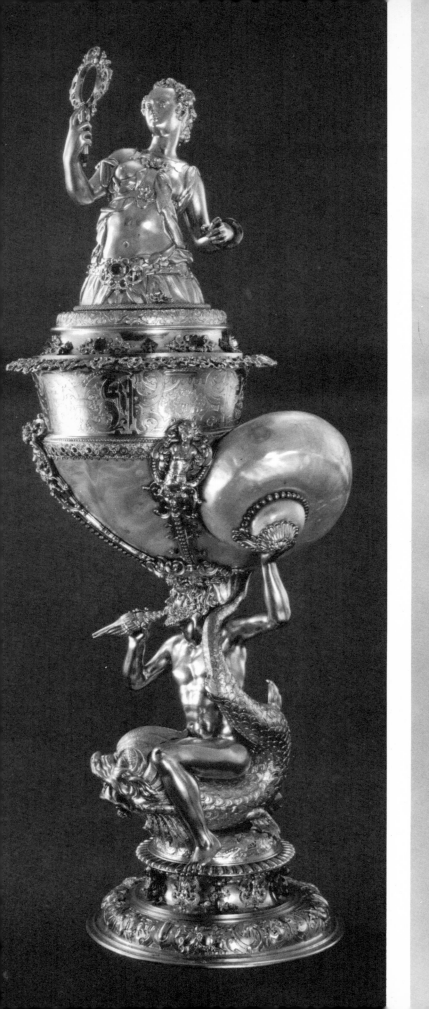

Hans Petzolt

(1551–1633)

On Wenzel Jamnitzer's death in 1585, Hans Petzolt (or Petzoldt) appears to have become the leading Nuremberg goldsmith. Born in 1551, he became a master craftsman in 1578 and was received as a Bürger in the following year. Like Jamnitzer he played a part in civic affairs. In 1591 he became a member of the greater Council. Twenty years later he was elected a *Ratsherr* (alderman) and sat on the Council until his death in 1633. Nothing is known of his private life or personality, but some forty works by him survive and his career may be documented by a number of commissions. From 1595 to 1614 he was intermittently employed in making pieces of silver for the Nuremberg Council to give to visiting notabilities and to people whose services to the city could not be rewarded with money; sixty-four lobed cups, eighteen cups of the type originally called *Traubenpokale*, from the similarity of the bowl to a bunch of grapes (though often called pineapple cups), and two salt-cellars. In 1604 he was summoned to Prague by Rudolf II who employed him to repair a fountain – perhaps Jamnitzer's table-fountain – and execute new works. While in Prague, Paulus van Vianen made a portrait medal of him. After having some difficulty in obtaining full payment from the Emperor he seems to have gone back to his native city in 1609. In 1616 Rudolf wrote to the Nuremberg Council asking them to allow Petzolt to return to Prague and he appears to have spent some months there, executing un-recorded works for the fee of 1,500 thaler.

Petzolt's virtuosity as a craftsman is displayed on a nautilus shell cup in the Museum of Decorative Arts, Budapest. It is supported on the figure of a triton riding a dolphin and blowing a conch. On the cover there is a half-length mermaid whose body emerges from the iridescent nautilus shell of the bowl; indeed, the shell is set in such a way that it seems to represent her curving tail. Another notable work is in the Royal Scottish Museum, Edinburgh: a cup delicately embossed with scenes illustrating the processes of mining and working silver.

All these works carry on the Jamnitzer tradition. But the majority of Petzolt's surviving pieces are in a strikingly different style. The most notable, perhaps, is the *Dianapokal,* once in the Esterhazy collection and now in the Kunstgewerbemuseum, West Berlin. Apart from the statuette of Diana on the cover and some fronds of antique style foliage, this cup is composed of elements associated with the early rather than the late six-teenth century. A silver double cup (two cups of identical design which may be joined at the rim so that one forms the cover of the other) in the Rijksmuseum, is still more obviously in the style of the early sixteenth-century Nuremberg goldsmiths. Several similar works by Petzolt are recorded, and other Nuremberg craftsmen – Leonhard Vorchamer, Hans Kellner and P. Weber – are also known to have reverted to this style in the last years of the sixteenth and first of the seventeenth century.

left Nautilus shell cup by Hans Petzolt. Museum of Decorative Arts, Budapest.

right The Diana Cup by Hans Petzolt, 1610–20. Standing nearly 80 cm. (31.5 ins) high, this cup is one of Petzolt's largest and most impressive works. Kunstgewerbemuseum, West Berlin.

87

Traubenpokal or bunch-of-grapes cup by Hans Petzolt, 1610–12. He is known to have made eighteen cups of this type for the city of Nuremberg. Kunstgewerbemuseum, West Berlin.

below Double cup by Hans Petzolt, made in the late sixteenth or early seventeenth century, but in a style which harks back to that of the Nuremberg goldsmiths of Dürer's time. Rijksmuseum, Amsterdam.

opposite Covered cup embossed with reliefs, illustrating the processes of mining and working silver, by Hans Petzolt. Collection of the Duke of Hamilton, on loan to the Royal Scottish Museum, Edinburgh.

Ostrich-egg cup with silver-gilt mount by Hans Petzolt, 1594. Minneapolis Institute of Arts.

Generally described as *Neugotik*, these works have been cited as manifestations of a precocious Gothic revival. They are not, however, connected with the religious Gothic revivals of the early seventeenth century – churches built in a simplified Gothic style for the Jesuits in the Rhineland, or churches and furnishings (including chalices of mediaeval pattern) commissioned by High Anglicans in England. And it is doubtful if Petzolt's cups would have appeared as Gothic to his contemporaries. Wenzel Jamnitzer had made at least one cup of this type in 1564 (now in the Germanisches Nationalmuseum, Nuremberg). 'Columbine' cups made to a pattern devised in the late fifteenth century were produced throughout the sixteenth century and often presented by goldsmiths as their masterpieces. Similarly, Petzolt's cups are not so much reminiscent of the Middle Ages but more of the period of the revival of the arts, or Renaissance, initiated in Germany by Dürer. They are, in fact, in the style of Dürer's designs for silver, and are manifestations not of a Gothic revival but of the Dürer revival greatly encouraged by Petzolt's patron, Rudolf II of Austria. It is significant that Petzolt was probably responsible for a medal of Dürer struck in Nuremberg in the late sixteenth or early seventeenth century. By the end of the sixteenth century Nuremberg had lost much of its earlier prosperity, and had already begun to live on its past. A backward glance to the period later called the *Dürerzeit* was thus coloured with poignant nostalgia.

But there may also have been artistic reasons for Petzolt's return to the designs of the early sixteenth century. Throughout Europe the Mannerist style in which Wenzel Jamnitzer excelled had come under heavy fire from theorists. A demand for unity rather than diversity, which was to culminate in the Italian Baroque style, had begun to manifest itself. Petzolt's *Dianapokal* is no less complex in form than cups by Wenzel Jamnitzer, but ornamental motifs are repeated in such a way that it appears the same from every viewpoint. His *Traubenpokale* composed only of embossed lobes are also made to fully integrated and unified designs. The beauty of their form and decoration may be appreciated in a single *coup d'oeil* – there is no need to turn them round and round to follow curving and interlacing elements or to 'read' figurative scenes of arcane significance. Although he may have derived inspiration from the goldsmiths of Dürer's age, and possibly from the drawings of Dürer himself, Petzolt seems also to have been striving after a new ideal.

Gaspare Mola

(1567–1640)

Plaque of silver-gilt and red jasper, designed by Johannes and Raphael Sadeler, and made by Gaspare Mola to commemorate the institution of the Gregorian calendar. Collection of Conte Vittorio Cini, Venice.

A large plaque made to celebrate Pope Gregory XIII's reform of the calendar is one of the most impressive pieces of Italian silver dating from the first years of the seventeenth century. An inscription reveals that it was made by Gaspare Mola to the design of 'Joan et Raph Sadeler'. Though Mola is recorded as a goldsmith, this is his only signed piece of silver which survives.

Gaspare Mola was born at Coldrè near Como in 1567. He is said to have been trained as a goldsmith in Milan and it is tempting to suggest that his master was the great sculptor, medallist and goldsmith, Leone Leoni. By 1599 he was in Florence working on the bronze west doors of Pisa Cathedral, for which he modelled the relief of the *Presentation in the Temple*, and a larger relief of the *Crucifixion* completed before 1604.

After working on the doors for Pisa Cathedral, Mola went back to Milan. But he returned to Florence in 1608 when he was appointed die-cutter to the Grand Ducal mint. In 1613 he was working for the mint in Modena and in 1614 for that of the Duchy of Guastalla. Little is heard of him for some years, but he had settled in Rome by the beginning of 1625 when he was appointed engraver at the papal mint. He was dismissed from this post by Cardinal Aldobrandini in 1631, but reinstated in 1633.

In 1637 Mola formed a partnership for the production of medals with Orazio Ghibellino and his own nephew (the son of his sister) Gaspare Moroni. He appears to have been known principally as the *medagliero del Papa* and it was as a medal engraver that he was elected to the Accademia di San Luca in Rome which still preserves a portrait of him. But the inventory of his effects drawn up after his death, on 26 January 1640, suggests that he had also been engaged in goldsmith's work until the end of his life. There were, for instance, seven copper crucifixes in his *bottega*. He also had boxes filled with pieces of lapis lazuli and other *pietre dure*, then so fashionable in Italy, besides such objects as an agate vase and a crystal cross mounted in gold. Other documents refer to his having elaborate *pietre dure* picture frames, notably one of *lapis lazuli*, cornelian, crystal, gold, ebony and other materials enclosing an *Annunciation* by Pirro Ligorio.

Few works apart from medals have been attributed to Mola. In the Museo Nazionale, Florence, there is a magnificent shield and helmet of silver partly gilt, crisply chiselled with grotesque motifs, identified as the work of Mola in a manuscript of 1642 which declares that it was 'regarded as a marvellous thing'. But the object to which he himself appears to have attached most importance was a sword with scabbard and belt which, as he said in his will, was 'a unique piece ... worthy of any king or emperor'. He left it to the hospital of San Carlo al Corso, suggesting that it should be sold, but there it remained for nearly two centuries. It is now in the Musée de l'Armée, Paris.

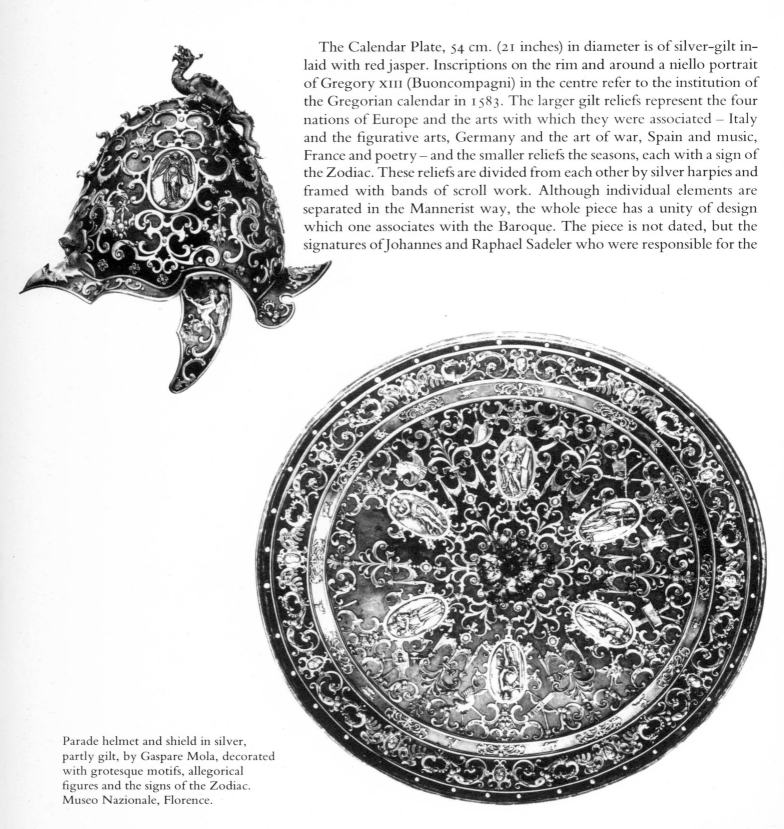

The Calendar Plate, 54 cm. (21 inches) in diameter is of silver-gilt inlaid with red jasper. Inscriptions on the rim and around a niello portrait of Gregory XIII (Buoncompagni) in the centre refer to the institution of the Gregorian calendar in 1583. The larger gilt reliefs represent the four nations of Europe and the arts with which they were associated – Italy and the figurative arts, Germany and the art of war, Spain and music, France and poetry – and the smaller reliefs the seasons, each with a sign of the Zodiac. These reliefs are divided from each other by silver harpies and framed with bands of scroll work. Although individual elements are separated in the Mannerist way, the whole piece has a unity of design which one associates with the Baroque. The piece is not dated, but the signatures of Johannes and Raphael Sadeler who were responsible for the

Parade helmet and shield in silver, partly gilt, by Gaspare Mola, decorated with grotesque motifs, allegorical figures and the signs of the Zodiac. Museo Nazionale, Florence.

design provide a clue – for Johannes died in Venice in August 1600 and Raphael appears to have gone from Germany to Italy in the following year. It therefore seems probable that Mola executed the plate in or shortly after 1601.

Mola is one of several metalworkers errant of the sixteenth and seventeenth centuries who passed from court to court, making medallion portraits, engraving dies for coins, cutting precious and semi-precious stones and sometimes working in gold and silver. They were essentially artists capable of producing small-scale sculpture in a wide range of media as distinct from silversmiths mainly engaged in making articles for domestic or ecclesiastical use. But they played an important part in the history of European silver.

Sword hilt by Gaspare Mola, who attributed great importance to this work, which he claimed to be 'worthy of any king or emperor'. Musée de l'Armée, Paris.

Ewer and basin by Paulus van Vianen,
executed in the year of his death, 1613.
The relief on the basin represents the
bath of Diana, and derives from a
painting of Poelenburgh. Rijksmuseum,
Amsterdam.

Paulus van Vianen

(c. 1568–1613)

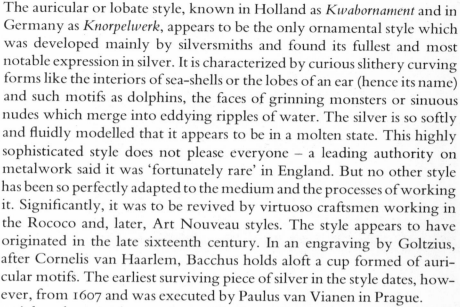

The auricular or lobate style, known in Holland as *Kwabornament* and in Germany as *Knorpelwerk*, appears to be the only ornamental style which was developed mainly by silversmiths and found its fullest and most notable expression in silver. It is characterized by curious slithery curving forms like the interiors of sea-shells or the lobes of an ear (hence its name) and such motifs as dolphins, the faces of grinning monsters or sinuous nudes which merge into eddying ripples of water. The silver is so softly and fluidly modelled that it appears to be in a molten state. This highly sophisticated style does not please everyone – a leading authority on metalwork said it was 'fortunately rare' in England. But no other style has been so perfectly adapted to the medium and the processes of working it. Significantly, it was to be revived by virtuoso craftsmen working in the Rococo and, later, Art Nouveau styles. The style appears to have originated in the late sixteenth century. In an engraving by Goltzius, after Cornelis van Haarlem, Bacchus holds aloft a cup formed of auricular motifs. The earliest surviving piece of silver in the style dates, however, from 1607 and was executed by Paulus van Vianen in Prague.

Adam, born in about 1565, and Paulus, a few years younger, were the sons of Willem Berstensz. van Vianen, whom Sandrart called 'ein sinnreicher Silberarbeiter zu Utrecht' – an ingenious silver-worker of Utrecht. They were probably trained by their father, though Paulus is said to have studied under a certain Cornelis Ellertz. as well. While Adam stayed in Utrecht, probably working in the father's shop, Paulus set off on his travels. According to Joachim von Sandrart (writing in the 1670s) he went to Rome where he executed excellent works, 'vases, figures and reliefs in silver' but fell foul of the Inquisition and was imprisoned for blasphemy. (Unfortunately there is no other evidence for this incident or even the visit to Rome.) By 1596 he had settled in Munich, where he was accepted as a master-craftsman in 1599, and made both silver armour and smaller objects for the Duke of Bavaria. In 1601 he was appointed court goldsmith to the Archbishop of Salzburg. But within two years he moved on to Prague where he became *Kammergoldschmied* to the strange, introverted and perennially fascinating Rudolf II. Apart from a return visit to Utrecht in 1610 he remained in Prague until his death in 1613.

Paulus seems to have been employed mainly in making silver reliefs of religious or (more rarely) mythological figures set in wide landscapes. His modelling is so fluid that these might almost be described as 'paintings' rather than sculptures in silver. Sometimes, indeed, he made use of paintings by other artists as the basis for his compositions and his *Bath of Diana* derives from a picture by Cornelis van Poelenburgh. But generally he appears to have worked to his own designs. One of his finest reliefs, dated 1610, represents the sleeping Argus with Mercury and Io, metamorphosed into a cow, in an Arcadian landscape. The exquisitely

97

Silver relief of the sleeping Argus, Mercury and Io by Paulus van Vianen; one of a series of reliefs of scenes from Ovid. A set of seven such reliefs in bronze was in the collection of Charles I. Rijksmuseum, Amsterdam.

nodelled body of Argus seems to be the result of a desire to 'display his knowledge of the nude' – as Vasari might have put it. The whole piece is, indeed, pervaded by the sophisticated – some might say precious – eroticism of the paintings which Bartolomaeus Spranger had executed for Rudolf's studio a few years earlier.

In other works of this date, Paulus began to develop the auricular style. At first he limited it to borders and cartouches where he treated the flat, leathery strapwork motifs, then so popular, with greater smoothness and fluidity. Motifs of the new type are given more prominence on the stem and foot of a tazza dated 1607, and the style is fully formed on a ewer and basin made in the year of his death, 1613. He clearly derived some inspiration from earlier ornamental designs, engravings by Virgil Solis

Tazza by Paulus van Vianen, 1607 with early auricular motifs on the base. Rijksmuseum, Amsterdam.

and, perhaps, Giulio Romano's drawings for silver which often included fishes, molluscs and similar elements. He must also have been aware of Wenzel Jamnitzer's slithering, wriggling reptiles so much in evidence in Rudolf II's treasure chambers. A jasper ewer with a gold cover from which a mermaid emerges, made by Paulus in 1608, is obviously indebted to the Jamnitzer tradition. The forms of nautilus shells may also have inspired him. It would, however, be rash to ascribe the invention of the style to Paulus alone. The Goltzius print, to which I have already referred, dates probably from the 1590s and cups like that held by Bacchus may well have been executed by Rudolf II's goldsmiths before Paulus reached Prague.

While Paulus was in Prague, his brother Adam was working in a

Ewer with a jasper body and gold mounts by Paulus van Vianen, 1608. Kunsthistorisches Museum, Vienna.

below Silver relief depicting Pan and Syrinx, by Paulus van Vianen, 1603, Rijksmuseum, Amsterdam.

fairly conventional late Renaissance style in Utrecht. But it seems that designs by Paulus were sent to Utrecht after his death. And it is surely more than a coincidence that auricular ornament appears in Adam's work for the first time in a tazza bowl dated 1613 and, more prominently, on a large ewer and basin of 1614. A tazza made in 1618 shows that Adam soon developed a bolder version of the style. Here a pair of kissing lovers seem to float on waves eddying out from a shellfish-like form in the centre, and the transitions are so smooth that it is impossible to say where one merges into another. Adam continued to execute representational

reliefs and even statuettes, including a figure of Prince Maurice of Nassau on horseback (1626) which has vanished. He also combined figurative reliefs with auricular motifs, as on a ewer with a veiled head peering out from beneath the lip and plaques of such insistently classical scenes as Mucius Scaevola, Cloelia, the Horatii and Curatii, and the beheading of the sons of Brutus, among the fishy motifs on the body. But he is distinguished mainly for auricular style works. As a craftsman he was a virtuoso, making no use of cast work but hammering each piece out of a single sheet of silver. (Paulus had occasionally used cast decorations attached by wires to the body of a plaque.)

Adam van Vianen was married in 1593 to Aeltgen Verhorst, who died young, and in 1598 to Catherina van Wapenveldt who bore him three children. He became a master-craftsman probably in 1593, certainly before his second marriage, was assayer of the Utrecht guild in 1606, 1607, 1610 and 1611 and dean in 1615. He died in 1627. His son Christiaen, born in 1598, served an apprenticeship under him. In 1635 Christiaen went to England and entered the service of Charles I, making seventeen pieces of plate for the royal chapel at Windsor, completed in 1639 but apparently stolen and destroyed three years later. He returned to Utrecht in about 1647 but was back in London in 1652 and again from 1660 to 1666. He worked in a style similar to that of Adam and used the same maker's mark. But his auricular forms tend to be less fantastic and he made greater use of figures, especially satyrs which serve as supports for salts and tazze. In 1650 he published a volume of his father's and his own designs for silver, engraved by Th. van Kessel and entitled *Modelles artificiels de divers vaisseaux d'argent*. The auricular style was taken up by

Two views of a tazza by Adam van Vianen, 1618. Adam was the elder brother of Paulus van Vianen, from whom he appears to have derived the auricular style in which this piece is wrought. Rijksmuseum, Amsterdam.

Ewer embossed with reliefs of scenes from ancient history by Adam van Vianen, 1621. Rijksmuseum, Amsterdam.

several other Dutch silversmiths, notably Thomas Bogaert and Johannes Lutma, some of whose designs were published in 1653 and 1654.

The appeal of the auricular style is hard to explain, especially to those who find it distasteful, for it is entirely sensuous. An admirer's eye caresses the smooth curves of these strange dishes and ewers, so softly modelled and yet so firm and cool. Though they are among the more astonishing feats of virtuoso craftsmanship, they betray no sign of labour or even of effort. Sometimes they have the inevitability of form of natural phenomena. But the appeal of the tazza with kissing lovers floating on its brim is not merely sensuous but almost explicitly erotic. And although we may doubt if either the van Vianens or their seventeenth-century patrons were consciously aware of sexual undertones in their table silver, those who know of the significance Freud put on watery forms can hardly fail to catch them.

Claude Ballin

(*c.* 1615–78)

Of the several goldsmiths employed by Louis XIV of France, Claude Ballin was probably the most highly esteemed for work on the grandest scale. In 1696 Charles Perrault included an account of him in his biographies of *Hommes Illustres*, declaring that he had 'carried the beauty of his art to a degree of perfection which had never previously been reached and will perhaps never be attained again'. By this date, however, all his secular works had been destroyed. In 1689 the King had ordained 'that throughout his realm all silver objects such as mirrors, fire-dogs, girandoles and all types of vases should be sent to the mint and melted down', and to set an example he ordered the immediate destruction of all royal plate, however well made, including even objects of filigree and the toilet sets of the princesses. In all, 20,805 Kg. (45,867 pounds) of silver went into the melting-pot. Ecclesiastical plate escaped only to be destroyed in the French Revolution a century later. These two holocausts of the works of Ballin and his contemporaries, not only deprived us of many fine pieces of silver but created at the centre of the history of European decorative arts a gap that can only partly be filled by drawings, paintings and contemporary descriptions.

Claude Ballin was born in Paris in about 1615, the son of a goldsmith, Pierre Ballin, from whom he learned his craft. It is said that he also studied the figurative arts and copied works by Poussin. At the age of nineteen he made four large dishes, decorated with figures representing the four ages of the world, which were bought by Cardinal Richelieu who ordered four vases 'in the antique style' to go with them. In 1637 he was received as a master by the silversmiths' guild and in 1640 he married. There is no further record of him until 1654 when he made a bust reliquary of Saint Remi given to Rheims Cathedral at the coronation of Louis XIV, for whom he is said to have provided a sword of enamelled gold and a finely wrought silver breast plate. He may have been working in Paris from 1640 to 1654, but it is tempting to suggest that he visited Rome, the artistic capital of Europe at this date. The registers of the Roman goldsmiths' guild record among the craftsmen working in the city in 1647–8 and in 1653, a Frenchman named 'Pietro Balino', which might just be a mistake for Claude di (son of) Pierre Ballin. There can, however, be no doubt that whether he went to Rome or not he adopted the classicizing Baroque style evolved there.

His works for the French Crown are well documented from 1665 when he was paid 75,760 livres on account for some large pieces of silver enriched with figures – bowls, vases and *brancards* (stands on which large vessels might be carried and displayed). In 1666 another payment was made to him for *brancards* and silver vases for orange trees. Two years later the balance of his account, amounting to the very considerable sum of 237,146 livres, was settled – nearly £12,000 in the English money of

Detail of a tapestry woven at the Gobelins factory to the design of Charles Lebrun. Claude Ballin made several large silver *brancards* like that carried by the men in the foreground of this tapestry.

Design for a silver chandelier by Claude Ballin, one of the several drawings acquired by the Swedish minister in Paris in 1693. National Museum, Stockholm.

the day. He was also allowed 1,000 livres to construct a workshop and a forge in the galleries of the Louvre. In 1676 he was made director of the Paris mint in succession to Jean Warin, and engaged in making medals. He died on 22 January 1678.

One may obtain a visual impression of Ballin's massive silver vessels from the work of the court painter Charles Lebrun. One of his cartoons for the *Maisons royales* tapestries depicts basins and vases carried on *brancards* much like those described in the inventory. Another *brancard* is shown in the foreground of Lebrun's famous tapestry of Louis XIV on his visit to the Gobelins factory. These pieces may indeed have been designed by Lebrun who exerted close control over the Gobelins and the production of all decorative objects for the royal palaces. He had included

Design for a fire-dog by Claude Ballin; the arms are those of the Colbert family. National Museum, Stockholm.

similar pieces of silver in his early painting of *The Entry of Alexander into Babylon*. And it is perhaps significant that among his numerous designs in the Louvre there are twenty-four for basins and vases similar to those described as the work of Ballin.

Ballin had, however, begun his career as a goldsmith before Lebrun finished his studies as a painter and was probably responsible for the design of silver he made for patrons other than the King. In 1693 Daniel Cronström, the Swedish minister in Paris, obtained seven drawings which he sent to the architect Nicodemus Tessin in Stockholm, writing: 'they are really by Ballin. Ballin, that is to say all and you know who he was'. They are now in the National Museum, Stockholm – three for chandeliers, two for fire-dogs with flame finials, one for a torchère or

Design for a *guèridon* by Claude Ballin. National Museum, Stockholm.

guèridon supported by a Moor, and one for a table. The absence of royal insignia shows that these designs were made for private patrons and, indeed, the fire-dogs bear the arms of the Colbert family. But they are fairly typical essays in the Louis XIV style and give no more than a faint idea of Ballin's abilities.

To judge from the inventory descriptions and Lebrun's paintings, the silver vessels Ballin made for the Crown belong to the tradition established in sixteenth-century Italy. Both forms and ornaments were derived from the Antique – with improvements and enrichments of course. Whatever Perrault may have thought, they must have derived their striking effect as much from their massiveness as from the refinement of their workmanship. The descriptions reveal that, in comparison with Mannerist works, the symbolism of their decorations was restricted and relatively simple. These gargantuan pieces, which needed special stands to support them and two men to carry them, were not made for the studio of a connoisseur – they were intended to give an immediate impression of princely magnificence which would overawe the most arrogant courtier and the proudest foreign emissary.

It may have been for financial as much as aesthetic reasons that when silver came back into general use after the great melting down, pieces of greater lightness and delicacy were demanded. Claude II Ballin, the son of Claude Ballin's brother Michel, was one of the several notable silversmiths who produced such works. He was born in 1661, began by studying under Claude I but was not received as a master until 1688, ten years after his uncle's death. In 1703 he was given apartments in the Louvre. His first recorded work was a monstrance for Notre Dame executed in 1708 to designs by the architect de Cotte and the sculptor Bertrand. As *orfèvre du roi* he supplied the crown for the coronation of Louis XV in 1722. Time has dealt little more kindly with his works than with those of his uncle, for there was a second great melting down of French royal plate in 1789, just a century after the first. But a large Louis XIV style basin made for the Elector Maximilian Emanuel in 1712-3 survives in the Residenzmuseum, Munich, and a table-centre in the Hermitage Museum, Leningrad.

Claude II Ballin died at the age of 93 on 18 March 1754. The obituary published in the *Mercure* commented on the elegance of contour he gave to all his works and declared that 'he was often heard to complain that good taste would be lost and beautiful forms spoiled by substituting for the sensible ornaments of the ancients lobsters and rabbits which, he said, were not suitable for the decoration of silver vessels'. This suggests that he had clung to the artistic ideals of his youth and disapproved of the work of such silversmiths as the Germains, even though the centre-piece in the Hermitage is in a style we should now call Rococo. It would be interesting to know if his later works showed a more earnest attempt to return to the Louis XIV style which began to enjoy a kind of revival in the mid-century.

Table-centre made by
Claude II Ballin
in 1726. Hermitage Museum,
Leningrad.

Silver dish by Claes Baerdt.
Naturalistically-rendered flowers of
this type enjoyed great popularity
throughout Europe in the later
seventeenth century. Fries Museum,
Leeuwarden.

Claes Fransen Baerdt

(c. 1628/9–after 1691)

The great efflorescence of painting in seventeenth-century Holland can hardly be explained by social and economic factors alone. But there can be little doubt that the riches of the Dutch, distributed fairly evenly through a large bourgeois public, greatly contributed to the excellence of the silverwork produced at the same time.

It is significant that there was no one centre particularly distinguished for the production of silver in the United Provinces. The van Vianens worked in Utrecht; Johannes Bogaert and Johannes Lutma in Amsterdam; a distinguished Nuremberg silversmith, Hans Coenraadt Breghtel, in the Hague. Each of the principal cities had its silversmiths' guild whose members were capable of work as accomplished as that made anywhere in Europe at the time.

Claes Baerdt was born and spent his life at Bolsward in Friesland – a small town in one of the less prosperous Provinces – and apparently worked only for patrons in the vicinity. Although he made no stylistic 'break-through', he became one of the best masters of embossed work in what may be termed the floral style. The few known facts of his life are briefly summarized. He was born in 1628 or 1629, the son of a silversmith, Frans Rienckes, and Lyuwckien Claesd. Alingha. At the age of eleven or twelve he began his apprenticeship and was accepted as a master of the Bolsward guild in 1654 when he married Siouck Harckd. No more than a dozen pieces of plate either signed by him or bearing his mark (a crescent between three stars) are recorded. The earliest is an oval alms-dish of 1677 in the Roman Catholic church of St Francis of Assisi at Bolsward, embossed round the rim with cherubs holding liturgical objects and musical instruments amongst a profusion of flowers. The latest is a circular alms-dish of 1691, decorated with cherubs, garlands and numerous insects, in the Dutch Reformed Church at Makkum. These are among his larger works – the dish at Makkum is 45·5 cm. (17·75 inches) across – but he also worked on a smaller scale, executing a little oval plaquette of men and women grouped round a turbanned Oriental 8·4 cm. (3·25 inches) high, and the back of a small brush decorated with a relief of a battle between Turkish and, apparently, Roman cavalry, in an oval 6 × 9 cm. (2·33 × 3·5 inches) (both in the Rijksmuseum). The date of his death is not recorded.

Baerdt's finest work is perhaps a dish of 1681 in the Friesmuseum, its broad rim embossed with cornucopia spilling a rich hoard of flowers and fruit – grapes, hops, hazel-nuts, wheat-ears and heads of Indian corn – with here and there a tiny insect. Flowers no less exquisitely rendered – daffodils, tulips and carnations – appear one by one on the rim of another bowl, the centre of which is decorated with two cherubs, one plucking a harp, the other blowing a flute.

Descriptions of these pieces might well read like those of the works of

left Silver dish by Claes Baerdt of Bolsward in Friesland, 1681. Fries Museum, Leeuwarden.

below Pair of salt cellars decorated with compositions of flowers, fish, shell-fish and insects on their bases, by Claes Baerdt, 1689. Rijksmuseum, Amsterdam.

Wenzel Jamnitzer, but the objects themselves could hardly be more different. The various naturalistic elements are rendered with the scrupulous accuracy of a miniature painter but without any regard to relative scale. A head of Indian corn is no larger than an ear of wheat, a dragon-fly no bigger than a snail. The demand for realism in scale is sacrificed to the richness of the general design. And, of course, these pieces by Baerdt were made not for display in the treasure chamber of some highly sophisticated prince, but for use either in a burgher's house or a small and simple church.

Giovanni Giardini

(1646–1721)

Giovanni Giardini was until recently an almost entirely forgotten figure. Even the most exhaustive histories of Italian seventeenth-century art ignore him. Yet he was the leading Roman goldsmith of his day, and although the majority of his works were destroyed during the Napoleonic Wars – when Cellini's famous morse was also melted down – enough survive to reveal that he more than maintained the high standards of craftsmanship set in sixteenth-century Rome. For his originality as a designer he deserves a place among the masters of the late Baroque style. It is more than probable that he also exerted a formative influence on French Rococo silversmiths, notably Thomas Germain who was working in Rome when Giardini was at the height of his career.

He was born at Forli in the Romagna on 24 June 1646 and went to Rome before he was twenty. From 1665 he was employed in the workshop of Marco Gamberucci, recently appointed 'Argentiere di Nostro Signore', who supplied plate for the Vatican and for Cardinal Francesco Barberini (nephew of Pope Urban VIII). He was accepted as a master silversmith and granted his patent in 1675. Next year he and Marco Ciucci took over the direction of Gamberucci's workshop, forming a company in which Gamberucci invested 5,000 scudi (£1,250 of the day). One of their first patrons was Cardinal Benedetto Pamphilj, for whom they made a large salt described in an inventory as having 'four triton shells and four snails to hold oil, vinegar and sauces'. They made a quantity of plainer table silver for the same Cardinal, also silver baskets and decorative dishes called *guantiere* (not necessarily intended to hold gloves).

The partnership with Ciucci was dissolved in 1680 but Giardini, who had been joined by his younger brother Alessandro (born in 1655), stayed in the workshop opposite the church of Santa Lucia. In 1686 he was elected fourth Consul of the *Congregazione degli Orefici e Argentieri* (corporation of goldsmiths and silversmiths) of which he was to be *Camerlengo* or chamberlain on three occasions, in 1692, 1703 and 1716 – an indication of the esteem in which he was held by his colleagues.

In 1689 he was given a commission as macabre as it was unusual – to make a silver mask to cover the face of Queen Christina at her lying in state and in the tomb. The Queen had expressed a wish to be buried 'without exhibition of the corpse and forbidding any funeral pomp and all other such vanity'. But Pope Innocent XI ordered the most elaborate funeral at his own expense, probably to show that his old quarrel with her had been healed. She died in Rome on 19 April, lay in state for four days in Palazzo Riario, was then exposed in the Chiesa Nuova and finally entombed in St Peter's. A contemporary records that despite embalming, the flesh of her face decayed and had to be hidden beneath a silver mask. When her corpse was exhumed a few years ago, the mask

Papal mace of silver made by Giovanni Giardini in about 1696. Victoria and Albert Museum, London.

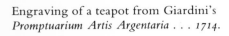

Engraving of a teapot from Giardini's
Promptuarium Artis Argentaria . . . 1714.

was intact and she was found to be wearing a silver crown and clasping a sceptre which had been made by Giardini some years before her death.

Very few of Giardini's secular pieces have survived, the most notable being a large plate so delicately engraved with rinceaux and shells that the surface has the appearance of silk damask. Ecclesiastical works include a reliquary made for a church in Gubbio in 1696, a papal mace of about the same date, now in the Victoria and Albert Museum, London, a large crucifix in the church of San Francesco at Matelica in the Marche, and a very handsome altar set comprising a crucifix and pair of candlesticks of malachite mounted in silver, signed and dated 1720, now in a private collection in Pavia. His mark appears on a large two-headed eagle with spread wings, originally the upper part of a lamp, in the Cathedral at

Holy-water stoup of silver, gilt bronze and lapis lazuli, almost certainly by Giardini. Minneapolis Institute of Arts.

Todi: it bears the arms of Monsignor Pianetti who was Bishop of Todi from 1673 to 1709. In 1711 he made a porphyry tabernacle with a frame of gilt copper and gilt copper angels enclosing a rock crystal urn mounted in silver gilt, for the high price of 2,400 scudi. This appears to be identical with a piece presented by the Archbishop of Milan to the Emperor Charles VI, inscribed 'Giovanni Giardini da Forli fec, inv. Romae', now in the Kunsthistorisches Museum, Vienna.

References to other works by Giardini have been found in the records of the papal archives, notably for holy-water stoups. There can be little doubt that he was the author of an exceptionally fine (but unmarked) stoup of silver, gilt bronze and lapis lazuli now in the Art Institute at Minneapolis. Its central relief of the Holy Family recalls the works of

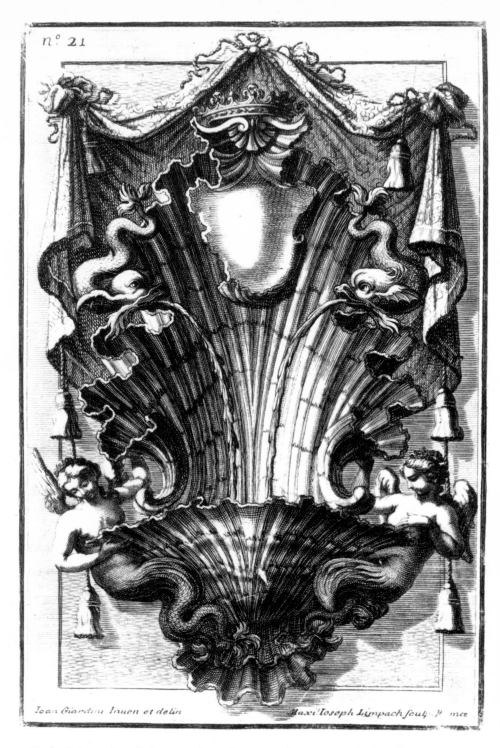

n.º 21

Ioan Giardini Inuen et delin

Maxi. Ioseph Limpach sculp. P. mæ

Carlo Maratti and the two kneeling angels seem to derive from Bernini by way of the leading sculptor of early eighteenth-century Rome, Camillo Rusconi. But the design as a whole, in a late Baroque style, trembling on the verge of the Rococo, is clearly the work of a silversmith with a highly developed feeling for the potentialities of his medium. It has, indeed, strong similarities to several of the designs for silver published by Giardini.

On 10 August 1712 Giardini signed a contract for Maximilian Joseph

no. 80

Ioan. Giardini Inuen. et delin.   Maximilianus Ioseph Limpach sculp. Romæ

Engravings from Giovanni Giardini's
Promptuarium Artis Argentaria . . . 1714.
left a shell-shaped stoup; *right,* a teapot.

Limpach of Prague to engrave one hundred of his designs for silver. These were published two years later. The designs for ecclesiastical plate are in a rich late Baroque style with an abundance of such characteristic motifs as kneeling angels, heads of cherubim, shells, garlands of flowers, luxuriant acanthus leaves, broken pediments scrolling inwards and outwards. But fantasy breaks lose in the secular pieces. There is a fantastic clock adorned with allegorical figures and strange birds and even stranger masks among a wealth of richly-scrolled architectural ornament. The

Tabernacle of porphyry, silver-gilt copper and crystal, made by Giovanni Giardini in Rome in 1711. Kunsthistorisches Museum, Vienna.

less richly ornamented designs are, however, still more arresting: curious fabrications which support fruit baskets, a tea-pot or a coffee-pot. The clouded backgrounds and low viewpoint give these objects a gargantuan super-human scale and anticipate the devices Giovanni Battista Piranesi was to use some forty years later in his views of the ruins of Rome.

Like so many other notable Italian goldsmiths, Giardini made use of hard stones like lapis lazuli, and base metals as well as gold and silver. In 1698 he was appointed bronze founder to the Papal government and in this capacity was responsible for casting a hundred bronze mortars for the defence of the Castel San Angelo. He was also given the task of casting J.-B. Théodon's reliefs for the monument to Queen Christina in St Peter's, begun in 1698 and finished in 1702.

Giardini was prosperous enough to buy a large vineyard at Tor di Quinto in 1702. And the inventory of his effects made after his death, on 31 December 1721, reveals a comfortable way of life. His house was well furnished and amply supplied with such luxuries as cushions covered in Lucchese silk. He had a collection of prints by Dürer, Stefano della Bella and others, several pictures including a portrait of Bernini, a Pietà by Domenichino, works by Benedetto Luti and Filippo Zucchetti and several pieces of sculpture – models for the monument to Queen Christina, a relief of putti by François Duquesnoy and a clay *bozzetto* of St Sebastian by Camillo Rusconi. A large quantity of silver is mentioned in the inventory. But, for the historian of silver, his most interesting possession was a pair of large low reliefs of gilt metal and lapis lazuli, modelled by Angelo Rossi and executed by 'Monsù Germano' – who may surely be identified with Thomas Germain.

Anthony Nelme

(fl. 1681–1722)

A very large number of pieces of silver survive bearing the mark of Anthony Nelme – a cursive *AN*. They are all of conspicuously high quality whether they are richly ornamented or severely plain. Nothing is known of Nelme personally, but he was clearly one of the leading London silversmiths of his time and probably at the head of a fairly large workshop. Extending from the early 1680s to the early 1720s, his career spanned a revolution in taste from the new St Paul's Cathedral to Colin Campbell's vast Palladian mansion, Wanstead Park. He saw his compatriots disentangle themselves from their flirtation with the Continental Baroque and settle down to a long period of staid Palladian domesticity which was to be enlivened only occasionally by a brief, if passionate, intrigue with the Rococo. And these changes in taste are sharply reflected in his silver.

Nelme's earliest works are in the Restoration style which, in silver as in furniture, derived from Holland. A covered cup of 1681 is delicately embossed around the base with acanthus leaves, the knob of the cover is similarly leafy, and the two gently springing handles are adorned with little human heads. It is of a type very popular during the reign of Charles II. Most of his other works of the period are also made to standard patterns, like a pair of sugar casters of 1683 now in the Manchester City Art Gallery.

In 1685 Nelme set up his shop at the sign of the Golden Bottle, Amen Corner, Ave Mary Lane, in the heart of the City. Here he was to work for the rest of his career, though he is known to have had a second shop in Foster Lane in 1691. He had clearly established himself in a position of some prominence among the London silversmiths. Significantly, he was given an important royal commission, for a pair of large silver gilt altar candlesticks for St George's Chapel, Windsor. These are the most impressive objects made in his workshop – more than 1 metre (40 inches) tall with richly balustered stems on boldly scrolling bases adorned with cherub heads, the emblems of the Order of the Garter and reliefs of St George and the Dragon. The authorship of the design is not recorded, but the cherub heads are close in style to the work of Grinling Gibbons, who was royal sculptor in wood at the time and might well have been called on to produce a model for such an important work. For although Nelme made several richly sculptured pieces in the 1690s none is comparable with the Windsor candlesticks. Others include a pair of domestic candlesticks supported by female figures, made to a design which originated in the 1660s and, curiously enough, came back into fashion a hundred years later. He also made at least two pairs of candlesticks supported by kneeling black slave boys which have an almost Venetian Rococo sophistication.

In the 1690s the London silversmiths were much concerned by the

above Silver-gilt altar candlestick made by Anthony Nelme for St George's Chapel Windsor, in 1694. The base is decorated by emblems of the Order of the Garter, and reliefs of St George and the Dragon.

opposite Silver tankard of 1683 by Anthony Nelme. Honourable Society of the Inner Temple.

Pair of candlesticks, supported by kneeling black slave boys, made by Anthony Nelme in 1697.

influx of Huguenot refugee craftsmen. According to Nelme and the royal goldsmiths, George and Francis Garthorne, and others who signed a petition to the King in 1697, the refugees used great quantities of solder in their wares (thus falsifying their weight in silver) and had persuaded certain venal English craftsmen to take their works to Goldsmiths' Hall and have them assayed as if they had been made by freemen of the Company. Such acts, the document states, 'will in all probability lead to the beggary and impoverishment of your petitioners'. But although these grievances were not entirely righted, and although the London silversmiths continued to complain of the decline in trade and the intrusion of foreigners, Nelme appears to have staved off the beggary he feared. He made plate for several of the greatest families of the realm. Between 1697 and 1704 he was employed to make silver articles for the Board of Ordnance – notably sets of snuffers and candlesticks, some of which still survive in higher government offices. And he secured the patronage of Queen Anne soon after her accession in 1702.

Although he protested at the invasion of Huguenot craftsmen, Anthony Nelme was by no means immune to their influence. Indeed, much of his surviving work is in what is known as the Huguenot style and he may well have employed French journeymen in his workshop. These pieces are decorated with cast (rather than embossed) ornament and cut card work (smooth bands and leaves which look as if they had been cut out of cardboard and stuck to the surface of the vessel). His most impressive performances in this manner are a pair of wine bottles, called 'Pilgrim bottles', of 1715 at Chatsworth. In 1703 he made in the same style a very handsome soup tureen which has been claimed as the

One of a pair of silver 'pilgrim' wine bottles made by Nelme in 1715. Chatsworth House, Derbyshire.

The head of a silver toaster made by Nelme in 1705 for Queen's College, Cambridge.

first produced in England. Nelme also appears to have been ready to make objects which normally lay outside the repertory of London silver-smiths – a saucepan, now at Trinity Hall, Cambridge; a toaster for toast-ing bread, also in a Cambridge College; and a censer shaped rather like an enlarged sugar caster.

But the most appealing and memorable of Nelme's works are those made during the last fifteen years of his career in the stark and almost aggressively simple Queen Anne style. His patrons probably demanded this plainness as a reaction against the richness of Baroque silver. A cult of simplicity began to manifest itself at the very beginning of the eighteenth century in England. And this desire for simplicity was by no means limited to the middle classes – Sarah, Duchess of Marlborough declared that she liked things to be 'clean and plain, from a wainscot to a lady's face'. Simplicity came to be regarded as a peculiarly English virtue in contrast with the frippery of France. Few silversmiths answered the

Inkstand made by Nelme in 1717.
Manchester City Art Gallery.

demand for plate of sterling solidity and simplicity, truth and lack of pretentiousness better than Nelme. His many teapots, hot-water jugs, inkstands, and even such larger objects as looking glasses, have an easy elegance of form and a beautifully smooth coherence which more than compensates for a want of applied decoration. The national qualities of English silver are seen at their best in such pieces, and it is hardly surprising that they have exerted so strong an appeal to English collectors.

In 1721 Anthony Nelme formed a partnership with his son Francis, who had become a freeman of the Goldsmiths' Company in 1719. When he died next year, Francis succeeded him, continuing to work at the sign of the Golden Bottle until 1727 when he moved to St Martin's, Ludgate. Francis made use of his father's patterns but is better known for more elaborate pieces, notably an enamelled gold cup of 1731 (in the Louvre) though its decorations may be later. He is recorded for the last time in 1759.

127

John Coney

(1655–1722)

John Coney was born on 5 January 1655, the eldest son of a John Coney who had been born in Boston, Lincolnshire, taken to America as a child by his mother and step-father and trained as a cooper in Boston, Massachusetts. Nothing is known of his early years, but he was almost certainly apprenticed to one of the two silversmiths then working in Boston, John Hall or Jeremiah Dummer whose sister-in-law he was later to marry. He had completed his training by the time he was twenty-one, and on 6 April 1676 a covered cup of his making was presented to the church of the First Parish in Concord, where it may still be seen. Next year he joined other 'Handycraftsmen, a very considerable part of the town of Boston' in signing a petition which demanded trade protection. At about this time he married his first wife, Sarah, who bore him two children both of whom died in infancy.

According to the Rev. Thomas Foxcroft, who preached his funeral sermon, Coney 'was a humble man; reserved and retired from the world in no little degree'. He played but a shadowy part in the life of the colony. The few scraps of available biographical information may be briefly summarized. By 1679 he is known to have been taking apprentices – a sure indication that he was fully employed. He married for the second time in 1683 and five years later was living in Court Street in Boston, near what is now Scollay Square. Light is thrown on his religious position by the presence of his name in 1689 among the subscribers for the King's Chapel which was described as 'a Church for God's worship in Boston, according to the constitution of the Church of England as by law established'. After the death of his second wife, who had four children, only one of whom survived infancy, he married in 1694 Mary Atwater, widow of John Clark and sister of Hannah who had married Jeremiah Dummer in 1672. She bore him a further six children. In 1699 he moved with his increasing family to a house near the town dock.

It is probable that Coney engraved the plates from which the first American bank notes were printed, and he was certainly responsible for those issued in 1702. That he should have been entrusted with this task reveals the esteem in which he was held: it also suggests his prosperity. A constant trickle of apprentices appears to have passed through Coney's workshop. The most interesting was the son of a couple of Huguenot settlers who arrived in Boston late in 1715 or early in 1716 – Apollos Rivoire, later to anglicize his name to Revere and father the more famous Paul. In 1717 Coney moved again, buying a house in Anne Street for the fairly large sum of £845.

John Coney died on 20 August 1722. In his funeral sermon the Rev. Thomas Foxcroft declared 'that he was a very blameless Liver, and that not many pass thro' the World with fewer Stains upon their reputation than he has done ... and I do believe him to have been an Israelite indeed,

Chocolate-pot inscribed on the base as the work of the Boston silversmith, John Coney. Museum of Fine Arts, Boston, Massachusetts.

I mean, a real & thoro' Christian; not one of those whose Religion lies in an empty Profession or in unregenerate Morality'. He also said that Coney 'had often spent much Time in serious Reading. His Bible was very much his study'.

The inventory of Coney's belongings drawn up after his death shows that he lived in comparative ease and comfort by the standards of Massachusetts Bay. His total estate was valued at £3,714 2s. 11d. including house and lands worth £2,516. In addition to his silversmith's equipment he had a stock of wrought plate assessed at £309 7s. 6d. besides gold worth £100. The contents of his wardrobe were valued at only £20 which suggests that he dressed with truly Puritan simplicity. But his house was well furnished. His bed had curtains, valence and bases of fustian worked with crewels, valued at £15, and he had two sets of damask curtains and valences (£26 10s. 0d.). Other furnishings included a clock-case (£18), a writing table, a walnut chest of drawers and table (£6), one large easy chair (few middle-class houses of the period had more, even in Europe) and many cane chairs.

Many pieces of silver made by Coney survive. The majority are drinking vessels, especially solid, squat tankards. His finest known work is the

above Tea-pot engraved with the arms of Jean Paul Mascarene, by John Coney. Metropolitan Museum, New York.

right Covered cup made for William Stoughton and engraved with his arms, by John Coney, *c.* 1692–1701. Harvard University.

Stoughton Cup given to Harvard University by William Stoughton who died at Dorchester, Massachusetts, in 1701. Stoughton was the lieutenant governor of Massachusetts from 1692 to 1701 and president at the trial of the Salem witches. Jean Paul Mascarene, who settled in the colony in 1709 and later became a major-general and lieutenant governor of Nova Scotia, appears to have been another of Coney's clients: his arms are engraved on a teapot by Coney now in the Metropolitan Museum. He also made candlesticks, coffee-pots, sugar casters, salvers, inkstands and sugar or sweetmeat boxes.

Stylistically all these pieces of silver derive from England. The simple tankards and sugar casters might easily be mistaken for English pieces. And even the more elaborate objects repeat English patterns. Sugar or sweetmeat boxes by Coney in the Boston Museum and the Currier Gallery of Art, Manchester, New Hampshire are very close indeed to one made in London in 1676. Like his contemporaries in the provincial cities of England, Coney appears to have been content to copy the silver made in the capital – and there can be little doubt that his clients wanted such imitations.

Sugar box by John Coney, who used this design, derived from an English prototype, on more than one occasion. Currier Gallery of Art, Manchester, New Hampshire.

Johann Zeckel

(c. 1660–1728)

When the travel writer Maximilian Misson, visited Augsburg in 1687 he noted that the craftsmen of the city were no less ingenious than those of Nuremberg, 'and even they excel particularly in Clock and Gold-smith's-work'. Augsburg was indeed maintaining its reputation as a centre for the production of *objets de luxe* which had been established in its more prosperous sixteenth-century hey-day when its leading citizens, the Fuggers, were probably the wealthiest bankers in Europe. It had been a very important trading city but, to quote Misson again: 'the Trade of Augsburg decay'd as that of Holland increas'd'. By the late seventeenth century Augsburg was owing its economic survival mainly to its crafts-men, especially silversmiths, whose delicate and sometimes very elaborate works were diffused throughout Europe.

Augsburg was an Imperial Free City with its own government and – what was very important in the seventeenth century – its own religious regulations. Half its senators were Lutherans and half Roman Catholics, and the various civic offices were held by members of each sect alternat-ively. Even the goldsmiths and silversmiths seem to have been divided between the two sects. The Roman Catholics specialized in ecclesiastical work. Lutherans – like members of the Biller family and the Drentwett family (one of whom made the showy silver throne for Queen Christina of Sweden, still in Stockholm) – naturally confined themselves to secular plate.

Johann Zeckel was one of the leading Roman Catholic silversmiths in the city. Born at Woykowitz (Waynganitz) in Moravia, he served his apprenticeship under Johann Veibyl in Vienna. He appears to have gone to Augsburg in about 1697 or 1698, and is said to have worked as a journeyman in the shop of Michael Mair for three years. Mair, who hailed from Thierhaupten near Neuburg an der Donau, had arrived in Augsburg in about 1670, worked under Philipp Saler until his death and then married his widow, thus obtaining admission to the guild. Among his assistants Mair employed Franz Ignaz Stadler who became an inde-pendent master, but died young. In 1691 Zeckel married Stadler's widow, Anna Maria, who was a member of the Saler family. It was by such complicated ties of marriage that the Augsburg silversmiths were bound together. But Anna Maria died and he married again in 1694. Zeckel soon became a prominent member of the goldsmiths' guild, serving as *Geschaumeister* (assay master) in 1703, 1706 and 1724–6, and as *Vorgeher* (president) from 1709–12 and again in 1715–16.

His most prominent work is a large monstrance more than 1 metre (40 inches) high made for the Bürgerkongregation of Ingolstadt in 1708 and still in the Bürgersaal of St Maria Victoria, Ingolstadt. This small church is a minor masterpiece of Bavarian Rococo with a ceiling painting – highly complicated in its iconography – by C.D. Asam.

Silver statue of St Joseph by Johann Zeckel, with enamels by Samuel Wolfgang 1709–10. Cathedral of Freiburg-in-Breisgau.

At first sight one might suppose that the monstrance was designed to fit it, but in fact the Bürgersaal is some twenty-five years later and was not begun until 1732. Similarly, it might be supposed that the very rich decorations on the monstrance were merely ornamental; but closer inspection reveals that it represents a hard fought naval battle – the battle of Lepanto – with Don John of Austria's banner flying high and the ship of the Turkish admiral floundering. Ships and men, guns, masts and rigging are all modelled with an astonishing attention to detail. Originally the monstrance was mounted on the back of a suitably abject kneeling Turk of solid gold adorned with pearls (the present rather ugly base dates from 1892). Various suggestions have been made about the authorship of the design and it seems likely that the painter Johann Rieger was responsible.

Silver reliquary bust of St Aquilinius made for the Marienkapelle, Würzburg, in about 1715.

Monstrance made by Johann Zeckel for the Bürgerkongregation of Ingolstadt in 1708. The relief depicts the battle of Lepanto. The base is late nineteenth century. St Maria Victoria, Ingolstadt.

Zeckel made several other monstrances though none as elaborate as that at Ingolstadt. One was in the Matthiaskirche in Breslau until World War II, others are in the Cathedral treasury at Mainz, at Fulda and at Beuggen. He also made such pieces of liturgical plate as silver covers for missals (a fine example of 1694 is in the Kreuzkirche at Augsburg) and, of course, chalices, patens, and ewers for wine and water. There are two ewers with an oval basin, of about 1714–16, in the Kreuzkirche Augsburg. These are all fine examples of late Baroque silver but no more distinguished than hundreds of others made in the same period. Zeckel is of interest mainly on account of his larger works.

In 1709–10 he made a silver statue of St Joseph one metre (40 inches) high for the Münster (Cathedral) of Freiburg in Breisgau. Standing in front of a sun-burst, the Saint holds his emblematic lily in his right hand and a shield in his left. The shield bears enamelled plaques of a view of Freiburg, the coats of arms of the Cathedral and State, and portraits of the reigning Emperor Joseph I and his brother King Karl, by the Augsburg enameller Samuel Wolfgang. It has been suggested that the figure was made after a model by Franz Xaver Hauser, a member of a family of sculptors working in Freiburg. Another prominent work by Johann Zeckel is a half-length figure of St Aquilinus made as a reliquary bust in about 1715 for the Marienkapelle, Würzburg. It is life-size and almost disturbingly life-like, with elegantly expressive hands and a knife sticking into his throat. The treatment of the ruffled linen sleeves and the fine brocade of the vestment is remarkably delicate. For the Catholic congregation of Fribourg in Switzerland, Zeckel made in 1716 a large silver crucifix, a statue of the Virgin and a set of six candlesticks, now in the Collège Cantonal St Michel.

Johann Zeckel died on 26 October 1728. Several Augsburg silversmiths of the name of Zeckel are recorded later in the century. Johann Michael, who married in 1722 and died in 1782, was perhaps his son. Johann Michael's son, Felix Anton (1730–93), was the father of Franz Xaver Zeckel, who was born in about 1770 and was making church plate in a classicizing style in the early years of the nineteenth century.

David Willaume

(1658–1741)

Wine cistern and fountain by David Willaume, 1708. Made for the 5th Earl of Meath but bought for George II when Prince of Wales. Collection of the Duke of Brunswick.

David Willaume, one of the most prolific and successful of the Huguenot refugee silversmiths in England, was born in 1658. There is some confusion about his place of birth, generally said to be Metz in Lorraine, though the registers of the church of La Patente in Soho describe him as *marchand orfèvre de la ville de Mers* – that is to say Mer en Blaisois between Orléans and Blois. It is not known when he left France or by what route he travelled to England. He is said to have arrived in 1674, and he almost certainly reached London some years before 1687. For in 1686 James II had already initiated measures against Huguenot refugees and his violently pro-Catholic policy would hardly have encouraged immigrants. But Willaume may well have owed the letters of denization granted him in December 1687 to the City's wish to oppose the King. In 1688 he registered his maker's mark – the initials DW with the fleur-de-lys which was incorporated in the marks of several other Huguenots, probably as a reminder of their French origin. He was admitted to the freedom of the Goldsmiths' Company in 1693. According to Sir Ambrose Heal he was trading at the sign of Windsor Castle, Charing Cross, between 1686 and 1690, and at the sign of the Golden Ball, Pall Mall, from 1697 to 1712. By 1720 he had moved to the Golden Ball in St James's Street where he also 'kept running cashes' – that is to say engaged in banking.

The fact that neither Willaume nor any of his dependants was obliged to draw a pension from the Royal Bounty Funds, established to help French refugees, suggests that he was from the beginning rather more prosperous than other Huguenot craftsmen. In 1690 he married Marie Mettayer. daughter of Samuel Mettayer, the minister of the French church in Crispin Street, Spitalfields. Marie's sister, Anne, was married to the engraver Simon Gribelin who had emigrated to England from Blois, worked as an engraver on gold and silver, published volumes of ornamental designs and also contributed illustrations to several books. Louis Mettayer, a son or grandson of the minister, was later apprenticed to David Willaume and became a silversmith of some note.

The most impressive pieces of plate which bear David Willaume's mark are a wine-cooler and fountain made for the fifth Earl of Meath in 1708, but later bought for the use of George II when Prince of Wales, and now in the collection of the Duke of Brunswick. They are exceptionally handsome examples of work in the Huguenot style with richly gadrooned borders and finely modelled cast-work – sea-horse handles on the cistern and lion masks on the fountain. Three other wine cisterns by Willaume have survived and he seems to have made something of a speciality of these weighty objects which were so popular in the early eighteenth century, though the majority were subsequently melted down. Among other large pieces there is a ewer and basin of 1706

Ewer made by David Willaume in
1706 for the Fishmongers' Company,
London.

Basin made by Willaume in 1706, to accompany the ewer reproduced on page 139. Fishmongers' Company, London.

belonging to the Fishmongers' Company.

Willaume's workshop was equally successful producing silver on a smaller scale. In the Victoria and Albert Museum there is a delicate helmet-shaped ewer of 1700 with cut-card decoration on the body and a sinuous mermaid as a handle. Sometimes the decorations are rather too heavy for the objects to which they are applied – as on a teapot of 1706 in the Manchester City Art Gallery – but a nice balance is generally maintained. The workshop also made much very simple plate, especially salvers and knives, forks and spoons. And the craftsmen probably gave much of their time to still more humdrum tasks. A long bill detailing work done for Lady Irwin of Temple Newsam in 1726 refers mainly to repairs and engraving of pieces of older plate: 'ingraving 2 soop Dishes 7s. Each ... 0:14:0, straitning boyling & burnishing 5s. Each ... 0:10:0'.

By 1709 David Willaume had amassed enough capital to buy a country place, Tingrith Manor in Bedfordshire, which he acquired from Sir Pynsent Chernock Bart., who had nearly ruined himself by contesting county elections with the Russell family. His son David seems to have been mainly in charge of the workshop at the sign of the Golden Ball from about 1716. The elder David Willaume appears to have died towards the end of 1741 and his will was proved on 22 January 1742.

DAVID WILLAUME

Teapot of 1706, with heavy cut-card decoration. Manchester City Art Gallery.

Knife, fork and spoon produced by Willaume's workshop in the first decade of the eighteenth century. Manchester City Art Gallery.

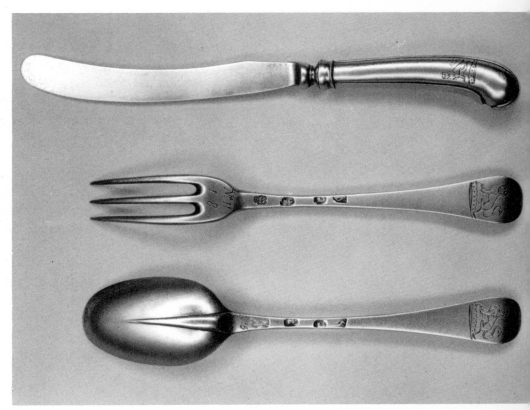

Johann Melchior Dinglinger (1664–1731)

In the Grünes Gewölbe (Green Vaults) in Dresden the visitor's eye is caught by what are probably the most extraordinary technical feats ever performed by a goldsmith – the works of Johann Melchior Dinglinger. They have been astounding visitors for two and a half centuries.

Dinglinger might well be described as the greatest of European goldsmiths. He is the last of those who worked successfully and on a large scale in the tradition established in the sixteenth century by Cellini and Wenzel Jamnitzer. And although he is usually called a Baroque craftsman, his works are closer in feeling to those of the Mannerists than to any paintings and sculptures by late seventeenth- or early eighteenth-century artists. He was much more fortunate than his predecessors in that all the major works he is known to have executed still survive intact. But as they are all in Dresden he has seldom received, outside Germany, the attention he merits.

The son of a cutler, he was born at Biberach an der Riss near Ulm, in Swabia, on 26 December 1664. He thus grew up in a land slowly recovering from the devastation of the Thirty Years War. In 1680 he was apprenticed to Johann Georg Schopper in Ulm. As son of a master craftsman he had to serve no more than four years' apprenticeship, to be followed by a period of *Wanderschaft* when he was a journeyman in the literal as well as the metaphorical sense of the word. It is not known where he went at this time. A visit to Paris has been suggested; but this is improbable as he was a Protestant and the persecution of non-Catholics was raging in France at that moment. He may, however, have gone to Vienna, then a notable centre for the goldsmith's craft, where his younger brother, Georg Christoph, was later to be trained.

By 1693 Dinglinger had settled in Dresden. He installed himself in the goldsmiths' guild by marrying in 1696 the daughter of the court goldsmith Moritz Rachel, a man who, after working in many places throughout Germany and visiting France and England, became *Hofgoldschmied* (court goldsmith) to a succession of four Electors of Saxony. It is fairly clear that Dinglinger was more prosperous than most journeymen. The year after his marriage he bought a house in the Frauengasse from his father-in-law for 4,000 thalers and was promptly entered in the Dresden *Bürgerbuch*. In 1698 he was appointed *Hofjuwelier* (court jeweller) by Augustus the Strong, for whom he was to work for the rest of his life.

There seems to have been a bond of sympathy between the Elector and the goldsmith. One can hardly doubt that the fantasies which Dinglinger realized in gold and enamel and precious stones and on which Augustus lavished such vast sums of money were the result of long and perhaps euphoric discussions between them. The extravagance of the Elector was notorious; it was said that his passion for Chinese porcelain brought the state to the brink of ruin.

Portrait of Johann Melchior Dinglinger, engraved by J. G. Wolffgang after A. Pesne in 1722. Kupferstichkabinett, Dresden.

Dish of gold set with jewels and ivory depicting dwarves playing with a goat. Grünes Gewölbe, Dresden.

So far as is known, Dinglinger made no attempt to rival his master's famous progeny – 365 bastards. But in five marriages he fathered no fewer than twenty-six children. Portraits suggest that he had the appearance of a court functionary rather than a craftsman. That painted by Antoine Pesne in 1722 shows him dressed in fur hat and fur-trimmed coat, fat and prosperous with eyes as bright as the jewels he so dexterously set in gold. In his left hand he holds, and with his right he points proudly to, one of his more portable, but hardly less extravagant creations, the *Dianabad*. Portraits of his last two wives make them look like high court ladies, dressed in eddying swirls of silk or satin.

Documents amply confirm the impression given by the portraits. His first wife, on her death in 1705, left a quantity of personal jewellery – rings, crosses, diamonds and especially pearls. His house in the Frauengasse, with a splendid Baroque fountain in the courtyard, was handsomely furnished. The rooms were tapestried and filled with objects. He had a large collection of shells, then very fashionable, two cupboards full of prints and a library rich in the classics as well as pattern books and travel books, many of which included accounts of the Orient. Czar Peter the Great of Russia visited Dinglinger here in 1711 and was so taken with the house that on returning to Dresden next year lodged with him for a week, accompanied by a guard of twelve and their corporal. The Czar called it 'the perfect specimen of a commodious dwelling house' and had a wooden model of it sent to Russia. But he may well have been more impressed by the gadgets than the planning.

Dinglinger was clearly fond of gadgets. On the top of his house, to quote Keyssler, there was 'a cistern, which one man, by means of a machine placed below in the yard, fills with water in a very short time; and from this reservoir the water is distributed all over the house. On the staircase at every landing there is a brass cock with two leathern buckets, so that in case of fire there is water at hand to be carried into any part of the house where it is wanted.' In the early years of the eighteenth century such a household water-supply was very rare if not unique. The leads of the house served as an observatory and Dinglinger kept a collection of telescopes and mathematical instruments in an upper room.

Few other goldsmiths or jewellers of the day can have lived in such style as Dinglinger. Yet unlike the majority of his successful contemporaries – David Willaume in England or even Thomas Germain in Paris – he clearly owed his position more to his own manual dexterity than an ability to manage a large workshop and satisfy a wide variety of clients. He worked exclusively for the Elector and his production was consequently limited.

His earliest recorded work is a little pendant of St George and the Dragon, of enamelled gold set with precious stones, made for the Elector

The golden coffee set – Dinglinger's first major work for the Elector Augustus, in 1701. It includes ivory statuettes, enamelled cups and crystal flasks. Grünes Gewölbe, Dresden.

Johann Georg IV on whom the Order of the Garter had been conferred by William III of England in 1692. He was to make other pieces of jewellery throughout his career: sword-hilts, buckles, aigrettes, pendants and so on. But in the last years of the seventeenth century he seems to have been employed mainly on *Kabinettstücke* objects of precious materials made for display in the treasury. Several covered cups and flasks of hard stone set in enamelled gold date from this period. He also made gem-encrusted gold waistbands and feathered hats for two ebony statuettes of Moors and an ebony black boy leading an ivory camel, carved by the court sculptor Balthasar Permoser.

Dinglinger's first major work for the Elector Augustus was executed in 1701 and is modestly called 'the golden coffee set' – a Baroque mountain of silver gilt on which are perched, among ivory statuettes, a set of enamelled gold cups, dishes, sugar-basins, crystal flasks and, at the summit, a preposterous coffee-pot with a dragon spout and snakey handle. The superstructure may be removed to reveal a group of Turks enjoying a coffee party. Each of the four cups and saucers is painted inside and out to simulate porcelain (though no porcelain of such fineness had yet been made in Europe).

right Detail from *The Grand Mogul's Birthday Party* started in 1702 by J. M. Dinglinger. It shows one of the potentates bringing his birthday gift to the Grand Mogul. Grünes Gewölbe, Dresden.

opposite Detail from the base of the 'Bath of Diana'. Grünes Gewölbe, Dresden.

below The 'Bath of Diana', an ornamental cup executed in 1704 by J. M. Dinglinger, incorporating an ivory statuette of Diana by Balthasar Permoser. Grünes Gewölbe, Dresden.

As soon as the coffee service was finished he began work on *The Grand Mogul's Birthday*, a decorative group of 132 exquisitely modelled figures of men and animals not to mention 33 vases, cups and other objects, all set in an architectural framework of stairs and balustrades and arches. It occupies a square metre and is made of gold and silver-gilt, enamels, precious and semi-precious stones. So far as it represents anything other than a vision of oriental splendour, the group shows potentates bringing to the Grand Mogul their birthday presents, each of which is carried by a pair of African or Asian servants. Dinglinger derived designs for individual details from a number of books of travels, but the general conception derives from his own, and probably the Elector's, imaginative fantasy. It is a masterpiece of chinoiserie – the realization of a European dream of the riches and oddity of the East, in which Chinese, Japanese, Indian and even Egyptian motifs are jostled together with an engaging disrespect for cultural frontiers. Dinglinger's brothers, Georg Friedrich and Georg Christoph, were among the assistants he employed on this work.

While the Grand Mogul piece was being fabricated, Dinglinger made his *Dianabad* in 1704. Though no more than 38 cm. (15 inches) high it is incredibly rich, consisting of an ivory statuette of Diana by Permoser and a chalcedony bowl set in a mesh of enamelled gold and silver studded with diamonds and hung with pearls. The bowl is supported on the curving horns of a stag's head: there are dogs and dolphins, bullrushes and other plants. In subsequent years Dinglinger made several other objects of this type. One has as its main motif Hercules wrestling with the Nemean lion, another a group of Callot-like dwarves cavorting around a goat. He also set a particularly fine antique cameo of Tiberius on a plinth, at the base of which he posed ivory statuettes by Balthasar Permoser.

opposite and below The Obeliscus Augustalis, completed by Dinglinger in 1722. In the centre of the base, he incorporated an enamel portrait of Augustus the Strong. Grünes Gewölbe, Dresden.

overleaf The Grand Mogul's Birthday Party, an exotic fantasy made of gold, silver, enamels and precious stones by J. M. Dinglinger for Augustus the Strong. Grünes Gewölbe, Dresden.

The 'Obeliscus Augustalis' which Dinglinger finished by 1722 is one of his most successful productions. It is 228 cm. (89 inches) high consisting of a slender obelisk faced with engraved gems by C. Hübner on a base incorporating sphinxes, Negro busts and a riot of architectural motifs with an enamel portrait of Augustus the Strong by Georg Friedrich Dinglinger in the centre. On either side stand two pieces of chalcedony set with antique and modern gems, and in front statuettes of Orientals and seated soldiers derived from the prints of Salvator Rosa. On a somewhat smaller scale there are three cameos set in elaborate mounts and representing the three ages of man as spring, high summer and winter. Most of the imagery is classical but the central piece incorporates monkeys somewhat in the style of Jean Bérain and such *Commedia dell'Arte* figures as harlequin and columbine. The cameos were carved by C. Hübner and G. Kirchner to Dinglinger's design.

left The Apis Altar – an Egyptian fantasy – J.M. Dinglinger's last work for Augustus. Grünes Gewölbe, Dresden.

His last work is in some ways the most extraordinary of all – an Egyptian fantasy called the Apis Altar. It is in the form of a casket, adorned with cameos, statuettes, funerary vases and flat enamel paintings, surmounted by a tall obelisk closely covered with hieroglyphics. He derived the design of details from engravings in travel books and archaeological works, some of which he followed very closely. But once again he combined them in an entirely fantastic manner. The Apis Altar is, indeed, the most elaborate and – if one excludes Piranesi's later Egyptian room in the English Café in Rome, known only from engravings – the most successful eighteenth-century essay in *Egyptiennerie*.

below A detail of the centre of Apis Altar showing a sacrificial animal being transported by boat.

Dinglinger made his will on 5 March 1731, and died next day. He was buried with appropriate pomp in the Bohemian cemetry. Augustus the Strong survived him by no more than two years.

Thomas Germain

(1673–1748)

Voltaire immortalised the name of Thomas Germain in one of his best known poems, *Les Vous et les Tu*, listing

> *… ces plats si chers que Germain*
> *A gravés de sa main divine*

among objects then in the height of extravagant fashion – Savonnerie carpets, *vernis-martin* cabinets, Japanese vases, diamond ear-rings – which he valued less than one of the kisses 'Philis' had given him when she was young. The context could hardly be more appropriate. Germain was a consummate master of the Rococo style which so often evokes the charms of a society devoted mainly to the pursuit of love and kisses. But although it has an element of delicate eroticism, the Rococo – like the early work of Voltaire – also has its more serious side. For it was not simply the product of a distaste for pomposity and desire for frivolity but an expression of fundamental aesthetic demands: hence its enduring appeal and fascination. The career of Thomas Germain, who might be called one of the 'creators' of the Rococo, helps to show how it developed.

Born in 1673, he came from a family of goldsmiths. His father, Pierre Germain, was born in 1645, became a maître in 1667, but died young in 1684. Though employed to make grandiose pieces of silver for Louis XIV, Pierre lived very modestly. An inventory reveals that the richest of his rooms was hung with a common 'verdure' tapestry and furnished only with six chairs and one tapestry-covered armchair. He owned seven pictures valued at no more than twenty-seven livres. But he also had a collection of prints and some illustrated books which may have exerted some influence on the young Thomas: they included Serlio's treatise on architecture, a volume mysteriously described as a 'livre d'architecture de Léonard de Vincy', and a volume of designs of vases in the antique taste by Jacques Stella and Georges Charmeton. Pierre left no fortune and Thomas was taken under the care of his maternal grandfather who was a hatter.

French silversmiths were faced with great difficulties as commissions from the Crown fell off in the 1680s. It may have been for this reason that Thomas began his artistic career studying under a painter, Louis Boullogne the younger. But he was soon sent to Rome, probably by the minister Louvois, who is said to have 'protected' him. The date of his journey is uncertain but he probably travelled with Pierre Bedeau, a protégé of Louvois, who was certainly in Rome before 1687 and possibly before the end of 1685. (The earliest biographical account of Germain, in the 1719 edition of Orlandi's *Abecedario*, states that he went to Rome in 1685 at the age of twelve.)

La Teulière, the director of the French Academy in Rome, in a letter of 15 January 1692 told the Marquis de Villacerf – the *Surintendant des*

Surtout de table made by Thomas Germain in 1730, but later altered by his son, François-Thomas Germain. It was made for a very rich Portuguese nobleman, the Duke of Aveiro, whose property was sequestrated by the King of Portugal in 1750, when he was barbarously executed for treason. Museu Nacional de Arte Antigua, Lisbon.

155

THOMAS GERMAIN

Bâtiments – that Germain was able to draw and model quite well but did not paint at all and was working under a goldsmith in Rome. He recommended that Germain should be given a pension in Paris where *orfèvrerie* was on a better footing. In Rome, this stern opponent of the Baroque declared, 'tous les beaux-arts languissent'.

But Germain stayed on in Rome. By 1695 he was recorded in the house of a Bavarian goldsmith, Giovanni Paolo Bendel, for whom he may well have been working earlier. He was among the very large number of artists – more than a hundred in all – employed on the elaborate altar of St Ignatius in the Church of the Gesù. In December 1695 La Teulière said that Germain and another Frenchman, Antoine Cordier, were to 'réparer' the bronze decorations which suggests that they were responsible for chasing and finishing them after they had been cast. The archives of the church reveal that he collaborated with F. Reiff on the silver, bronze and hardstone crucifix, that he assisted in making a portable ladder of silver, and that he worked on the bronze relief of the liberation of prisoners (by P.-E. Monnot) and the very handsome lamps on the balustrade.

Little is known about his other works in Rome, though he was active as an independent silversmith from 1697 when he agreed to make a monthly payment to the guild church of St Eligio as a foreigner working in the city. His only surviving works in silver which date from this period are two reliefs which he made in 1700 for the reliquary of St Lupus in Sens Cathedral: they show the saint curing the sick and stopping the burning of the city of Melun. Possibly because they were made for France, they are in a much more restrained style than the bronze decorations on the altar of St Ignatius. But like that other creator of Rococo ornament who was in Rome at the same time, G.–M. Oppenordt, he had obtained first-hand experience of the late Baroque style which served as the base for his subsequent development.

Germain returned to France by 1706 when he made a silver censer for the chapel at Fontainebleau. Though Louis XIV's ban on the use of silver in private houses was not strictly enforced, commissions for domestic silver must still have been limited and Germain seems to have specialized in ecclesiastical work. His most important pieces of this period were a silver-gilt monstrance and a gilt copper altar set (crucifix and six candlesticks) for Notre Dame in Paris. At the end of January 1720 he was received as a *maître orfèvre* and three months later married Anne Denise Gauchelet, daughter of a goldsmith. Apartments in the Louvre were granted him in 1723 when he was listed with Nicolas Besnier and Claude II Ballin as *orfèvres du Roi*.

For the coronation of Louis XV in 1722 Germain made a large monstrance for the young King to give to Rheims Cathedral. It was destroyed in 1790 but a glowing account of it published in the *Mercure de France* in 1722 reveals that it incorporated symbols of the four Evangelists and statuettes of two angels holding the royal crown and sword.

From this time until the end of his life Thomas Germain was extensively employed in making silver and gold objects for the King, who declared early in his reign that he wished to be served at table with as much pomp as his grandfather. The inventories show that from 1728 Germain supplied a few pieces practically every month – golden mustard pots and the small covered dishes called écuelles, silver candlesticks, sconces, plates, dishes, even chamber-pots (engraved with the legend *Enfans de France*) in glittering profusion. Whenever the royal *ébénistes*, Gaudreau or Joubert, delivered a bureau, Germain had to provide an inkstand to go with it. Every time a prince or princess was born, Germain made its rattle. When Marie Leczinska arrived as Queen in 1726, Germain produced her silver-gilt toilette. Ten years later when the

Écuelle by Thomas Germain 1733–4. Although he is best known for more exuberantly Rococo pieces of silver, Germain appears to have produced many simpler articles of this type. Musée du Louvre, Paris.

left Wine cooler by Thomas Germain, one of a pair made in 1727–8. Musée du Louvre, Paris.

right Salt-cellar by Thomas Germain, one of a pair made in 1734–6. The naturalistically rendered tortoise, scallop and crab recall the works of Wenzel Jamnitzer, executed one hundred and fifty years earlier. Musée du Louvre, Paris.

Dauphin passed from the hands of the court ladies to a tutor, Germain supplied the silver for his apartment – seventy-nine pieces in the first batch with a canteen of cutlery to follow. The inventories dwell almost lovingly on the details of decoration on these hundreds of objects – shells and shellfish, leaves and flowers, lion-masks and lion-feet.

He did not, however, work exclusively for the King. One of his most celebrated pieces was a gold chalice with figures in relief, made for the Elector of Cologne and inspected by his nephews, the princes of Bavaria, in Germain's workshop in 1725. He made toilettes for the King of Portugal in 1725, the princesses of Brazil in 1727, the Queen of Spain in 1728 and the King and Queen of Naples in 1732–3. Nor did he limit his services to royalty; the Viscount Bateman was among his clients and a teapot he made for him is now in the Louvre.

The King of Portugal was the most notable of his foreign patrons. In the early years of the eighteenth century the Portuguese had bought domestic silver in England and church plate in Rome. He received his first order from the King of Portugal in 1728 and in the course of the next forty years some 3,000 pieces of silver are said to have been sent from the Germain workshop to the palace in Lisbon. Germain also supplied other Portuguese patrons, notably the very rich Duke of Aveiro for whom he made a magnificent *surtout de table* (that is to say a table-centre which was primarily decorative but might also include receptacles for sweet-meats, sugar, oil-bottles and so on), decorated with greyhounds and hunting horns and putti, which was seized by the King, subsequently altered and is now in the Museu Nacional de Arte Antigua, Lisbon – perhaps the finest surviving eighteenth-century piece of its kind.

Portrait of Thomas Germain and his wife, by Nicolas de Largillière, 1736. Gulbenkian Foundation, Lisbon.

In addition to directing his workshop, which must have been fairly large, Germain played an active part in the civic life of Paris. He was elected a city councillor and alderman in 1738 and re-elected in 1741 but was then ennobled and styled an *écuyer*. In 1741 he began to build to his own design and at his own expense a small church which was dedicated to St Louis du Louvre and consecrated in 1744. It had a relief by the sculptor Pigalle over the door and ornaments carved by Jean-Baptiste Robillon. Blondel published a full description and engravings of the church in 1754, but it was pulled down in 1810.

In addition to his apartments in the Louvre, said to be the best of those occupied by artists, Germain had a separate workshop in Paris which he bought in 1743 on the corner of rue des Orties and rue de Matignon. He was clearly prosperous and a portrait by Nicolas de Largillière shows him and his wife to be well dressed though distinctly bourgeois. But he seems to have lived nearly as simply as his father. His apartment was modestly furnished and hung with a few pictures including a pair of views of Rome. He had a large collection of prints and a library of 450 books, including a volume of prints of the *Loggie* in the Vatican and Juste-Aurèle Meissonnier's famous set of designs. Yet at his death on 14 August 1748 he left hardly any fortune. He may well have spent all his savings on the church of St Louis du Louvre where he was buried.

The direction of the Germain workshop passed to his fourth son, François-Thomas (b. 1726), who was promptly made a master of the guild, allowed to take over his father's apartment in the Louvre and appointed *sculpteur orfèvre* to the King. Work continued on major commissions which had not been completed, notably a very elaborate lamp for the church of St Geneviève (1744–54). Supplies for the Crown were kept up – tablewares, chandeliers, inkstands, chapel furnishing and more rattles for royal babies. Among the more elaborate pieces there was a *surtout de table* and set of tureens for the King to give to the Nabob of Golconda. According to a contemporary, the covers of the tureens were decorated with artichokes 'negligently thrown down', leaves which 'perfectly imitated nature' and other ornaments 'aussi riches que recherchés'.

These vast quantities of silver could not have been produced without the assistance of a large staff. François-Thomas is said to have employed between sixty and eighty workmen at a time. And, of course, many tasks like gilding and engraving were executed by independent craftsmen. It therefore seems probable that Thomas Germain, at the height of his success, and later François-Thomas limited their own activities to designing and overseeing. Only one of the important pieces, and no more than a handful of simpler objects, executed under Thomas have survived. But a comparison between these and the very much larger number of pieces marked with the initials of François-Thomas reveals little difference in quality and less in style.

Biscuit box, in the form of a ship, made for the King of Portugal by François-Thomas Germain, who took over his father's workshop in 1748, and continued to use some of his patterns. Museu Nacional de Arte Antigua, Lisbon.

Despite the change in taste, the demand for Germain silver in the Rococo style seems to have shown no sign of slackening. François-Thomas declared that his turnover in 1765 amounted to more than 2,500,000 livres. He was, none the less, faced with financial difficulties. And although he attributed his plight to the machinations of rivals, there is little doubt that he was himself largely responsible. He lived extravagantly. And, like the stock libertine of fiction, combined profligacy with parsimony. Police records reveal that for a time he enjoyed the favours of Mlle Hughes of the Comédie Italienne. She was followed by the less expensive Mlle Maisonville, daughter of a second-hand dealer, whom he kept on a miserable allowance of ten louis a month. In 1763 he tried to save the situation by marrying an heiress who brought him a *dot* of 80,000 livres – but this was not enough. Initial extravagance had driven him into the hands of money lenders whose demands for interest sank him still deeper in debt. Although he floated a company in a final attempt to save himself he was declared bankrupt on 27 June 1765, owing 2,400,000 livres. As a result he was turned out of his apartments in the Louvre and dismissed from his post as a royal goldsmith. Perhaps encouraged by the change in taste, he began to produce copies of antique vases made of a glassy substance which resembled various hard stones – but without much commercial success. In 1768 he went to try his fortune in London. He was back in Paris in 1772 appealing to the King and the minister, Marigny: both were inexorable. Pathetically in 1776 he wrote to Voltaire who had immortalized his father – but Voltaire, describing himself as 'an old man of eighty-two, overwhelmed by illness and ready to quit the miseries of the world' could do nothing. Three years later he was living in the Marais vainly trying to regain some furniture he had left in the Louvre. Then he sank into complete obscurity and no more was heard of him until his death on 24 January 1791.

Paul de Lamerie

(1688–1751)

Paul de Lamerie is the best known English silversmith and some of the finest pieces of English Rococo silver were made in his workshop. But he was very prolific and, in fact, many of the objects which bear his mark are in no way superior to those produced by several of his contemporaries. He was a highly typical rather than an outstanding figure and his well-documented biography is of interest for the light it sheds on the London silver trade in general as much as for the information it provides about him as an individual.

He was born in 1688 (baptized on 14 April) at 's Hertogenbosch in Holland, the son of Huguenot parents who spelt their name de la Marie and had apparently left France as religious refugees in the early 1680s. His father, Paul Souchay de la Marie, belonged to the *petite noblesse* and having served as an officer in the French army was accepted in the service of the United Provinces in 1686. The family moved to England in the wake of William III and had settled in the parish of St James's, Westminster, by 1691. Ten years later the father was receiving half-a-crown a day pension from the Royal Bounty Fund for French Refugees. He dropped the Souchay from his name, which he now spelt Delamerie, but did not abandon his pretensions to aristocracy.

On 6 August 1703 Paul, now aged fifteen, was articled to 'Peter Plattell Citizen and Goldsmith of London for the term of seven years'. Platel, who waived the fee normally paid by a father on having his son apprenticed, was similarly a Huguenot and a member of the minor nobility. Having completed his apprenticeship, Paul de Lamerie was made free of the Goldsmiths' Company 'by service' and a freeman of the City of London on 4 February 1712. Next day he registered his mark declaring that his shop was in Windmill Street, near Haymarket, where he was to remain until 1738 when he moved to Gerrard Street.

From 1712 onwards de Lamerie's life seems to have been that of a successful London tradesman. In 1716 he was appointed a goldsmith to the King. Next year he married Louisa Juliott, the daughter of another member of the Huguenot nobility. He was now rated for two houses in Windmill Street, one of which was presumably his dwelling and the other his workshop. Also in 1717 he was admitted to the Livery of the Goldsmiths' Company, of which he was to become a member of the governing body in 1731, serving as fourth warden in 1743 and second warden in 1747. The dishonesty of an apprentice involved him in a legal action in 1722 from which it emerges that he kept an open shop and dealt in jewellery as well as plate.

Some indication of de Lamerie's financial position is given by the Sun Insurance Office assessment of his property in 1728. His stock in trade of wrought plate was valued at £800, his household goods at £200 and wearing apparel at £100 (presumably including the clothes of his wife

Silver-gilt cup and cover made in 1737 by Paul de Lamerie, who made use of the same design on at least one other occasion. The Fishmongers' Company, London.

and children). Five years later he began to invest in real estate. His mother lived with him but his father appears to have been estranged and when he died in 1735 was buried as a pauper. Of his six children only three girls survived infancy. One, Susanna, married in 1750 Joseph Debaufre, the son and grandson of Huguenot refugee watchmakers. Another, Mary, stayed at home and was rewarded with £500 in de Lamerie's will. De Lamerie made his will on 24 May 1751 and died on 1 August.

As he had no son or colleague to succeed him, de Lamerie directed that his stock should be sold by auction. Two sales were held and the advertisement for the first, on 27 January 1752, lists: 'Tables, Terreens and covers, Bread-Baskets, Sauce-Boats, Tea-Kettles, Tea-Chests, Cannisters, Coffee-pots, Figure and other candlesticks, Girandoles, Cases of Knives, Forks and spoons, Cups and covers, Tankards, Mugs, Salts, Tea-spoons &c. all enriched and finish'd in the highest taste'. Watches and jewellery were also included in the sale. Brief as it is, the list gives some indication of the range of de Lamerie's production (though it is, of course, possible that some of the articles had been made by other silver-smiths and were merely being marketed by de Lamerie).

Wine cistern made by Paul de Lamerie for the 1st Earl Gower in 1719. More than a metre (about 40 ins) wide, this is one of de Lamerie's largest surviving works. Minneapolis Institute of Arts.

The sale list and also the insurance assessment of 1728 show that de Lamerie kept a large supply of wrought silver in stock. This is of some interest for it reveals that whereas most continental silversmiths were still working mainly to fulfil commissions given them either by individual clients or by middlemen, de Lamerie and his contemporaries in England were already practising a system which was to facilitate the industrialization of the trade. This practice may also have had some influence on the design of silver and account for the stylistic conservatism of the vast majority of pieces made in eighteenth-century England. For the silversmith working for stock rather than to order is bound to play safe. It seems probable that de Lamerie's more ornate and, of course, largest pieces were made to answer specific orders, while the very large quantity of simpler plate which bears his mark was intended for sale over the counter to the casual buyer.

De Lamerie began by working in the two styles popular in early eighteenth-century England – the starkly unornamented Queen Anne fashion and the Huguenot style with much gadrooning, cut-card ornament and heavy cast work. Within a decade he began to attract commissions from some of the richest noblemen. His most impressive work of this period is probably the vast wine-cistern made for the first Earl Gower in 1719 and now in the Minneapolis Institute of Arts. Seven years later he made a wine cistern of similar proportions for the fourth Earl of Scarsdale, now in the Hermitage Museum, Leningrad. Though slightly old-fashioned by Parisian standards, these pompously magnificent works show that de Lamerie, like other Huguenot craftsmen, had kept up with artistic developments in France after their exile. Both pieces must have been ordered and made to designs approved by the clients.

The simpler pieces of plate made in de Lamerie's workshop throughout his career conform to designs established early in the eighteenth century – tankards, teapots, coffee-pots, salvers, communion vessels. But many of them are decorated with engravings which gave them a more fashionable appearance. Such work was, of course, executed by independent engravers. And the elaborate allegorical engraving on the finest of de Lamerie's salvers – that made from the second Exchequer seal for Sir Robert Walpole and now in the Victoria and Albert Museum in London – has plausibly been attributed to William Hogarth. But if de Lamerie did not himself execute the engraved decorations on his plate, he presumably selected the engraver and approved his design. And as the asymmetrical scrolls and shells of the French Rococo make one of their earliest appearances in England on a fruit dish by de Lamerie hallmarked 1734, he may be given some credit for introducing the style. (Unless, as is possible, this dish was engraved some years after it was assayed.)

Tankard made by Paul de Lamerie, 1716. He continued to make vessels nearly as simple as this throughout his career.

By the 1730s, however, de Lamerie was producing cast and embossed plate in an individual version of the Rococo style. His most interesting works in this manner are covered cups, one of which is dated 1737 and belongs to the Fishmongers' Company in London. Though distinctly Rococo in general appearance, its decorative motifs derive from three earlier sources. The guilloche band running down the front comes from Roman architectural ornament, possibly by way of late seventeenth-century French pattern books. The alarmingly realistic snakes weaving their scaly bodies in and out of the bowl to serve as handles are reminiscent of the sixteenth-century 'rustic' style and especially the work of Wenzel Jamnitzer. But the smooth decorations on the cover and base are in the auricular style of the van Vianens.

Ewer by Paul de Lamerie made in 1724 and engraved with the arms of George Treby. It forms part of a large toilet set.
Ashmolean Museum, Oxford.

above Fruit dish by Paul de Lamerie, 1734. Ashmolean Museum, Oxford.

left Ewer by Paul de Lamerie, 1741, one of several pieces made for the Worshipful Company of Goldsmiths to replace older plate that had been melted down. Goldsmiths' Company, London.

Covered cup by Paul de Lamerie, 1742. De Lamerie made use of this design on more than one occasion; there is another in the collection of Mr and Mrs Joseph S. Atha, Kansas City. Minneapolis Institute of Arts.

Ewer and dish by Paul de Lamerie, 1740. There is a gilt bronze dish made to the same design in the Cleveland Museum of Art. Collection of Viscountess Galway.

A group of covered cups dated from 1739 to 1742 is rather closer in feeling to French work of the same time. Yet here the very rich decorations seem to have been applied to mask as much as to embellish vessels of standard early eighteenth-century form. De Lamerie was rather more successful with a very rich ewer and basin made for the Goldsmiths' Company in 1741, especially the ewer which has a finely modelled triton handle and a richly scrolled base reminiscent of Meissonnier. But overall design is wholly integrated with decoration only on a delicately asymmetrical plate in the form of a low-relief seascape with a triton emerging from the waves and blowing his horn (collection of the Viscountess Galway, Dorchester).

Most of de Lamerie's products of the later 1740s are decorated, if sometimes rather sparsely, with Rococo motifs. A tea-kettle and bread basket of 1745, apparently made for David Franks of Philadelphia (now in the Metropolitan Museum, New York), are good examples of his work at this time. But he does not appear to have made any pieces as bold or as rich as those dating from the years on either side of 1740. One is therefore bound to ask whether the most interesting pieces which bear his mark – like the Goldsmiths' ewer – were not the work of some exceptionally gifted assistant, possibly a foreigner. Several very able foreign silversmiths were active in London at this time, notably Charles Kandler, a somewhat mysterious figure known only by a few pieces of Rococo silver of uninhibited fantasy. But whereas Kandler's works are wholly Continental in feeling, de Lamerie's usually display a touch of English gaucherie – hence, perhaps, their perennial appeal to English collectors.

Juste-Aurèle Meissonnier

(1695–1750)

Wine-cooler, engraving by Huquier after a design by Juste-Aurèle Meissonnier, the earliest of the dated designs in Meissonnier's book.

When, in 1754, Charles-Nicholas Cochin launched what is certainly the wittiest as well as the most deadly of attacks on the Rococo, he singled out for special blame the goldsmith, architect, ornamental engraver and – in all senses of the term – master of fireworks, Juste-Aurèle Meissonnier.

Born in Turin in 1695, Juste-Aurèle Meissonnier was the son of Stephen Meissonnier, a goldsmith of Provençal origin. A document of August 1705 lists Stefano Mesonier aged forty-five, his wife Antonia aged thirty-three, and their son Giust' Aurelio aged ten, living in casa Quaglia, isola San Gaetano, Turin. Little is known of the father except that in 1723 he was mentioned as a native of Aix in a list of foreign craftsmen active in Turin. In 1727 he was working on a set of candlesticks presented by the King of Sardinia to the Pope, and in 1734 he was paid for a monstrance made for the church of Superga. The last reference suggests that he was one of the craftsmen employed by Filippo Juvarra, the director of all artistic enterprises at the Piedmontese court from 1714 until 1735. Juvarra, who came from a family of Sicilian silversmiths, was not only an architect – the greatest of his day in Italy – but also an interior decorator, and designer of both furniture and silver, working in a highly developed Baroque style which hovers with dragon-fly lightness on the verge of the Rococo. There can be little doubt that he exerted a profound and lasting influence on the work of Juste-Aurèle Meissonnier.

Juste-Aurèle's earliest recorded works were dies for coins for which he was paid 300 lire on the 6 April 1715. (The documents which provide this information describe him as an 'engraver in steel'; but Italian coin engravers were usually silversmiths as well.) The coins in question are no more distinguished than others minted by the House of Savoy at the same period and hardly indicate the direction in which the young artist's talents were to develop. He left Turin for Paris in about 1720 and it is tempting to suggest that he may have accompanied Juvarra, who made a journey to Lisbon, London and Paris in 1719–20.

In Paris he seems to have established himself very quickly. His published works include an engraved design for a wine-cooler made for 'M. le Duc' in 1723 (presumably Louis Duc d'Orléans, son of the Régent). In 1724 he was admitted to the mastership of the goldsmiths' and silversmiths' guild, by patent as a royal goldsmith working at the Gobelins. In December 1725 he succeeded the younger Bérain as *Dessinateur de la chambre et du cabinet du roi.* . . . The design he presented on this occasion, and on the merits of which he was appointed, was for a grandiose firework display to celebrate the young King Louis xv's recovery from an illness. Three years later Meissonnier designed a firework display to mark the birth of the Dauphin. The Duc d'Antin, *directeur général des bâtiments*, said that it was 'très belle et de fort bon goût'.

D'Antin described Meissonnier as an 'orphèvre', and this was still his

Engraving of the monstrance made by Juste-Aurèle Meissonnier in 1727 for the Carmelites of Poitiers. The base represents the ark of the Old Covenant and the grapes and wheat-ears on the stem allude to the elements of the Mass.

main occupation. The *Mercure* article giving an account of the fireworks for the King's recovery also described a fine monstrance he had made for the Carmelites of Poitiers. 'This piece is entirely in the taste of the famous Pietro da Cortona and Puget, whose school has always been the object of the author's studies', the anonymous writer declared. The monstrance has vanished – probably destroyed at the time of the Revolution – but an engraving of it was included in Meissonnier's works.

Apart from a single snuff-box, no example of his work as a goldsmith

Silver three-branched candlestick made by Claude Duvivier in 1734–5 after a design by Meissonnier. Musée des Arts Décoratifs, Paris.

is known to survive. But Meissonnier published many of his designs for silver and there are several silver and gilt-bronze candlesticks based closely on them. The most interesting, perhaps, is a silver three-branched candlestick with stem and foot composed of spirally eddying curves scattered with roses. It bears the maker's mark of Claude Duvivier and the Paris date stamp for 1734–5. The wonderful fluidity of this piece can hardly be paralleled in any silver apart from that made by Adam van Vianen and Jan Lutma in early seventeenth-century Holland.

It is not known when Meissonnier began to publish his designs which were probably issued a few at a time. The fourth group has a title-page dated 1734. And in that year a brief but complimentary review of it appeared in the *Mercure de France*. The writer stated that the prints were in the style of Stefano della Bella, the mid-seventeenth-century Florentine engraver, and, he went on, ought to stimulate the curiosity of the public and all who are interested in 'the best taste'. 'They include fountains, cascades, ruins, *Rocailles* [pieces of rock-work] and *Coquillages* [pieces of shell-work], examples of architecture which have effects which are bizarre, unusual and *pittoresque*, by their piquant and extraordinary forms, in which often one part does not correspond to the other, though

CHANDELIERS DE SCUPLTURE EN ARGENT.
*Invanté par J. Maissonnier Architecte en 1728.
Avec Privilege du Roy.*

Duplesis Sculpsit

Three views of a candlestick made by J.-A. Meissonnier in 1728.

the subject appears no less rich and agreeable.' Here the word *pittoresque*, which was to be applied to the whole high Rococo style in France, seems to have been used with reference to the decorative arts for the first time.

Meissonnier's engraved designs are, indeed, extraordinary: and not least those for silver objects. All of them are boldly three-dimensional and any figures that appear are solidly sculpturesque even when they are intended to be rendered only in relief. His feeling for the third dimension was so strong that he needed to reproduce designs of one candlestick taken from three points of view to indicate its intricacy of form. The designs for candlesticks which look as if they had been twisted out of puff-pastry by a cook of genius are perhaps the most appealing of all.

177

Projet de Sculpture en argent d'un grand Surtout de Table, et les deux Terrines qui ont été executée pour le Millord Duc de Kinston en 1735.
A Paris chès Huquier rue S.t Jacque au coin de celle des Mathurins CPR.

above Design for a *surtout de table* incorporating two tureens, made by J.-A. Meissonnier for the Duke of Kingston in 1735; one of the most elaborate manifestations of the *genre pittoresque*.

below Design for a tureen by J.-A. Meissonnier.

A *surtout de table* crowned by a group of putti and dolphins, one tureen decorated with shell-fish and another with a still-life of dead game were made, so the inscription reveals, for the Duke of Kingston in 1735 and must have been among the more elaborate examples of eighteenth-century silver. (They were last heard of when they passed through a sale room in 1909.) Similar motifs recur on several other pieces. But many of the designs are free compositions of curves, abstract forms of the greatest subtlety.

He is said to have given up work as a silversmith in 1735 to devote himself exclusively to architecture and interior decoration. At this moment he was at the height of his fame. But after little more than a decade, taste began to turn against the style of which he was a master. The first mutterings of discontent are heard in 1745 when the abbé Leblanc protested against the vogue for asymmetry, and fantastic combinations of shell-work, rock-work and so on, calling for a return to the style of the 'century of Louis XIV'. Two years later the abbé inveighed against these 'extravagances' again, mentioning Meissonnier, Germain Boffrand and Thomas Germain as the main culprits. It is unlikely that the haughty Meissonnier heeded these barbs, and it was not until after his death – on 31 July 1750 – that the attacks became more numerous and telling. The obituary published in the October issue of the *Mercure* (perhaps written by Mariette) is distinctly hostile. He had abandoned all symmetry, the obituarist remarked, he had sacrificed everything to the pursuit of novelty. And, to make matters worse, he had attracted imitators all over Europe.

Inkstand made by Philip Syng in 1752,
and used at the signing of the
Declaration of American Independence
in 1776. Independence Hall,
Philadelphia.

Philip Syng

(1703–89)

The silver standish or inkstand used at the signing of the Declaration of American Independence on 4 July 1776, and now kept in Independence Hall, Philadelphia, is an historical relic of more than ordinary interest. That it is also one of the most elegant pieces of American eighteenth-century silver is no more than a coincidence. It was made for the Provincial Assembly of Pennsylvania in 1752 (for the price of £25 16s. od.) when independence from Great Britain would have seemed neither necessary nor desirable to most of those who used it. Similarly, it is a coincidence that its maker, Philip Syng, was a close friend of Benjamin Franklin, a member of his 'Junto' and one of those men who created the climate in which independence became an intellectual as well as an economic necessity.

Philip Syng was of Irish origin, born at Cork on 29 September 1703. His father, Philip Syng the elder, born in 1676 and probably trained in Dublin, was described as a 'Goldsmith and gentleman'. In 1714 the family emigrated to America and settled at Annapolis. But by 1720 they had moved to the more prosperous city of Philadelphia where the elder Syng established himself as a silversmith with a shop near the Market Place. A handsome, if rather austere, flagon belonging to Christ Church, Philadelphia, reveals the quality of his craftsmanship. In 1722 he and a certain Thomas Browne patented a tract of two hundred acres called The Partners' Adventury on the south side of the Susquehanna River – a land speculation which does not appear to have yielded any exceptional profits. After the death of his first wife, Abigail, he married Hannah Learnyng in 1724, and soon afterwards appears to have returned to Annapolis where he married for the third time in 1734. He died on 18 May 1739 leaving personal estate valued at £751 1s. 7d.

The younger Philip Syng took over the workshop in Philadelphia when his father returned to Annapolis. In 1730 he married Elizabeth Warner who is said to have borne him no fewer than twenty-one children. Only one son survived infancy and he died in 1758. Benjamin Franklin, writing to a Philadelphia friend, remarked 'I am grieved for our Friend Syng's loss. You and I, who esteem him, and have valuable sons ourselves, can sympathize with him sincerely.' Nothing is known of the extent of Syng's trade as a silversmith. But it must have sufficed to support him and his large family, allowing him time to engage in other pursuits as well.

In November 1731 Syng is recorded as a member of the Library Company of Philadelphia – Franklin's 'first Project of a public Nature'. Though Syng's junior by three years, Franklin had already gained a much wider experience. He had been to England, met Sir Hans Sloane and other notabilities, returned to Philadelphia in 1726, established a printing press and already begun to emerge as one of the leading lights of

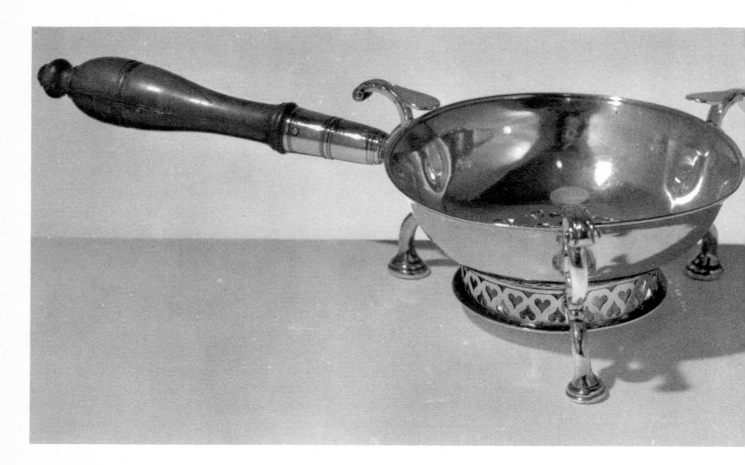

Silver brazier by Philip Syng.
Philadelphia Museum of Art.

the Colony. Syng was an Anglican, eventually a vestryman of Christ Church, Philadelphia, while Franklin was in every way a Dissenter. But both were Freemasons and in 1741 Syng became warden of the first Masonic Lodge in America, of which Franklin was a foundation member. As one of his most trusted friends, Syng witnessed the will which Franklin wrote in 1750. They shared a common concern for public improvements and a common interest in science. And it need hardly be added that, in due course, they both joined in the struggle for American Independence.

The second of the public projects with which both Syng and Franklin were involved was the Union Fire Company established in 1736 to supplement the city's wholly inadequate fire-fighting organization. This was no more than a mutual aid society. But in 1750 Syng was among those who, under Franklin's leadership, attempted to establish a fire insurance society, realized in 1752 as the Philadelphia Contributionship, of which Syng was a director and for which he made the seal with the emblem of 'four hands united'. In 1747 they both participated – Syng being one of the managers – in the scheme of the Philadelphia Lottery

Coffee pot by Philip Syng. Like the majority of American silversmiths of the period, Syng made use of English patterns. Philadelphia Museum of Art.

which was to raise the sum of £3,000 for public use. Two years later Syng became a founder and trustee of the Academy, agreeing to pay £6 a year for five years. This was the institution out of which the University of Pennsylvania was to grow. Syng continued to be active in public works after Franklin had left on his third and longest visit to Europe. In 1765 he was one of the signatories of the Non-importation Agreement which called for the repeal of the Stamp Act and indicated the growth of American opposition to government from England.

The Library Company, of which Syng was a member, was concerned with science as much as literature, but Syng's scientific discoveries have been overshadowed by those of Franklin. With characteristic generosity, however, Franklin acknowledged their importance in contributing to his own work, without explaining their nature very clearly. In 1747, for instance, Franklin told his London correspondent Peter Collinson that Syng had devised a machine to aid the generation of electricity. Three years later he alluded to 'Mr. Syng's Observations' on alum.

Neither of the subjects which Franklin names as objects of Syng's study had any bearing – at that date – on his craft as a silversmith. But

Franklin remembered both his scientific and professional interests in London in 1766 when he sent him a copy of William Lewis's book: *Commercium philosophicotechnicum, or the Philosophical Commerce of Arts* (1763–5). Syng's reply, written on 1 March 1766, is his only recorded letter:

Dear Sir, I received yours of the 26th September last, with your very agreeable Present Doctor Lewis's new Work. You judged very right that I should find in it entertaining Particulars in my Way – the Management of Gold and Silver is treated of in it better and more particularly than I have met with in any Author. The regard you have always shown me requires my acknowledgement, which I wish to make by serviceable Actions, because they speak louder than Words, but I fear I shall die insolvent. The Junto fainted last summer in the hot Weather and has not reviv'd, your Presence might reanimate it, without which I apprehend it will never recover.

Salver by Philip Syng. Philadelphia Museum of Art.

With debates in the Junto, scientific experiments and public works on his hands, Philip Syng can have given no more than a part of his time and thought to the making of silver. The relatively few pieces of silver that bear his mark are all more than competent essays in the styles fashionable in early and mid-eighteenth-century England, sometimes adorned with delicate, if subdued, Rococo ornaments. His activity as a manager of lotteries and treasurer of more than one organization suggests that he may, like several London silversmiths, have been a banker. But apart from being a landowner and a shareholder in the Philadelphia Linen Manufactory he is not known to have engaged in any other financially productive enterprise. There can, however, be no doubt that he prospered. At the time of his death, on 8 May 1789, he owned several houses in Philadelphia besides a large country place called 'The Prince of Wales Farm'.

Tankard by Philip Syng, engraved with the Maddox coat of arms. Yale University Art Gallery.

Christian Precht

(1706–79)

Christian Precht, one of the most notable of Swedish Rococo designers and a brilliant silversmith, was born in Stockholm on 30 October 1706. He was the son of a sculptor and cabinet-maker, Burchardt Precht, a native of Bremen who first went to Stockholm in 1674 to assist in decorating Drottningholm Palace. Four of his sons became craftsmen of some distinction. Johann Philip, the eldest, spent many years in England where he appears to have been trained as a cabinet-maker. The next, Burchardt, was a sculptor. The third, Gustaf, was also a sculptor, assisting his father and finally taking over his workshop. Christian was the youngest.

Christian was apprenticed in 1721 to the leading Stockholm gold-smith, Gustaf Stafhell the elder. In 1727 he qualified as a journeyman and in the same year he set off on his travels. He went first to England where he worked in London under the Augsburg jeweller, Augustin Heckel, who, according to George Vertue, was esteemed for the 'neatness and design' of his chasing on gold. At that period the world of London craftsmen was surprisingly cosmopolitan, including several Germans as well as the second generation of Huguenot emigrés. But Christian Precht soon moved on to Paris, the fountain head of artistic novelties. He did not spend much time in Paris, perhaps less than a year, but it was long enough for him to acquire artistic capital to last a life-time. Thomas Germain was already at the height of his powers. Meissonnier who had been created *architect-dessinateur* to the Crown a few years earlier had probably begun to issue engravings of his designs. That most exuberant sub-species of the Rococo style, the *genre pittoresque* was just burgeoning into its extravagant flowering. In the summer of 1730 Precht began to return to Sweden, travelling by way of Nuremberg and Augsburg, still two important centres for the production of goldsmiths' work. He was back in Stockholm in 1731.

Christian Precht's eldest brother, Johann Philip, died in 1736 and his father two years later, when the family workshop passed to Gustaf. At some time, probably about 1740, Gustaf and Christian used an engraved label which served as a joint advertisement. This might suggest that the brothers were in partnership. But in fact they seem never to have been formally allied in business and their relationship was often uneasy if not openly hostile.

In 1737 Christian obtained from the magistrates of Stockholm permission to carry on a silversmith's business without intervention from the guild. This meant that he was not permitted to stamp his products with a personal mark. And as no silver could be sold without a maker's mark, he was bound to pass all his wares – save those made for the royal palace – to some member of the guild for assaying. His works are thus much more difficult to trace than those of most other notable eighteenth-century

Baptismal ewer and basin bearing the maker's mark of Johan Colin, 1745, but probably the work of Christian Precht, who had no registered maker's mark. Eriksberg Castle.

silversmiths. And since all the documented pieces he supplied for the Crown were melted down or otherwise lost, his fame now rests on a few objects attributed to him and his drawings.

A very handsome baptismal ewer with a shell-shaped bowl held aloft by an animated cherub perching on the crest of a wave of Rococo scroll-work, in Eriksberg Castle, bears the maker's mark of Johan Colin and the date letter for 1745. It is a triumph of Rococo elegance. But as it differs in style and quality of execution from Colin's other marked works it has generally been attributed to Precht. A somewhat thornier problem is

right Design for a coffee-pot by Christian Precht. National Museum, Stockholm.

far right Coffee pot made by Michael Äström in 1764, probably after a design by Christian Precht. Collection of Fru Harriet Almquist, Stockholm.

presented by an elaborate coffee-pot, made by Michael Äström and dated 1764, in the collection of Mrs Harriet Almquist in the Nordiska Museet, Stockholm. It corresponds closely with a drawing which, so the inscription declares, was the design for the 'masterpiece' which Äström made for presentation to the silversmiths' guild. But Äström is not known to have produced any other piece of comparable quality, and the design is in a style so close to the drawings of Precht that there can be little doubt that he was responsible for it. A 'masterpiece' was, of course, intended to prove a silversmith's skill in his craft rather than his ability as a designer and there is no reason why he should not have availed himself of a design made by someone else.

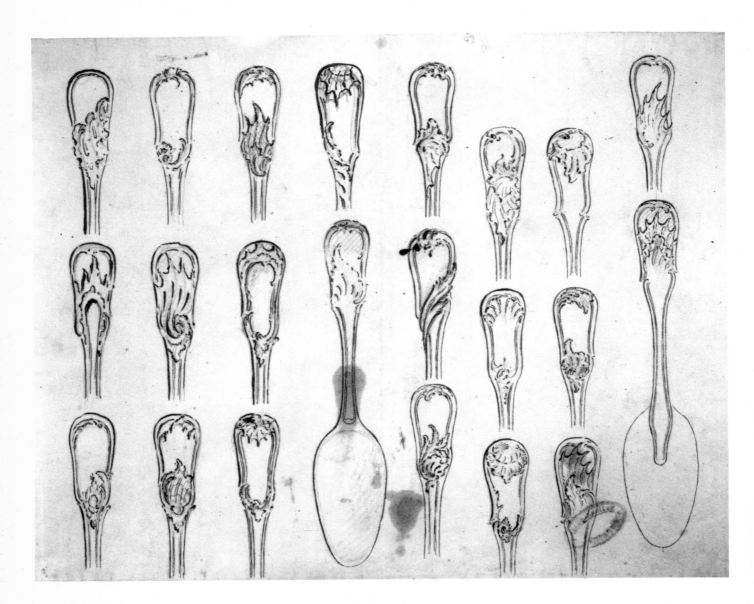

Design for spoon handles by Christian Precht, whose many drawings show the influence of French Rococo patterns. National Museum, Stockholm.

Happily, there is no doubt about the authorship of many designs for silver by Precht now in the National Museum, Stockholm. Deftly and lightly sketched, they reveal him as a master of Rococo ornamental design with a flair for abstract motifs reminiscent sometimes of falling water, and sometimes of the patterns made by frost on a window-pane. He was able to suggest the fragility of tiny flowers strewn or garlanded over the surface of his designs. Though inspired by Meissonnier, these drawings are no mere plagiarisms cut out of pattern books, but the essays of an original artist in search of ever more delicate novelties in both form and surface texture. One may, however, question whether such delicacy could ever have been realized successfully in any medium

Design for a tureen by Christian
Precht. National Museum, Stockholm.

as hard as silver. Even on Michael Äström's 'masterpiece' some of the
subtlety and freshness of the drawing has been lost.

In addition to working as a silversmith, Precht made at least two
bronze medals. He was active as a jeweller and also designed ceramics. In
1738 he provided drawings which were sent out to China for the guidance of makers of 'export porcelain'. It is interesting to note that these
are purely European in character and incorporate no chinoiserie motifs.
He may also have executed designs for the Marieberg pottery works in
Sweden where jugs, basins and tureens were made in close imitation of
Rococo silver vessels.

Jacques Roettiers

(1707–84)

Little is known of the ancestry and family background of most silver-smiths. Jacques Roettiers is an exception, for he belongs to a bewilderingly large and active family from Walloon Flanders, several of whose members achieved European fame as mint masters and coin engravers. At one time three of the Roettiers were being employed to engrave coins for the kings of England, France and Spain. Four members of the family held the lucrative post of 'graveur général des Monnaies de France' – Joseph from 1682 to 1703, Norbert from 1704 to 1727, Joseph-Charles from 1727 to 1753 and Charles-Norbert from 1753 to 1772. Although Jacques Roettiers was mainly a silversmith he preferred to describe him-self as a medallist and coin engraver – and as such he was admitted to the Parisian Académie des Beaux Arts which would not have accepted a mere *orfèvre* in its august company.

In 1745 Jacques Roettiers' aunts who were living in London provided a full, if somewhat confused, account of their family for that passionate collector of materials for the history of art in England, George Vertue. He wrote: 'When King Charles the 2d was beyond Seas in Exile being at Antwerp had occasion for moneys, was assisted by Mr. Roetiers of Antwerp at that Time a Goldsmith & Banker, who had several sons. Engravers of Medals. This favour so much obliged the King that he promised when he returned to his Kingdomes he would imploy them in his affairs of the Mint'. Charles was as good as his word and at the Restoration sacked the excellent engraver who had worked for the Commonwealth, Thomas Simon, and installed Jean and Joseph Roettiers in the English mint. From about 1683 Jean was assisted by his son Norbert. All went well until the 1688 Revolution when, to quote Horace Walpole (who extracted a coherent account from Vertue's notes);

no sollicitation could prevail on John the father to work for king William. This rendering him obnoxious, and there being a suspicion of his carrying on a treasonable correspondence, guards were placed round his house in the Tower, and lord Lucas, who commanded there, made him so uneasy that he was glad to quit his habitation. He was rich and very infirm, labouring under the stone and gravel, additional reasons for his retiring. He took a house in Red Lion Square. Norbert, less difficult, executed some things for the government.

But a coin struck by Norbert in 1694 caused trouble.

Some penetrating eyes thought they discovered a Satyr's head couched in the King's. [Walpole continues] This made much noise, and gave rise to a report that king James was in England and lay concealed in Rotier's house in the Tower. Norbert on these dissatisfactions left England, and retiring to France, where he had been educated in the Academy, was received and employed by Louis XIV where, whatever had been his inclinations here, he certainly made medals of the young chevalier.

Dinner service in silver, made by Jacques Roettiers for the 5th Earl of Berkeley, between 1735 and 1738. This enormous service consists of 168 pieces. Collection of S. Stavros Niarchos.

Norbert married Elizabeth Isard in England, but she appears to have died before he went to France. There he married Winifred Clarke, said to be a great-niece of the Duke of Marlborough. Their son Jacques was born at St Germain-en-Laye on the 20 August 1707 and baptized in the chapel of the château next day, with the Old Pretender and the Duchess of Perth as god-father and god-mother.

Jacques attempted to establish himself in England, according to George Vertue, in 1731. But he had returned to Paris by 1733 when he was admitted to the Goldsmiths' corporation by decree, although he had served no apprenticeship. The document recording his admission says that he had studied painting at the Académie and spent some time with 'les Sieurs Germain et Besnier orfèvres de S.M.'. He was promptly made a royal goldsmith and given apartments in the Louvre. Next year he married Anne-Marie, daughter of Nicolas Besnier, the chief Orfèvre du Roi. Besnier had, however, just been appointed director of the Beauvais tapestry factory and Roettiers seems to have taken over the management of his silver workshop. On 14 March 1735 he and Roettiers were paid jointly for plate supplied for the 'service du Roi'. Two years later Roettiers was granted the succession to Besnier's official post.

Tureen from the Berkeley dinner service by Jacques Roettiers. This piece is decorated by a cabbage modelled in silver. Collection of S. Stavros Niarchos.

Roettiers presumably took over Besnier's staff of craftsmen. As no important pieces made in the workshop in the early 1730s survive, it is impossible to say if and to what extent Roettiers changed its style. But a large dinner service made under Roettiers between 1735 and 1738 (consisting of 168 pieces weighing altogether three-quarters of a ton) includes some of the richest surviving pieces of Rococo silver, as fine as any surviving works by Thomas Germain. The service was probably made for Augustus, fifth Earl of Berkeley, and until 1960 was at Berkeley Castle in Gloucestershire.

There can be little doubt that Roettiers was a designer and workshop manager rather than a craftsman. For Pierre Germain's pattern book *Elements d'orfèvrerie* 1748, he supplied exuberant designs for three *flambeaux*, a tureen, a *pot à oille* (a special type of tureen), and a centrepiece crowned by supple nude female figures, representing wine and water, holding aloft two cupids on a sea-shell. Pierre Germain, who was no relation of Thomas, was a native of Avignon, spent much of his youth in Rome (whence he derived the nick-name Le Romain) arrived in Paris in 1736 and was officially apprenticed to Besnier, though Roettiers was

Candlesticks by Jacques Roettiers,
dated 1762–3. Metropolitan Museum,
New York.

probably in charge of the workshop by this date.

A *surtout de table* commissioned from Roettiers by the Elector of
Cologne was described at length in the *Mercure de France* in July 1749 and
appears to have been a masterpiece of Rococo naturalism and elabora-
tion – the object itself has, of course, vanished. But the days of such
extravagant fantasies were already numbered. Early in the 1750s the
Parisian world began to succumb to a fashion for what was called the
'goût grec' – objects decorated with rather heavy architectural ornaments
(Roman rather than Greek) and often similar to those of the Louis XIV
period. Roettiers supplied for the King a pair of gold sugar bowls which
were described as 'à la grecque' and were in the form of vases with
reliefs of little black boys on a sugar plantation. They can hardly have
been examples of what we now call Neo-classicism. But it is clear that in
the late 1750s Roettiers was abandoning the airs and graces of the Rococo
for a more solid and serious style. A pair of candlesticks dated 1762–3,
now in the Metropolitan Museum, New York, are soberly decorated
with antique architectural motifs and make a striking contrast with his
earlier productions.

These less fanciful pieces were probably designed not by Jacques Roettiers but by his son, Jacques-Nicolas who was born in 1736, accepted as a *maître* in 1765, and formally associated with him in royal commissions. The mark of Jacques-Nicolas appears on various liturgical vessels made in 1769–70 for the Chapelle of the Dauphin and now in the treasury of Troyes Cathedral. All his more grandiose works for the Crown were destroyed. But a pair of 'terrine' forks in the Louvre, hall-marked 1770–1, were probably made for a member of the royal family. With little satyr faces above the prongs, they answer the description of a set of four forks 'ornées de mascarons michelangesques' which he delivered for royal use in 1767.

The most notable of the surviving works by Jacques-Nicolas is the vast Orloff dinner service. It was ordered from him by Catherine the Great acting on the advice of the sculptor Falconet. The service was finished and sent to Russia in 1775, Catherine gave it to her favourite, Count Orloff, but bought it back after his death in 1783. Comprising 88 dishes, 650 plates, 103 covers, 16 wine coolers, 10 candelabras, 48 candlesticks, 22 tureens, 6 teapots, 7 chocolate pots, not to mention many smaller objects, it was dispersed after the Russian Revolution. A comparison with the Berkeley service shows how taste had changed in thirty-five years. The quest for novelty, grace and contrived contrapposto has been abandoned. The Orloff service is of an almost pompous solemnity and marmoreal monumentality. Wisps of asymmetrical foliage have been replaced by solid gadroons, paterae and guilloches borrowed from ancient architectural ornament. Yet some shell-shaped butter dishes which he made shortly afterwards are wrought with a delicate naturalism, and might easily be based on patterns evolved at the height of the Rococo. And a plate dated 1772 with a Vitruvian scroll running round its rim is stylistically indistinguishable from pieces made fifty years earlier and ascribed to Nicolas Besnier.

Jacques Roettiers retired in 1772. Next year he was admitted to the Académie des Beaux Arts as a medallist although – as Pierre-Jean Mariette pointed out – many years had passed since he last made a medal. He was also ennobled and able to style himself Jacques Roettiers de la Tour. He died in 1784. Jacques-Nicolas who succeeded as Orfèvre du Roi in 1772 retired with a fortune five years later. He appears to have turned his attention to sculpture and a marble bust of the Duc de Brissac at Versailles is signed *J. N. Roettiers de la Tour Eques. Fecit 1785*. In 1786 he is recorded in Madrid but nothing further is known of him. Jacques' younger son, Alexandre-Louis, returned to the family profession of coin engraving and became master of the Paris Mint in 1791. Although he ran into trouble with the Revolutionary government, he survived the Terror and died in the mid-nineteenth century.

above Chalice made in 1769–70 by Jacques-Nicholas Roettiers for the Chapel of the Dauphin. Troyes Cathedral.

right Soup tureen with cover and stands, from the Orloff service ordered from Jacques-Nicholas Roettiers by Catherine the Great. Metropolitan Museum, New York.

above Ewer and basin by Vincenzo Belli, made in Rome in the later 1740s for Portugal. The King of Portugal commissioned large quantities of ecclesiastical plate from Roman silver-smiths. Museu de Arte Sagra, Lisbon.

right Coffee service by Vincenzo Belli, probably *c.* 1770. Collection Fabrizio Apolloni, Rome.

Vincenzo Belli

(1710–87)

Vincenzo Belli was the founder of a family of craftsmen whose members made much of the best Roman domestic and church plate between the mid-eighteenth and the mid-nineteenth centuries. Born in Turin in 1710 – just fifteen years after Meissonnier – he grew up in a city visually enriched and architecturally ennobled by Filippo Juvarra. He appears to have been trained in the shops of no fewer than four Turin silversmiths – Antonio Serafini, Giuseppe de Mode, Pietro Cebrano and Pietro Busseroni – who later testified to his character and abilities. By September 1740 he had moved to Rome. Next year he married Angela, daughter of Bartolomeo Balbi, a Roman silversmith who seems to have specialized in making ecclesiastical vessels. This may have eased his entry into the Roman guild which accepted him as a master later in 1741. In 1759 the Piedmontese Minister in Rome referred to Belli as 'one of the ablest and most reliable silversmiths' in the city. He was elected Fourth Consul of the Guild in 1765 and *camerlengo* (chamberlain) in 1779 but refused this honour. His wife died in 1771 and he in 1787.

One of his most elaborate works is an ewer and basin in the Museu de Arte Sagra at Lisbon, probably dating from the later 1740s and one of the many pieces of ecclesiastical plate ordered from Roman silversmiths by John v of Portugal. It is in a very exuberant Rococo style with decorative scrolls which break into 'choppy' waves. Some years later, probably in 1780, he made a much more sober ewer and basin for Cardinal Francesco Antamoro, now in the Museo di Palazzo Venezia. Though its decoration is heavier, this ewer recalls a jug made by Thomas Heming in London in the 1760s. Salvers which bear Belli's mark are still more obviously like English work of the mid-century and one may wonder if he had not seen and admired pieces of English silver. But most of his works have a distinctly Roman presence – rich, bold and sometimes rather overbearing, despite the fantasy of some decorative motifs. A pair of handsome pot-bellied tureens in the collection of the Duke of Torlonia have a notably august splendour.

Vincenzo Belli's prosperity is indicated by the fact that he was allowed, under the sumptuary laws, the luxury of two horses and traps. He employed some twenty assistants and in his later years had the help of his son Giovacchino (b. 1756), who took over the workshop after his death. Giovacchino abandoned his father's Rococo style for a more rectilinear but not always plainer antique revival manner, making sugar bowls in the form of Grecian urns and oil lamps supported on the heads of term figures. In 1815 he completed silver models of the arches of Constantine, Septimus Severus and Titus which won the praise of the antiquary G. A. Guattani who published a pamphlet about them. In this work he had the collaboration of his son Pietro, born in 1780.

Pietro appears to have taken a leading part in the Belli workshop before 1820, when he cast a silver figure of Christ for a crucifix modelled by the sculptor Pietro Tenerani. This work is now in the church of San Stefano, Pisa. At about the same date he made a series of drawings of silver vessels, probably as a kind of catalogue. The designs are elegant, rather in the manner of English silver of the 1780s, but they must have looked curiously out of date to visitors to the city. Perhaps the writer of an English book about Rome, Mrs Eaton, had such pieces in mind when she wrote in 1818: 'If the fine arts prosper in Rome, the useful arts are in a woefully degenerate state. . . . Except in Paris or in London, you will meet with no handsome work in gold and silver'. But at least one English visitor, the fifth Earl of Jersey, patronized Pietro Belli's son, Vincenzo II, buying a large silver group after the antique statue of *Menelaus and Patroclus*. Vincenzo II took over the Belli workshop on Pietro's death in 1828 and lived on until 1859.

Ewer and basin made by Vincenzo Belli for Cardinal Francesco Antamoro *c.* 1780. Museo di Palazzo Venezia, Rome.

Thomas Heming

(*fl.* 1745–82)

In the Museum of Decorative Arts in Copenhagen there is a relic of one of the most unfortunate members of the House of Hanover – a silver toilet service made for Princess Caroline Matilda on her marriage to Christian VII of Denmark in 1766. She was a posthumous daughter of Frederick Prince of Wales, eldest son of George II, and was married at the age of fifteen to the profligate Christian, who was sinking fast into imbecility. The toilet service consists of thirty pieces which fit neatly into a leather box – a large looking glass, an ewer and basin, several boxes, bottles, brushes, a pair of candlesticks and a silver bell. The snuffer tray bears the mark ER for Emick Romer, and the candlesticks in a delicate Strawberry Hill Gothick style are probably also by him. But twenty-three of the pieces bear the maker's mark of Thomas Heming, official 'Goldsmith to His Majesty'.

Although he occupied a position of some importance, Thomas Heming is a very obscure figure. He is first recorded in 1745 when he registered his mark at Goldsmiths' Hall, London. On the accession of George III in 1760 he succeeded John Boldero as royal goldsmith. In this capacity he worked for the Jewel House which was responsible for providing the King with new silver as well as looking after the crown jewels, insignia of the garter and the plate in royal palaces. Before the establishment of the Bank of England in 1694 the royal goldsmith had often been a banker, like Sir Robert Viner. But in the eighteenth century he was either a merchant or a plate-worker with enough capital to supply the silver that was needed and patience to wait until his bills were paid. Boldero had no registered mark and does not seem to have been a working silversmith. Heming prepared the regalia and plate for the coronation of George III. During the next two decades he supplied plate to the Jewel House to the value of about £6,000 a year. This was a fraction of the sums spent on silver by the French king at the same time, but it has been suggested that Heming's prices were excessive. And when the Jewel House was abolished in 1782, he was not confirmed in his office of royal goldsmith.

Several pieces of church plate were included in the works Heming executed for the Jewel House. In 1764 he was given the order to supply communion plate for Anglican churches in the American colonies. Chalices and patens made on this occasion are still in Trinity Church, New York City, and Christ Church, Williamsburg, Virginia. They are very plain, made to a design standardized early in the century, which Heming repeated for a set of plate presented by the widow of the second Duke of Portland to the Portland Chapel, Marylebone, in 1765. Some years later, in 1779, he supplied communion vessels little less austere for the private chapel at Windsor Castle. But these ecclesiastical pieces are uncharacteristic of Heming's work.

Silver toilet service made by Thomas Heming for the English Princess Caroline Matilda on her marriage to Christian VII of Denmark in 1766. Kunstindustrimuseum, Copenhagen.

Thomas Heming's trade card of about 1765, when he moved to Bond Street.

Silver-gilt ewer from the toilet service of Princess Caroline Matilda. Kunstindustrimuseum, Copenhagen.

He began in the French-inspired Rococo style that was fashionable in England in the 1740s. Even on a trade card which he issued in or after 1765 there is an ewer copied precisely from an engraving in Pierre Germain's *Eléments d'orfèvrerie* of 1748. But although they are French inspired, his Rococo pieces could hardly be mistaken for the work of a French silversmith. They are more balanced in form and more restrained in ornament. His works in this manner include a toilet set made for the wealthy Williams Wynn family in 1768 – almost the double of that owned by the unfortunate Caroline Matilda. He often repeated the same

Vine-wreathed cup of 1753 by Thomas Heming. Collection of David H.H. Felix of Philadelphia.

designs, and a very delicate vine-wreathed cup of 1753, now in the collection of Mr David H.H. Felix of Philadelphia, is almost identical with another of 1760 in the Victoria and Albert Museum, London. A little porringer – rather like a French *écuelle* – crowned with the Prince of Wales's feathers and made in 1763 for Queen Charlotte who gave it to her eldest son must, however, have been specially designed. Sometimes his work is almost insistently English as, for instance, a tea-kettle on a subdued Rococo stand made in 1762 and engraved with the cypher of Queen Charlotte.

A covered cup made by Heming in 1771 and now belonging to Trinity Hall, Cambridge, is a curious document in the history of English taste. The basic form is that of a classical urn, but the handles are entwined with snakes of the type beloved by Paul de Lamerie. It is crowned by an infant Bacchus holding a bunch of grapes. On the front there is a relief of three bewigged men in early eighteenth-century costume carousing in a room with an Adam-style looking glass hanging on the wall behind them. Although the individual elements are classical, the effect is still distinctly Rococo.

Heming began his career with a shop in Piccadilly. In 1765 he moved to Bond Street. From 1773 until 1781, however, George Heming (presumably his son) is recorded as working at the Bond Street shop – the sign of the King's Arms – in partnership with William Chawner. It therefore seems probable that Thomas Heming had retired in 1773, though without relinquishing his post of royal goldsmith. His mark continued to be used until the early 1780s but was perhaps applied only to plate made for the Jewel House.

In 1775 George Heming and William Chawner received what must have been the largest commission given to an English silversmith by a foreign patron in the eighteenth century. On the advice of the Russian consul-general in London, who called them the best silversmiths in England, Catherine the Great ordered two complete dinner services and two dessert services. They are said to have employed some four hundred craftsmen on this task. It is interesting to note that this order was given in the year that the vast Orloff service had been completed by Roettiers. But it was apparently not the only, or necessarily the first, commission given by Catherine to the Heming family. The inventory of the Russian Imperial collection drawn up in 1907 refers to thirty-eight candelabra by Thomas Heming and these may well have been made earlier.

above Porringer crowned by the Prince of Wales's feathers. This piece was made by Thomas Heming for Queen Charlotte of England in 1763, to give to her eldest son. Collection of H.M. the Queen.

left Covered cup made by Thomas Heming in 1771. This piece is based upon the form of a classical urn, but with ornate Rococo handles and cover. Trinity Hall, Cambridge.

CAROLVS
THEODORVS
ABSENSPATRIAEMEMOR
BOIARIAESVAEDD.
MDCCLXXXIII

Luigi Valadier

(1726–85)

Late eighteenth-century Roman craftsmen like Vincenzo Belli are
completely overshadowed by Luigi Valadier, a silversmith of international fame and distinction. While Belli was old-fashioned, not to say
provincial, Valadier kept abreast of the latest fashions in Paris and
London. With a considerable staff of assistants – as many as one hundred
and eighty – Valadier seemed to anticipate the large scale manufacturing
silversmiths of the nineteenth century. But he was more strongly linked
with the past than the future. Although his workshop turned out simply
designed domestic plate in quantity, he is of interest mainly on account of
special decorative pieces executed in a variety of media which reveal how
fully he maintained the artist-goldsmith tradition established in sixteenth-
century Rome.

As his name suggests, he was of French extraction. A mid-nineteenth-
century writer states that his father, Andrea (b. 1695) came of a good
family from Aramont in Provence, and went to Rome in 1714. Andrea
is first mentioned in the records of the Roman silversmiths as a journeyman in December 1720. Three years later he was employed by Francesco
de Martini, a good and fairly prolific silversmith and bronze worker. He
was received as a master craftsman in 1725 and married Anna Tassel:
Luigi, born on 26 February 1726, was their first child.

Luigi began his career as his father's apprentice. But he was sent to
Paris to complete his studies in 1754, just when the reaction against the
Rococo was beginning to make itself felt. He was back in Rome by May
1756 when he married Caterina, daughter of Filippo della Valle one of
the leading Roman sculptors. Andrea died in 1759 and Luigi took over
the workshop. In 1760 he was received as a master craftsman by the guild
of which he was to be fourth consul from 1766 to 1769. In 1765 he was
elected to the artists' confraternity, the Virtuosi del Pantheon – a rare
distinction for a silversmith. His house and shop in Rome were at the
corner of what is now via del Babuino and vicolo degli Orti Alibert: and
here in 1775 he received a visit from Pope Pius VI who made him a
cavaliere in 1779.

As official silversmith to the Sacro Palazzo Apostolico Valadier was
employed on a variety of works – a gold shrine for relics of St Elizabeth of
Hungary, mounts for antique cameos in the Vatican museum, silver
vessels for the Pope's table. In 1780 he was commissioned to design and
make four vitrines of brazil wood with metal mounts for the display of
small antiquities in the Vatican library. He was also entrusted with the
task of casting a great bronze bell for St Peter's in 1783. Other works in
bronze included a set of twelve busts of librarians for the Vatican and a
copy of the *Apollo Belvedere*, dated 1770, now the property of the French
state.

The most splendid of his ecclesiastical works is the high altar of silver

right High altar of silver and gilt bronze made by Luigi Valadier in the 1760s for the Cathedral of Monreale.

right High altar of silver and gilt
bronze made by Luigi Valadier in the
1760s for the Cathedral of Monreale.

below Chalice by Luigi Valadier,
decorated with lapis lazuli. Musée du
Louvre, Paris.

and gilt bronze in the Cathedral of Monreale, outside Palermo. As Sicily suffered no Napoleonic invasion it has survived untouched – one of the few large-scale pieces of Roman ecclesiastical silver outside Portugal. The reliefs and statues of six saints which stand on it are in a chastened but still distinctly Baroque style and it is tempting to suggest that they were made to models by Luigi's father in law, Filippo della Valle, who died in 1768. A silver relief of the Crucifixion of St Peter in a frame decorated with lapis lazuli, by Luigi Valadier is in a similar style and probably dates from the same period.

Luigi's maker's mark – three fleurs-de-lys with the initials LV – was also used by his son Giuseppe. It is therefore difficult to tell which of the many pieces of domestic silver which bear it were made before Luigi's death in 1785. The output of the workshop included many coffee-pots, sugar bowls and so on, all of elegant shape and not unlike those made in Paris and London in the last three decades of the century. His lamps are more obviously Italian (because of their form), but they too are in the antique revival style. The workshop also produced complete table services, notably one made for Prince Borghese in 1784.

His reputation was however founded on decorative rather than useful works. In 1764, under the guidance of Giovanni Stern, he executed gilt bronze ornaments for the Salone d'Oro of the Palazzo Chigi in Rome in what would generally be called the Louis XVI style. One of his finest products was a two metre (6·5 feet) high model of Trajan's column incorporating a cylinder clock. This won the approval even of Goethe who described it as a precious and curious object. It was begun in 1774, finished in 1780, bought by the Elector Karl Theodore of Bavaria on a visit to Rome in 1783 and is now in the Residenzmuseum, Munich. Inscriptions reveal that Valadier made it in collaboration with two German assistants, Peter Ramoser and Bartholomäus Hecher.

He made something of a speciality in the creation of table-centres of the type called *desserts*. These are not to be confused with *surtouts de table*, which generally incorporated candlesticks, baskets for fruit and some-times holders for oil and vinegar bottles. *Desserts* were purely decorative, and those by Valadier were often little anthologies of antique sculpture and architecture: hence their popularity with the cognoscenti. One, made in 1778, incorporated models of the Arch of Trajan at Ancona and the Arch of the Argentari in Rome. He made others for the Archduke Ferdinand in 1780 and for the rich art-loving Maltese ambassador, the *bailli* de Breteuil. But the finest and largest was probably that made for Luigi Onesti-Braschi, Duke of Nemi, the nephew of Pius VI. Writing in the *Giornale delle Belle Arti* in 1784, G.A. Guattani said that it was so famous that no description was necessary, but nevertheless obligingly supplied one. It was more than five metres (196 ins) long and about seventy-five cm. (29 ins) wide, made of bronze, marble, amethyst and various hard stones and incorporated vases, cameos and statuettes – both antique and modern – set amongst colonnades, temples and triumphal arches. Accounts of it read like descriptions of some fantastic engraving by Piranesi. Unfortunately when the French occupied Rome in 1798 this *dessert* was seized and sent off to Paris where it appears to have been dis-membered and dispersed.

Though patronized by the greatest Romans and also by wealthy visitors to Rome Valadier does not seem to have prospered. On 15 September 1785 he committed suicide by throwing himself into the Tiber. The Lucchese ambassador who reported the tragedy to his government said that the 'celebre artefice' had gone out of his mind on account of the delayed payment of considerable sums owing to him.

Luigi's workshop was taken over by his son Giuseppe (b. 1762) who had already begun his career as an architect. He managed it until 1817. And, according to an account of 1788, jewellers, bronze founders, cameo-cutters, hard-stone workers, iron and brass workers as well as silversmiths were employed in it. Much domestic table silver seems to have been made under Giuseppe's direction, and also some notable ecclesiastical pieces – the reliquary of the Holy Crib for the Church of Santa Maria Maggiore, silver reliquary busts of St Peter and St Paul for the high altar of St John Lateran, a reliquary bust of St Gaudenzio for Rimini Cathedral and an altar frontal for Siena Cathedral. The workshop also continued to produce work in bronze, notably a table supported on figures of Hercules (modelled by the sculptor Vincenzo Pacetti) in the Vatican library. Luigi's younger brother Giovanni (1732–1805) was also a notable Roman silversmith and his three sons Filippo (b. 1770), Tommaso (b. 1772) and Luigi II (b. 1781) all followed his calling. None of them seem, however, to have produced any work as distinguished, either for design or craftsmanship, as the finest pieces executed under Luigi Valadier, the last great Roman artist-goldsmith.

William Faris

(1728–1804)

William Faris was a small-town silversmith, a figure of some importance in Annapolis, where he spent most of his life, and the writer of a diary preserved by his descendants. He was born in August 1728, probably in London, taken to America as a boy by his mother, and brought up in Philadelphia where he learned the art of clockmaking. In about 1756 he moved to the little sea-port of Annapolis and on the 7 March 1757 advertised in the *Maryland Gazette*: 'William Faris, Watch-Maker, from Philadelphia ... cleans and repairs all sorts of watches and clocks, as well and neat as can be done in any part of America ... He also makes Clocks, either to Repeat or not, or to go either Eight Days or Thirty, as the Purchaser shall fancy, as good as can be made in London, and at reasonable Prices.'

He does not seem to have turned his attention to the silver trade until 1760 when, still calling himself a 'Watch and Clockmaker', he inserted a notice in the *Maryland Gazette* saying that 'having procured an excellent Workman for that Purpose' he 'carries on the Silversmith's Business, Large, Small or Chas'd Work in the neatest, best and cheapest Manner. Also Jewelling of any Kind'. Nothing is known of the ability of this employee, but he was perhaps less well qualified than the 'very Compleat Silver Smith, who has served a regular Apprenticeship to that Business' whose arrival in his workshop he announced in 1763. Six years later he informed his fellow-townsmen that he had taken on 'two exceeding good workmen, (one of them has been a finisher for several years to the celebrated Mr. Allen)'. At the same date he embarked on furniture making and advertised that he had 'for sale several dozen of very neat black Walnut Chairs'.

It is clear that Faris was a merchant as much as a craftsman. The silversmiths who worked for him were probably journeymen from Philadelphia. But at least one member of his staff was a black slave. In 1778 he advertized in the *Maryland Journal*: 'To be sold, a very likely young negro fellow, by trade a silversmith, Jeweller and Lapidary; there are few if any better workmen in America. Any person inclined to purchase the said negro may know further by applying to the Subscriber living in Annapolis.' Why he wished to dispose of such a likely lad is something of a mystery unless he was now beginning to have the assistance of his three sons, William, Charles and Hyram, all of whom were trained as silversmiths.

Faris's account books indicate the prices he charged for silver in the 1770s, half a dozen tea-spoons at £1 12s. 0d., a pap-spoon at 15s., a silver snuff-box at £3 12s. 6d. (£1 7s. 0d. for the silver and £2 5s. 0d. for fashion). A set of silver coat buttons cost £1 11s. 6d. and a thimble 5s. For 'guilding the head of a cane' he charged £1 2s. 6d. Most of his income seems to have derived from other activities. He continued to

Sugar urn, cream jug and coffee pot,
made in silver by Charles Faris, the
son of William Faris, in the last quarter
of the eighteenth century. Metropolitan
Museum of Art, New York.

work as a watch-maker and some letters reveal that he was in touch
with a firm of London merchants – Messrs De Drusina, Ridder & Clark –
to whom he sent watches and clocks for 'finishing'. He charged various
citizens of Annapolis 30s. a year for winding their clocks. But it is clear
that during the last years of his life his workshop was engaged less in
making than repairing silver articles and time-pieces. Like several other
colonial silversmiths he was also an inn-keeper. In 1764 he announced
that 'having supplied himself with the best of Liquors, Hay & Oats . . .
he has now opened a Tavern'.

Only a few very simple pieces of silver made in Faris's shop are
recorded. But the Metropolitan Museum, New York, owns a handsome
coffee-pot, cream-jug and sugar urn made by his son Charles in about
1790. And the collection of Faris's diaries, account books and other
papers includes a series of nineteen working drawings for various types of

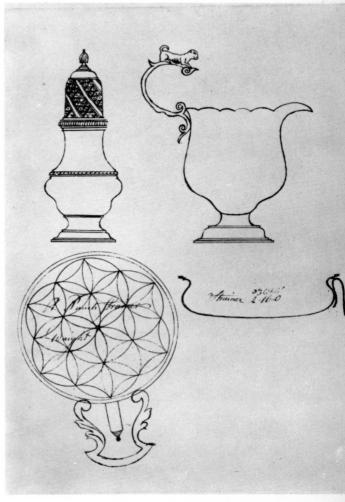

Designs for a tea-pot, and for a pepper-pot, cream jug and punch strainer. Though probably dating from the 1770s, these and other designs owned by Faris derive from silver patterns popular in England fifty years earlier. Maryland Historical Society.

silver ware – coffee pots, tea kettles, pepper-pots and so on. They are all in a simplified version of the English mid-eighteenth-century style which remained popular in America until the War of Independence. It is not certain whether these drawings were made by Faris himself, or by one of his assistants, or were acquired by him for use in his workshop. But they provide a valuable record of the repertory of a small-town silversmith towards the end of the Colonial period, complementing the more personal information in the diary he kept from 1792 until his death in 1804. The description of many quarrels with his sons and neighbours suggest that he was more than a little cantankerous. But he also chronicled the day to day events of Annapolis – births, marriages, illnesses, deaths, sermons, balls, horse-races, fires, disasters at sea, murders, public hangings and, as a recurrent theme, the care he bestowed on his beloved tulips.

Matthew Boulton

(1728–1809)

Portrait of Matthew Boulton by C.F. von Breda. Institution of Civil Engineers, London.

Silver jug by Matthew Boulton, Birmingham City Museum and Art Gallery.

Silver was only one of the many interests of Matthew Boulton and only one of the many products of his factory. Although he cannot be described as either a craftsman or a designer of silver, by transforming a large silver workshop into a 'factory' he was to revolutionize the silver trade in England, in Europe and in America. In his day London silversmiths had already begun to work for stock as much as to fulfil orders from individual clients, but had generally been wary of adopting new fashions. Boulton's factory specialized in the production of ready-made plate produced in large quantities and in the most up-to-date style. By using his experience as a manufacturer of base metalwork, he developed new machinery for making silver wares and new methods of marketing them.

He was born in 1728, the son of a Birmingham 'toy maker' – that is to say a manufacturer of such small metal objects as buttons and buckles. Matthew joined his father's business at the age of fourteen, became a partner seven years later, and took it over in 1759. It was a flourishing concern making buckles which were sold to Holland and Italy as well as on the home market. In 1762 he founded the famous Soho factory just outside Birmingham in partnership with John Fothergill, who was to act as sales manager and traveller, making extensive journeys across Europe. The factory was designed to look like a large country house in a landscaped park: he and his family were later to live in the central block, while the wings provided both workshops (on the ground floor) and apartments for the artisans. Over the years he gradually expanded the range of work done at Soho. To the making of buckles he added buttons, various types of steel jewellery, Sheffield-plated wares, silver, ormolu and so on. And, of course, he was to attain lasting fame by assisting James Watt in the completion of the steam engine and the production of heavy machinery.

Boulton's production of Sheffield plate provides an instance of the way in which he developed technical processes. This material had first been made – from copper sheets rolled between and fused with two films of silver – in about 1742 by Thomas Bolsover of Sheffield who used it for buttons and other small articles. Boulton probably began by adopting it for similar objects but soon realized that it was also suitable for making table wares and such vessels as coffee-pots and teapots. The main defect of the substance is that with frequent cleaning the silver surface is gradually rubbed away and the copper revealed. Realizing that this would happen first at the edges of a vessel, Boulton applied ribbons of solid silver wire at the places most liable to damage. He appears to have begun to make Sheffield plate in about 1762: in the last quarter of the eighteenth century the Soho factory was probably the largest as well as the best producer of plated wares in England.

216

By 1765 Boulton had also turned his attention to making solid silver wares. But he was immediately confronted with a serious difficulty. No object could be sold as silver unless it had been tested and marked at an official assay office, and the nearest to Birmingham was at Chester, seventy-two miles away. The silver was liable to damage either in transit or in the assay office (the silversmiths of Chester were anxious to discourage competitors in Birmingham). In a letter about one such incident Boulton remarked: 'altho' I am very desirous of becoming a great Silversmith, yet I am determined never to take up that branch in the Large Way I intended unless powers can be obtained to have a Marking Hall at Birmingham'. He thus set about presenting a petition to Parliament for a Birmingham assay office. After much wrangling and lobbying, an act was passed in May 1773 establishing assay offices in both Birmingham and Sheffield.

Boulton's open-mindedness freed him from the antiquated traditions of the silversmith's craft. In his silver workshops he established a system of divided labour similar to that evolved for the production of Sheffield plated articles which were necessarily made from independently wrought component parts. Fused plates cannot be cut by fret-saw without revealing the copper centre, so pierced work on Sheffield plate could be carried out only by means of a mechanically-operated fly-punch. And as this mechanism was able to repeat pierced designs more quickly and precisely than a craftsman's fret-saw, Boulton adopted it for the decoration of silver as well.

To carry out his work, he lured experienced artisans from Sheffield. But most of his employees had been trained at the Soho factory and as they had not been apprenticed in the normal way they were probably readier to accept new techniques than those who had inherited both the traditions and the prejudices which had been passed from master to apprentice for centuries. He took into his employment 'fatherless children, parish apprentices and hospital boys' for whom he provided accommodation, initiating a type of industrial paternalism that was to be developed, and notoriously abused, in the next century.

Supplying a dinner service to Mrs Montagu in 1776, Boulton remarked: 'I flatter myself its neatness, its simplicity and durability will be more agreeable to you than French finery or dirty richness'. And there can be little doubt he rated these practical qualities as high as the aesthetic merits of the plate made in his factory. When he began to produce plate, most of the London silversmiths were practising a somewhat tired version of the Rococo style, turning out wares on which the curves had lost most of their spring and the flowers all of their freshness. From the start, he adopted the antique revival style which had been recently popularized by Robert and James Adam, and seems to have appealed to him for a

above left Silver-gilt jug bearing the mark of Boulton & Fothergill, 1776. Museum of Fine Arts, Boston.

above right Sheffield plate candelabrum made at Boulton's Soho factory, 1797. Birmingham City Museum and Art Gallery.

below Sauce tureen, one of a pair bearing the maker's mark of Boulton & Fothergill, 1776. Birmingham Assay Office.

Patterns for sauce tureens made at the Boulton & Fothergill Soho Factory. Birmingham Reference Library.

number of reasons. In the first place, it was becoming highly fashionable among intellectuals, and Boulton must have foreseen that it would soon begin to appeal to a wider public.

Boulton must also have appreciated the practical advantages of the antique revival style from the manufacturer's point of view. Rococo silver derives most of its charm from the individual craftsman's ability to vary the texture of the surface, to twist ribbons into a delicately ir-regular knot or give to a spray of flowers 'a grace beyond the reach of art'. The new style demanded absolute uniformity of texture, precision of form and the exact repetition of ornamental motifs, which could better be obtained by the aid of machinery than by hand and hammer alone. Thus while the importance of the individual craftsman declined that of the designer increased. Occasionally Boulton obtained designs from the leading architects in London – the Adam brothers, Sir William Chambers and James Wyatt. Most of his silver seems, however, to have been designed by permanent employees. For their benefit, as well as his

Design for a tureen made in the drawing office of Boulton & Fothergill Soho Factory. Birmingham Reference Library.

own intellectual diversion, Boulton appears to have gathered a library of books about antiquities. The very large number of drawings executed by these draughtsmen testify to their ability. And the many silver wares that bear the mark of Boulton and Fothergill – not to mention numerous pieces of Sheffield plate – reveal the technical excellence of the machine-aided craftsmen in the Soho factory.

Matthew Boulton died on 17 August 1806. In his later years he had been concerned less with the departments making silver and Sheffield plate at Soho than with his iron foundry and steam-engine factory. In more than one way he was the precursor of the nineteenth-century industrialists. Yet he remained essentially a man of the eighteenth-century Enlightenment, and he clearly regarded the design of a piece of table silver, the perfection of a valve for a steam-engine, or the organization of a workshop, as problems which could all be solved by similar intellectual processes.

Robert-Joseph Auguste

(c. 1730–1805)

Robert-Joseph Auguste's early career is obscure: the date of his birth is not known and he appears to have served no regular apprenticeship. He is first recorded in 1756 as a *compagnon* or journeyman. Next year he was received in the Corporation as a *maître* by royal order, which suggests that he had already begun to work for the King or Mme de Pompadour. Before 1759 he married Louise-Elizabeth Barge, daughter of a master gunsmith, who in 1760 instigated legal proceedings for a financial separation on account of the disorder of his affairs. His embarrassment was caused by the bankruptcy of unnamed creditors and also his having gone surety for a royal jeweller named Rondé (presumably Claude-Dominique or Laurent).

Several of Auguste's recorded works might well be classified as jewellery. There were, for instance, two little statuettes, one of a sailor the other of a child with a sack, serving as a pepper-pot and salt-cellar – both of solid gold and made at a cost of 16,000 livres for Mme de Pompadour before 1764. In 1774 he made the gold crown, chalice and other regalia for the coronation of Louis XVI. All these precious objects have vanished. But a gold box by him survives, an exquisite trifle bought in Paris by the 1st Earl Spencer in 1769. He also worked in gilt bronze, making in 1760 decorations for a porphyry column designed by the architect Charles de Wailly for the Marquis d'Argenson. Gilt bronze decorations which he executed for the interior of Mme de Pompadour's Château de Choisy are recorded but have also vanished.

Auguste is best known for his table silver. Visiting Paris in 1768 Christian VII of Denmark bought six pieces which are still in the Danish royal collection – four tureens and two *pots à oille*, each provided with a lining, cover, stand and ladle. They are all inscribed *Auguste f à Paris* but stamped with a bewildering number of different date marks, ranging from 1756–7 to 1769–70. It seems that the *pots à oille* had been made in 1756, probably for a commission which had fallen through, and that reliefs of the Danish royal coat of arms were added when the tureens (hall-marked 1769–70) were made *en suite*.

Stylistically, the pieces in the Danish royal collection are still distinctly Rococo. But he soon abandoned this style and a three-branched candle-stick of 1767–8 in the Metropolitan Museum, New York is already more restrained. A dinner service he completed in 1775–6, now in the Swedish royal collection, is conspicuously antique revival both in the form of its various vessels and the ornaments. The tureens are of simple outline decorated with bold acanthus leaves which look as if they might have been chiselled out of marble. And the beautifully modelled putti who emerge from them to embrace – and serve as conveniently strong handles – clearly derive from Roman relief sculpture (while those on the Danish pieces are brothers to the smirking cupids who flutter about the

above Tureen from a dinner service made by Robert-Joseph Auguste 1775–6, for the Count de Creutz from whom it was acquired by Gustavus III of Sweden. Collection H.M. the King of Sweden.

below Gold snuff-box made by Robert-Joseph Auguste. An inscription reveals that it was bought by the first Earl Spencer in Paris in 1769. Collection of Earl Spencer.

Pot à oille – a special type of French tureen – by Robert-Joseph Auguste, engraved with the arms of Otto von Bloehme, Hanoverian minister at the French court, 1771.
Private Collection, Paris

paintings of Boucher). The tureens and *pots à oille* are inset with gold reliefs of notable events in the life of Gustavus III of Sweden and show him uniting the political factions, granting the constitution of 1772, protecting the arts and sciences and so on. They are said to have been executed after models by Pajou according to a programme provided by the Count de Creutz, who commissioned the service which was bought by Gustavus III in 1781.

Auguste made dinner services for Catherine the Great – whose appetite for table-ware seems to have been insatiable – for the King of Portugal and other royal patrons. He also worked for private clients, including the Earl of Findlater.

Despite his earlier financial difficulties, Auguste was obviously prosperous by the 1770s. Since the retirement of J.-N. Roettiers – whose house in the Place du Carrousel he had bought – he was unquestionably the leading silversmith in Paris. And the number of his employees reveals that he was working on the grand scale. At about this time he was also able to avail himself of the assistance of his son, Henri, born on 18 March 1759. Henri married on 7 September 1782 Madeleine Coustou, the daughter of an architect and descendant of the famous sculptor. The painter Joseph-Marie Vien was a witness at the wedding: the court painter Jean-Baptiste Pierre and the architect Jacques-Germain Soufflot both signed the register. Their names may indicate the artistic milieu in which the Augustes lived. In 1785 Henri obtained the succession to the official appointment held by his father who probably retired at this date. In 1788 Robert-Joseph was made supplier and manager of the Paris mint. He survived the Revolution and died on the 23 Ventose An. XIII (1805).

Henri Auguste continued to make grandiose dinner services until the Revolution. One, made for a Neapolitan ambassador, was acquired by George III in 1787 and is still in the English royal collection. It is much less smoothly designed than Robert-Joseph's services, with angular, almost chunky, handles to the tureens, and has the massiveness one associates with silver made by Paul Storr and others in London after 1800. But Henri's most distinguished works are in the full-blown Empire style. They include an ewer and swan-handled basin used at Napoleon's coronation and a *surtout de table* given by the City of Paris to Napoleon on the same occasion.

Despite Imperial patronage, Henri Auguste fell into financial difficulties. Owing 1,500,000 livres, he fled from Paris but returned to face his creditors who agreed to allow him eight years in which to put his affairs in order. In the autumn of 1809, however, he tried to smuggle no fewer than ninety-seven cases of silver out of France, was caught, bankrupted and deprived of his rights of citizenship. The silver was, of course, sequestered by the State. He crossed to England, then went to Saint Domingo and after a roving life died at Port-au-Prince in Haiti on 4 September 1816.

left The Empress's nef, made by Henri Auguste for the Empress Josephine in 1803. Château de Malmaison.

right Oil and vinegar stand by Robert-Joseph Auguste, 1775–6. The design is similar to that of the *huilier* in the dinner service made by Auguste for Count de Creutz and acquired by Gustavus III of Sweden. Musée du Louvre, Paris.

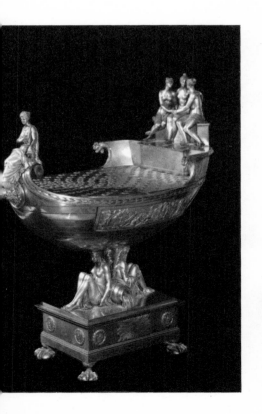

Paul Revere

(1734–1818)

Every American and English schoolboy knows – or used to know– the story of Paul Revere's ride, in lilting verse by Henry Wadsworth Longfellow. In England this only too easily memorized ballad has done as much harm to Longfellow as to Revere, obscuring the genuine gifts of the poet and the ability of the silversmith. The English have glibly and unjustly tended to dismiss the interest of American collectors in Revere's silver as little more than sentimental chauvinism. He certainly owes much of his fame to his activities during the War of American Independence, but the greater part of his life was, naturally, devoted to his craft and various industrial pursuits.

He was a second generation American. His father, Apollos Rivoire, was born at Riaucaud, near Bordeaux, in 1702 of a Huguenot family, left France in 1715, crossed the Atlantic from Guernsey and reached Massachusetts Bay late that year or early in 1716. Apollos was apprenticed to John Coney who died before he had finished his articles, and he may have served the rest of his term under another Boston silversmith. He had probably begun to work independently before 1729 when he married Deborah Hitchbourn, daughter of the owner of Hitchbourn Wharf in Boston. At about this time he anglicized his name and in 1730 announced in *The Weekly News Letter* that 'Paul Revere, Goldsmith is removed from Capt. Pitts at the Town Dock to North End over against Col. Hutchinson'.

His son, Paul Revere, was born in 1734 and baptized on 1 January 1735. He was probably educated at the North Writing School and trained in his father's workshop which made table silver in a solid, forthright, unornamented, but not inelegant, early Georgian manner. Apollos died in 1754 but was survived by his widow until 1777.

Like many other young New Englanders (including the cabinet maker, Benjamin Frothingham), Paul Revere served in the war against the French in Canada, enlisting in 1756 as a volunteer in Richard Gridley's regiment in which he was commissioned as a second lieutenant. He served in a campaign, rather like that which provides the background to James Fenimore Cooper's *The Last of the Mohicans,* until November when the approach of winter made further fighting impossible. Next year he married Sarah Orme who was to bear him eight children, only one of whom survived him. A few months after her death in 1773 he married his second wife, Rachel Walker.

In about 1765 the young John Singleton Copley painted the portrait of Paul Revere who had supplied him with silver miniature frames. It shows him clutching one of his own pear-shaped teapots. But these were lean years for those engaged in the luxury trades in Boston. A severe financial depression led to rioting. In 1765 Paul's estate was attached for a debt of only £10. He was, however, owed as much as this

above Tea service by Paul Revere, 1792–3. Minneapolis Institute of Arts.

below Two tureens by Paul Storr, 1806–7. I.D. Freemans.

Portrait of Paul Revere by John Singleton Copley, painted in about 1765. Museum of Fine Arts, Boston.

by Josiah Flogg, a jeweller, with whom he collaborated in publishing *A Collection of Psalm Tunes*. Obliged to find other means of earning a living, Revere turned his ability as an engraver to account in print making. But if he was well able to engrave arms or formal patterns on silver, he was rather less successful with figurative work and his prints are distinctly naïve. He also tried dentistry and one hopes that he was more expert in this line.

In 1760 Revere had become a Freemason and was later to be elected Grand Master of his Lodge. Although Freemasonry was by no means as free-thinking and libertarian as it was to become in the nineteenth century, it undoubtedly attracted many malcontents in the Colony. Membership would have brought Revere into close association with several of those most bitterly opposed to the British government. He showed his political colours more clearly in 1768 when he made for the Sons of Liberty a gallon punch-bowl in honour of the ninety-two members of the Massachusetts General Court who had refused to pay the new taxes. It was engraved with suitable symbols and legends – caps of liberty, 'No. 45' (alluding to John Wilkes), 'Magna Carta' and 'Bill of Rights'. At the same time he engraved a print – inspired by an English political caricature issued in a different context – showing the seventeen members who had accepted the taxes marching into the jaws of hell.

As tension mounted in 1773 Revere was one of the five Bostonians chosen by their fellows to find out if they would be backed by Sons of Liberty elsewhere. He travelled to New York and Philadelphia and brought back encouraging reports. This was just before the notorious Boston Tea Party in which members of two associations to which he belonged – the North Caucus and the St Andrew's Masonic Lodge – played an important part. The following spring and summer were deceptively calm. But, as he later wrote, 'In the fall of '74 and the winter of '75, I was one of upwards of thirty, chiefly mechanics, who formed ourselves into a committee for the purpose of watching the movements of the British soldiers and gaining every intelligence of the movements of the Tories. . . . In the winter, towards spring, we frequently took turns, two and two, to watch the soldiers by patrolling the streets all night.' And it was, of course, on 19 April 1775 that he made his great ride to Lexington to warn the country that the regulars were out. Next morning British and Colonial troops faced each other and the first shot of the war was fired.

At this time Revere would have found few calls for the services of a silversmith even if he had not been otherwise engaged. But with American Independence established and the return of peace, Revere went back to work in silver. One of his clients was the wealthy Elias Haskett Derby of Salem who was buying furniture from Samuel McIntyre at the same time. He also dealt in imported clothing, paper, pencils and large quantities of Sheffield plate. He began a foundry for casting bells – previously imported from England – and also bolts, spikes and so on for

Porringer made by Apollos Rivoire, a French immigrant who settled in Boston, anglicised his name as Paul Revere and was the father of the more famous Paul Revere. Metropolitan Museum, New York.

Tankard, a characteristic example of the simple and sturdy vessels made by Paul Revere before the War of Independence. Metropolitan Museum, New York.

Tea-pot by Paul Revere made for Moses Brown of Newburyport in 1789. As soon as the War of Independence was over, Revere's workshop began to produce plate in the most recent English style. Museum of Fine Arts, Boston.

ships. These several ventures seem to have prospered and in 1800 he moved to a grander house on Charter Street. In the same year he set up a rolling mill for sheet copper. He made his will in November 1816, disposing of property valued at about 30,000 dollars and died on 10 May 1818.

Though he is said to have worn to the end of his life breeches and hose of the type normal in his youth, he showed no such conservatism where silver was concerned. Before the War of Independence he worked in the plain early Georgian style which remained popular in Boston (though less so in the South) until the 1770s. But as soon as the war was over he picked up the latest English fashions, making delicately fluted, almost fragile, vessels very lightly engraved with feathery swags, and salvers perched on pretty little tip-toe feet. The Templeman tea-set of 1792–3 (now in

Tankard by Paul Revere, engraved with the coat of arms of the Jackson family. Museum of Art, Rhode Island School of Design, Providence.

Minneapolis Institute of Arts) is a fine example of his work in this manner. One is, nevertheless, bound to ask how much he contributed to the works made in the last two or three decades of his life, and to what extent his employees were responsible for the elegance of their design and refinement of their craftsmanship. He was engaged in so many concerns that he can have had little time to work with the silversmith's hammer and graver. And there can be little doubt that the fortune he left was derived less from his work as a silversmith than from his enterprise as an industrial manager.

231

Martin-Guillaume Biennais (1764–1843)

Martin-Guillaume Biennais, perhaps the best known of French Empire silversmiths, owed his prosperity to the dissolution of the Parisian *corporations* or guilds during the Revolution. The *Corporation des orfèvres* had been one of the six *grands corporations* of Paris (a group that included no furniture-makers), proud of its position and jealous of its privileges. It was limited to three hundred *maîtres*. Any candidate for membership who was not the son of a *maître* had to serve an apprenticeship of eight years, wait for a vacancy and then pay a fee of 1,350 livres. The dissolution of the guild opened the door to the entrepreneur. And Biennais was one of the first to exploit the opportunities offered by the new situation. This may be one reason why he succeeded while Henri Auguste, brought up in the old tradition, so miserably failed.

Biennais was the son of a peasant family, born at Lacochère (Orne) in 1764. But he must have gathered some capital by about 1789 when he established himself at the sign of the *Singe Violet* in the rue Saint Honoré in Paris, as a *tabletier* – that is to say a maker and vendor of such small objects as table games, and cane handles made of ivory, tortoise-shell, ebony or other woods. His stock also appears to have included the travelling cases called *nécessaires de voyage*. There is a charming story that

left Desk candelabrum made by Biennais in 1809 for Napoleon, but altered for Louis XVIII after 1815, when the original Napoleonic emblems were replaced by Bourbon insignia. Musée du Louvre, Paris.

right Nécessaire de voyage made in silver by Martin-Guillaume Biennais between 1810 and 1814. The box is made of mahogany inlaid with leather. Private collection.

The contents of the *nécessaire de voyage* reproduced on p. 233. *above*, tray with tea-pot, sugar-bowl and cream-jug: *below*, a cup and bottles in crystal mounted in silver-gilt, tea and coffee caddies, a chocolate heater and cutlery. Martin-Guillaume Biennais made this piece for Napoleon to give to his second empress, Marie Louise. Private collection.

at the time of the Napoleonic campaigns in Egypt and Italy, Biennais supplied *nécessaires* on credit to several indigent young officers who not only paid him on their return but patronized him ever more lavishly as they ascended the ranks of the army. Froment-Meurice who recounted this went on to say that Biennais 'was a complete stranger to *orfèvrerie*: not even the pieces of silver in the *nécessaires* he sold were made on his premises'. But in a very short time he found himself at the head of the most important goldsmith's and jeweller's business in Paris, employing some six hundred workmen.

It is easy to account for the success enjoyed by the *nécessaires* which

Silver-gilt tea-urn made by Martin-Guillaume Biennais and Joseph-Gabriel Genu in about 1800. Private collection.

Biennais produced, each composed of numerous pieces of exquisitely wrought silver which fit together in their leather case, as snugly as a child's box of bricks. Of the several that survive the finest is one completed for Napoleon in 1806 and, after many travels, presented to the Louvre in 1969. It includes a shaving bowl, boxes for soap, sponge and opiates, eye-bath, tooth brushes, tongue-scrapers, razors, scissors, bottle for eau de Cologne, an inkwell, compasses, pen-holders and candlesticks, not to mention a table service with plates, teapot, coffee-pot and so on – in all 86 pieces in a box only 14 cm. high, with a top measuring 54 cm. by 35 cm. (roughly $5\frac{1}{2} \times 21\frac{1}{2} \times 14$ inches). Other objects supplied by Biennais

235

for Napoleon included table services, candlesticks and swords. Though larger and slightly richer in decoration, the pieces of table silver have the same neatness as the objects in the *nécessaires*.

Napoleon set aside 100,000 francs a year for silver, most of which was purchased from Biennais and his only serious rival in Imperial favour, Jean-Baptiste-Claude Odiot. But this was seldom enough for his needs. In 1809 he bought from Biennais six of the shaded candlesticks called *flambeaux de bureau* at 7,000 francs apiece, not to mention many other objects. Special quantities of silver were needed for Napoleon's marriage to the Archduchess Marie-Louise in 1810. Biennais supplied the liturgical plate for the ceremony and also such pieces as a tea-service with an urn 80 cm. (31 inches) high. But the busiest and most profitable year for Biennais must have been 1811 when, to mark the birth of the King of Rome, he supplied the Imperial household with silver to the value of 720,199 francs – including 38 girandoles, 10 soup tureens, 46 dishes, 62 covers, several hundred plates and quantities of knives, forks and spoons.

Biennais worked for the other members of the Imperial family, especially Queen Hortense. He also supplied silver for the Russian Imperial family, notably a large dinner service for Michael Pavlovitch, brother of Alexander I. Special orders included the crowns, orb, sceptre and sword made for the coronation of the first King of Bavaria in 1806. But a very large number of his pieces bear no special emblems and appear to have been made for less distinguished clients both in France and elsewhere. He also did a brisk trade in military decorations and other insignia. On his writing paper he described himself as 'Orfèvre de S.M. L'Empereur et Roi' and declared that his goldsmith's and jeweller's workshop *Au Singe Violet*, rue Saint-Honoré 283, provided all French and foreign insignia.

Biennais was not himself a craftsman and it is unlikely that he was a designer. Although he probably called on Charles Percier and Pierre-François-Léonard Fontaine for designs for the grander pieces of Imperial plate, he seems to have employed a staff of draughtsmen capable of working in their style for more run-of-the-mill productions. His talent was for the organization of labour. In his workshop – as in Matthew Boulton's some years earlier – stylistic aims happily coincided with the practice of industrial production.

Biennais kept his position as official goldsmith to Napoleon until the end of the Hundred Days. The Empire style in which his silver was made remained popular in France long after 1815. But in 1819 Biennais retired and sold his business to Charles Cahier, goldsmith to Charles X of France. He died in 1843.

above Crown made for the coronation of the first King of Bavaria in 1806. *below* Sword made in 1804 for Napoleon, who gave it to his step-son, Prince Eugène Beauharnais. Both pieces are the products of the Biennais workshops. Schatzkammer der Residenz, Munich.

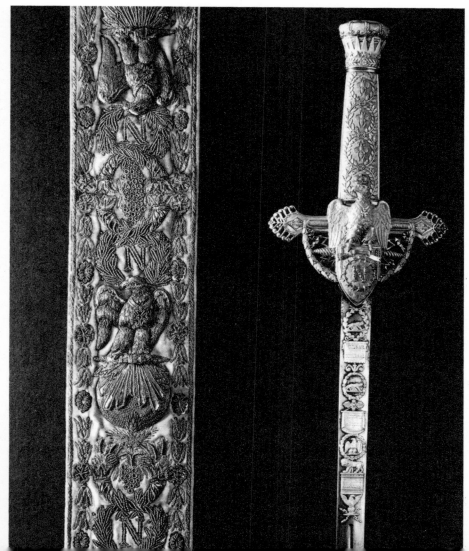

Paul Storr

(1771–1844)

The story of Paul Storr's life vividly illustrates the change in the status of the plateworker brought about by the industrialization of the silver trade. When he was born, in 1771, nearly all the more prominent London goldsmiths had been trained as craftsmen. When he died in 1844, the leading members of the trade were essentially merchants like Robert Garrard or manufacturers like George Richards Elkington. Ironically, the Industrial Revolution which made it possible for men from all walks of life to become captains of industry tended to favour the unskilled man (whether he came from a humble or middle class background) to the skilled craftsman who was tied by early training to a single last.

Paul Storr's father, Thomas Storr was a silver chaser who turned innkeeper or victualler of Tothill Street, Westminster, in 1788. At the age of fourteen Paul was apprenticed to a plate-worker of Swedish origin, and obtained his freedom in 1792 when he went into partnership with William Frisbee. This association was dissolved in 1796 when Storr began on his own with premises at 20 Air Street, in the Soho area. In 1801 he married Elizabeth Beyer, daughter of a German pianoforte and organ maker, who was to bear him ten children who, in turn, fathered and mothered fifty-four grand-children. From a social point of view it is interesting to note that Paul's eldest son was sent to Harrow and Oxford and then ordained in the Church of England.

In 1808 Storr moved from Air Street to 53 Dean Street Soho. Although he styled his firm 'Storr & Co.' he appears to have been working mainly for the jeweller and dealer in silver, Philip Rundell, with whom he entered into a formal partnership in 1811. This association also included John Bridge, Edmund Waller Rundell and John Theed, but there can be no doubt that Philip Rundell was the guiding spirit – if one may use that term for a character of Dickensian villainy.

By this time Rundell was already a successful businessman. Born in Bath in 1743, he had been apprenticed to a jeweller, went to London in 1767 and worked as a shopman for Theed and Pickett, goldsmiths and jewellers of Ludgate Hill who took him into partnership five years later. In 1781 Pickett's daughter was burnt to death while dressing for dinner and Rundell – always quick to take advantage of the misfortunes of others – played on his unhappiness to buy him out. With money borrowed from his brother (a doctor who married a rich patient), Rundell obtained sole command of the business in 1786. Two years later he took into partnership John Bridge, the brother of a successful west country farmer who had been consulted by George III on agricultural problems. Bridge had been working in the shop for some time and had presumably proved his ability to deal with rich and important clients. According to G. Fox, an assistant of the firm, he was employed in 'beating the bush to drive the game to Ludgate Hill'. It was due to his efforts that Rundell &

Silver cup made by Paul Storr and presented to Nelson by the Turkey Company to celebrate his victory at the Battle of the Nile in 1799. National Maritime Museum.

Bridge were appointed jewellers and goldsmiths to the Crown and given warrants by the Prince of Wales, the Duke of York and other members of the Royal family. Bridge was 'naturally of a timid quiet disposition', Fox wrote. 'To anyone and to every one by whom he expected to gain anything he was apparently the most humble and obedient person that could well be imagined, his back was exceedingly flexible and no man in London could bow lower or oftener than could Mr. Bridge'.

Rundell was, to quote Fox again, 'of a violent disposition, very sly and cunning and suspicious in the extreme. Avarice, covetousness and meanness were so deeply rooted in him that it affected every feature of his face and entered into every action of his life'. Yet he was at the same time 'naturally what the world calls a gay fellow and he might be seen at his shop door early of a morning with his jockey cap, scarlet coat, buckskin smalls, booted and spurred waiting the arrival of his groom with the horses that he might go and follow the chase to settle himself down a little after a night spent over the bottle or the card table.' He never married but kept a mistress on a pittance.

Profiting from the French Revolution, Rundell and Bridge acquired plate and jewellery brought to England by the emigrés, apparently at cut prices. The business was extended and in 1808 they took into partnership William Theed, a sculptor who had previously worked as a modeller for Wedgwood. The firm was joined next year by Rundell's nephew. All that was now needed was an accomplished silversmith who could act as workshop manager – and there were few in London better equipped than Paul Storr. Theed died in 1817 and the fact that his widow had to apply to the Royal Academy for financial assistance shows how little he had profited from the firm. Storr left in 1819. But by this date the Rundell organization was so rich and large – with agencies in Paris, Vienna, St Petersburg, Constantinople, Baghdad, Calcutta, Bombay and various towns in South America – that it could well afford the loss of partners.

While in partnership with Rundell, Storr continued to use his own mark on silver made under his direction. These pieces range from the simplest teaspoons and cruet frames to the largest and most elaborate centre-pieces and chandeliers. The smaller works are often very attractive, if no more distinguished than those produced at the same time by Benjamin Smith and a host of less well-known London silversmiths. But Storr made his name with silver on the grand scale. The earliest of his large works antedate his connection with Rundell by several years. A large christening font with figures of Faith, Hope and Charity which he made for the Duke of Portland is dated 1797–8. In 1799 the Governors and Company of the Merchants of England Trading into the Levant Seas commissioned from him the 'Battle of the Nile Cup' for presentation to Nelson. This was the beginning of the great age of presentation silver and Storr made many of the best pieces.

The majority of Storr's works are richly and boldly decorated with antique figures and ornaments both in relief and in the round. Some are as

Theocritus cup made by Paul Storr in 1812, after a model by the sculptor, John Flaxman. Collection of H.M. the Queen.

delicate as the Theocritus cup in the English Royal collection, after a model by John Flaxman. Others have a marmoreal massiveness. Surprisingly, Storr seems to have been among the first to draw inspiration direct from ancient Roman silver. For although eighteenth-century craftsmen had often based their designs on marble or pottery urns, none seems previously to have adapted the delicate vine-leaf border found on pieces of Roman silver.

In the same years Storr was also producing silver in a revived version of the Rococo style – rather heavy, perhaps, in comparison with the work of Thomas Germain but none the less richly encrusted with shell-work and rock-work and exuberant sea-horses. There seem to be two explanations for this early revival of the Rococo. As we have already seen, French emigrés brought silver, probably including early and mid-eighteenth-century pieces, with them to London: and Rundell was among those who bought from the emigrés. At the same time, the antique revival, especially in its more advanced form, had come to be associated first with the Revolution and secondly with Napoleon. The Prince Regent, a great lover of French decorative arts, said that he chose to build and decorate the Pavilion at Brighton in a mixture of exotic styles lest his furniture be accused of Jacobinism. Once the vogue for 'second' Rococo silver had been established in London it suffered no set-back and in the course of time contributed to the still more richly florid early Victorian manner.

Two-handled cup in silver made by
Paul Storr in 1806. Cleveland Museum
of Art.

After leaving Rundell's in 1819, Storr set up on his own in Harrison
Street, off Gray's Inn Road. Three years later he went into partnership
with John Mortimer, previously a salesman and chief assistant to a goldsmith with a shop in New Bond Street which they took over. Over-
buying brought them to the brink of ruin, averted by a nephew of
Storr's wife, John Hunt, who invested £5,000 in the concern and became
the third partner. All appears to have gone well until 1838 when Storr
and Mortimer quarrelled over the terms of the partnership. Next year

Centrepiece made for Sir Arthur Wellesley, later first Duke of Wellington, by Paul Storr. Victoria and Albert Museum, London.

Storr retired and lived at Hill House, Tooting, until his death on 4 March 1844. His estate was valued at only £3,000 which makes a striking contrast with the £1,500,000 left by his former partner Philip Rundell in 1827. The firm of Storr, Mortimer and Hunt continued after 1839 under the name of Mortimer and Hunt and then from 1842 as Hunt and Roskell. It continued to produce presentation silver, much of which was shown at the 1851 Exhibition in London when Hunt and Roskell vied with Messrs Robert Garrard in the fabrication of vast trophies, candelabra and vases.

243

Robert Garrard

(1793–1881)

Robert Garrard was born in 1793 almost literally with a silver spoon in his mouth. His father, Robert Garrard the elder, was a partner in a prominent firm of London silversmiths which he was later to inherit and develop into one of the most prosperous in all Europe. The history of this firm, recently elucidated by Mr A.G. Grimwade, is of considerable importance for an understanding not only of the career of Robert Garrard the younger, but also of the development of the silver trade in England.

In 1735 a silversmith named George Wickes established himself in Panton Street, London, at the sign of 'The King's Arms and Feather', and in 1747 went into partnership with Edward Wakelin, who had served an apprenticeship under the Huguenot silversmith John Le Sage. The firm dealt in both jewellery and silver. By 1792 Edward Wakelin's son, John, was in sole charge and went into partnership with Robert Garrard who had been working for the firm for a short while, though he had been apprenticed to a hardwareman and had no training as a silversmith. On Wakelin's death or retirement in 1802, Garrard obtained complete control of the firm which was run by his descendants until 1952, when it was amalgamated with the Goldsmiths' and Silversmiths' Company of Regent Street.

Ledgers reveal that the firm was involved less in making silver than in selling the works of various manufacturing silversmiths. From 1766 it ran accounts with nearly seventy plateworkers each of whom seems to have specialized in certain types of object. In the decade between 1766 and 1775, to quote Mr Grimwade, it 'bought candlesticks and waiters from Ebenezer Coker, salt and teaspoons from James Tookey, spoons from William and Thomas Chawner, salt-cellars from David and later David and Robert Hennell, miscellaneous plate from Daniel Smith and Robert Sharp, cruets from Thomas Piercey,' and so on. The firm bought from jewellers, ringmakers, watchmakers, and pearl stringers. It also dealt in plated goods supplied by Matthew Boulton of Birmingham and Roberts, Cadman & Co, of Sheffield. The same type of trade was maintained in the early nineteenth century under Garrard's direction and Paul Storr is recorded as supplying some beehive-shaped honey-pots.

It is probable that other firms of London silversmiths with shops in fashionable quarters – Thomas Heming for example – functioned in much the same way. But the example of Wakelin and Garrard is enough to show that the development of the silver trade from craft to industry was brought about not only by the creation of larger and better organized workshops but also by the division of makers from retail sellers. Both developments favoured what we now call the 'organization man' at the expense of the craftsman who, with a few rare exceptions, sank to the level of an artisan.

The elder Robert Garrard served an apprenticeship as a hardwareman,

Tureen made in 1824–5 by Garrards who specialized in the production of such weighty pieces of table silver. Campbell Museum, Camden, New Jersey.

but his sons stepped into business on the top floor. On Garrard's death in 1818 his three elder sons, Robert, James and Sebastian inherited the greater part of the concern with its shop in Panton Street and leasehold premises in Haymarket. Though only twenty-five years old, Robert seems to have taken immediate command of the firm which he controlled until his death on 26 September 1881 – a reign as long as that of Queen Victoria herself. Unfortunately there are no ledgers to chart the firm's progress over these many years. Other sources reveal that Garrards succeeded Rundell and Bridge as Royal goldsmiths in 1830 and became official Crown jewellers in 1843. Their royal commissions ranged from the provision of Waterman's badges and regalia for the Garter King of Arms and nine heralds at Queen Victoria's coronation, to making inkstands for the War Office, a jewelled pendant for Florence Nightingale and table-centres to the Prince Consort's own design. In 1852 they were charged with the task of cutting the Koh-i-noor diamond – the first facet being cut by the Duke of Wellington. They were patronized by other crowned heads, including the Czar of Russia. They made chains of office for mayors of English boroughs. The fact that Robert Garrard left personal estate valued at more than £109,000 indicates how very profitable his various activities had been.

Table-centre showing the 1st Duke of Marlborough writing a despatch on the battlefield at Blenheim, executed after a model by Edmund Cotterill and bearing the mark of Robert Garrard, 1846. Collection of the Duke of Marlborough, Blenheim Palace.

Much of Garrard's prosperity must have derived from ordinary day to day trade in silver wares for the dinner table, tea table and study, small objects of jewellery and the like. Executed in the usual range of Victorian styles, they seem often to have been designed to make their sterling solidity, their weight and consequently their value, immediately apparent. Although they were made for the purse-proud – like most other table silver – these pieces are showy but generally too stolid to be called vulgar. Standing on gleaming mahogany or set off by double damask, Garrard tureens and dishes still have considerable appeal – they seem redolent with the flavour of the turtle soup and stewed ortolans of Victorian England.

But if Garrard's made their fortune out of useful wares, they derived their reputation from objects both fanciful and useless. With Hunt and Roskell, they were the leading purveyors of presentation silver. They made the silver that the Liverpool Committee gave to Huskisson in 1825. They furnished race cups for Ascot and Doncaster, the Gordon Bennett Mediterranean yachting trophy, the America Cup. And they fabricated innumerable table-centres. Such pieces now look as if they were made to be given away. But many opulent Englishmen commissioned them to decorate their own tables. The Marquis of Exeter, for example, ordered a series of solid silver models of his prize bulls.

Moorish table-centre bearing the mark
of Robert Garrard, designed by
Edmund Cotterill, possibly working
from a sketch provided by the Prince
Consort. Collection of H.M. the
Queen.

Table-centre designed by the Prince Consort and made by Robert Garrard in 1842. Four of Queen Victoria's dogs are portrayed on it. Collection of H.M. the Queen; on loan to the Victoria & Albert Museum, London.

One of the most striking of Garrard's table-centres was made in 1842 to a design by the Prince Consort. Its decorative motifs are derived from sixteenth-century Italy and Germany with the addition of four models of the Queen's dogs. The Prince Consort also seems to have had a hand in designing a centre-piece in the Moorish style with Arabs and prancing horses. He was, of course, very interested in the improvement of the decorative arts and like many others of the time supposed that this could be achieved simply by engaging artists to design for industry.

In 1833 Garrard's had secured the services of Edmund Cotterill as head of their design section. Significantly, he was not a goldsmith but a sculptor who had been trained at the Academy Schools. A writer in the *Illustrated London News* remarked in 1842 that he 'deservedly stands at the head of the class of artists who model for silversmiths and his productions, annually exhibited at Messrs Garrards, have earned for that house a celebrity which no other can equal'. He specialized in racing trophies which another – or perhaps the same – writer in the *Illustrated London News* described as a 'national art and a national manufacture' comparing them favourably with earlier race cups. 'In former days, what were called Racing-cups were Cups, and nothing more – mere awkward vessels, fit for the rugged squires who contended for the possession of them; and of so rude and inelegant appearance, that, when seen in these days, they excite curiosity at the rusticity of our ancestors and derision at their total want of taste'. Cotterill's trophies included the Ascot Cup of 1842, representing an incident in the Battle of Crécy; the Queen's Cup for Ascot, 1848, a Mexican lassoeing a wild horse; and again for Ascot, in 1860, a statuette of Richard Coeur de Lion. In 1839 he modelled a testimonial given to the Earl of Eglinton as a record of the famous tournament. Another represents the death and treeing of a fox – an unappetizing subject which has a history in silver going back by way of Roettiers to the sixteenth century. In early 1850s Cotterill visited the East and, in the words of a contemporary, 'had many opportunities of seeing Oriental scenery and costume' which enabled him to produce 'figures truthful and accurately characteristic', like the group of Arab horsemen at an oasis which served as the Goodwood Cup in 1854.

Cotterill died in 1860 and was succeeded at Garrard's by W.F. Spencer who seems to have been rather less ambitious. Spencer was probably responsible for the elaborate table ornaments made for the Maharajah Duleep Singh and shown at the International Exhibition of 1862. The principal group, according to the catalogue, 'represents the late Maharajah Rinjeet Singh seated in his houda on an elephant, receiving a famous horse which he desired to possess'. But the number of people who 'desired to possess' such fantastic objects in silver was soon to decline rapidly. New notions of what constituted 'good taste' were abroad and soon the 'rustic' cups which the writer in the *Illustrated London News* had scorned were to be preferred to the richest and most elaborate examples of Victorian silver.

George Richards Elkington (1801–65)

The patenting of the electro-plating process by Elkingtons of Birmingham in 1840 revolutionized the silver trade. With the hindsight of history we can now see that the time was ripe for such a development. The industrialization of the silversmiths' workshop had already been effected. As a result of the fluctuation and decline of the price of the ingot, silver had ceased to be regarded as a good investment and had come to be valued mainly for its glitter and, of course, as a status symbol. And for the increasingly large middle class demanding the elegance of table silver, Sheffield plate was as good as sterling – until tell-tale glints of copper began to show through the surface. Electro-plated articles proved much more durable than Sheffield plate supplying, as Elkingtons proudly remarked in 1847, 'all the advantages of silver, in utility and beauty of effect, and at very much less cost to the consumer'. Although Elkington had not aimed at providing a substitute for Sheffield plate when he began to experiment in electrolysis, he was quick to realize the potentialities of his discovery and exploit them.

George Richards Elkington was born in Birmingham on the 17 October 1801. From his father, James Elkington, he inherited a gilt toy and spectacle manufactory which he developed in partnership with his cousin Henry Elkington. In 1830 he began experiments to discover a method of gilding less dangerous than the mercury process. The first of his many patents, taken out in 1836, was for 'an improved method of gilding copper, brass, and other metals or alloys of metals' by a process which in fact involved electrolysis, though it is doubtful if he was aware of its physico-chemical niceties. In 1839 he exhibited jewellery and bronze objects 'gilt without mercury' in Paris, giving an address in the rue du Temple. But by this time he had already begun to turn his attention to silver plating. In the same year he wrote to the London silversmith Benjamin Smith: 'the four candlesticks you ordered are now ready for silvering and shall be done as richly as possible upon the method we have in use. It is uncertain how soon we can complete the improvement we contemplate, but ultimately I have no doubt of effecting it'. Three days later he reported 'sufficient progress to speak positively as to the success'. On 24 March 1840 he took out a patent for plating by means of a galvanic current.

His discovery was a by-product of a series of experiments carried out by scientists in different parts of Europe. Alessandro Volta had discovered in 1799 that a current of electricity may be generated by bringing two or more metals into contact with a suitable fluid. Various chemists then found that an electric current passed through a conducting liquid decomposed its ingredients and set their elements free at the immersed electric poles. In 1801 Dr William Hyde Wollaston succeeded in coating a piece of silver with copper and in 1805 Brugnatelli gilded two silver

medals by electrolysis. But the process would have had little practical value if it had not been discovered that the alloy variously known as German silver or nickel silver – an alloy of about forty parts copper, twenty spelter and twenty nickel (a metal first discovered in the eighteenth century) – provided the best base on which to deposit silver by electrolysis. The next problem which faced the metallurgists was to obtain even, thick and durable deposits of a good colour. The Elkingtons in collaboration with Alexander Parkes – a scientist whom they employed – and John Wright, a Birmingham surgeon whom they took into partnership, found that this could be done by the addition of cyanides of silver to the liquid. The objects thus plated were, however, coated with a film of frosty white silver which had to be burnished. It was not until 1847 that two of Elkington's employees showed that the addition of bisulphide of carbon to the solution would cure this defect.

Elkingtons had begun to enlarge their premises in Birmingham before the discovery of the electro-plating process, building a new factory

The Milton Shield of silver and damascened iron, designed by Léonard Morel-Ladeuil, and made in Elkington's factory. It won a gold medal at the Paris Exhibition in 1867. Victoria and Albert Museum, London.

which was begun in May 1838 and partly ready for use by the end of the year. Indeed, they seemed at first to have intended keeping to the toy business and profit from their invention by licensing out the patent. Thus they took out patents in various European countries. In 1841 they issued a licence to gild photographic prints. And, as we shall see, they licensed Charles Christofle in France to use their silver-plating process in 1842. Their records show that they were interested in various types of manufacture. In 1841 they began to buy designs from one of the more curious artists of the time, 'Sir' Benjamin Schlick, who had come to England after working in Germany, France and Italy. It seems probable that these were intended for the production of solid silver articles made by the complex electrotype process which they had developed and patented in 1841. In 1845 they bought an 'invention' for making Chinese gongs – for the modest price of £50 (200 dollars). But soon they were wholly committed to making silver and silver-plated articles. Gradually mechanization took command of the factory. In 1852, for instance, they installed a large steam-operated apparatus to stamp out the nickel-silver objects which had previously been raised mainly by hand and hammer and soldered together.

A catalogue issued in 1847 states that Elkington's electro-plate had already withstood 'the most severe test of wear in the vessels of the Royal Mail Steam Packet Company, the Peninsular and Orient Company, and numerous Club Houses, Hotels and Private houses in every part of the kingdom'. But doubts were expressed about the durability of the new ware. While commending the electro-gilding process, because it was safer for the artisan, the jury of the 1851 Exhibition was less than confident about the silver plate. In 1862, however, the exhibition jury pronounced that 'there is no limit to the art which may be employed in the production of plated goods by the new process of electro deposit, and for articles in daily use it is now found to be quite as durable as the old process'. The great advantage of electro-plate was, however, that worn articles could be cheaply and easily replated.

As the 1847 catalogue reveals, the firm's first wares were in the range of styles used at the same time for solid silver objects. If anything, they were rather more elaborately fussy as if to demonstrate how they had overcome all technical difficulties. The only austere items are a chalice and 'pocket communion service' of a severity to appeal only to Evangelicals. The range of table wares embraces all the usual objects as well as such Victorian specialities as marrow scoops, asparagus tongs and sugar tongs. Prices are higher than might be expected – £32 (128 dollars) for an engraved tea-tray, £30 (120 dollars) for a candelabrum, £16 5s. od. (64 dollars) for a plain tea-kettle and £17 10s. od. (70 dollars) for an engraved one. Table forks of ordinary quality cost no more than £2 4s. od. (8·8 dollars) per dozen. These prices were greatly reduced in subsequent years, but the fact they began rather high may have helped to establish the commodity among those who affected to despise the 'cheap and nasty'.

Teapot with rivets, designed by Christopher Dresser and produced in Elkington's factory, c. 1898.

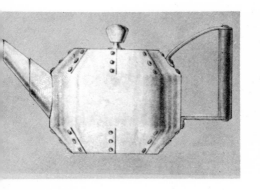

The fortunes of Elkington were made by the mass-production of useful wares, and especially those made for use in hotels and restaurants. But the Victorian industrialist was expected to live not by bread and butter alone. The firm thus set out to rival Garrards and Hunt & Roskell in the production of decorative pieces in solid silver which would catch the eye of exhibition jurors and increase their prestige. They used the electrotype process to make silver replicas of natural objects – doing chemically what Jamnitzer had achieved by a process of casting many years before – and also for the reproduction of earlier masterpieces of silver and other metals.

For the design of both ordinary and ornamental pieces, Elkingtons employed a succession of French sculptors. The first was Aimé Chesneau (the master of Carrier-Belleuse). He was succeeded by Pierre Emile Jeannest who signed a five year contract in 1853. He specialized in Renaissance and classical style work, sometimes with a touch of auricular ornament, but also modelled a statuette of Lady Godiva, commissioned by the Prince Consort, a group of Queen Elizabeth and the Earl of Leicester and another showing Charles I meditating on the corpse of a standard-bearer after Edgehill. Albert Wilms, who had previously worked for Christofle and Froment-Meurice in Paris was taken on in 1855 and was responsible for work in Gothic and Byzantine styles, besides a rather fussy Pompeiian dinner service. But the most successful of the Elkington modellers was Léonard Morel-Ladeuil who worked for them from 1859 until his death in 1888. His masterpiece was the Milton shield which won a gold medal at the Paris Exhibition in 1867.

Jeannest was paid £450 (1,800 dollars) a year; Morel-Ladeuil began at £400 (1,600 dollars). They were clearly the most highly remunerated members of the staff. A draughtsman who had completed his apprenticeship seems to have received about 60 shillings (12 dollars) a week, an electro-depositor and a polisher 30 shillings (6 dollars) – that is for a sixty hour week. By 1865 when G.R. Elkington died, the firm was employing more than one thousand men and women. He left a fortune of £350,000 (1,400,000 dollars) which suggests that the enterprise was still more profitable than Robert Garrard's trade in solid silver.

The death of the founder did little to alter the nature of the firm which continued to prosper and grow. Only one subsequent event demands special mention – the purchase of designs in about 1880 from Christopher Dresser, one of the most interesting of the artists involved in the decorative arts in the nineteenth century. His silver designs not only made a complete break with historical styles but were intended exclusively for industrial production. But the rarity of these pieces suggests that they were made in small numbers and achieved little popularity at the time. They may well have seemed too revolutionary to win much support either from the intellectual aesthetes who called for arts and craftsmanship, or from the general public who still demanded that silver plate should provide them with some of the status reflected in solid silver.

François-Désiré Froment-Meurice (1802–55)

The name of Froment-Meurice is familiar to attentive readers of Balzac's novels, though few may realize that he was not a fictitious character. He was perhaps the most fulsomely praised of all nineteenth-century craftsmen. Balzac bought the works of his 'cher aurifaber'. Gautier eulogized him. Victor Hugo addressed him as 'ouvrier magicien' in an ode. Eugène Sue began letters to him: 'Mon cher Benvenuto'. Indeed, few of those who apostrophized his works failed to compare him with Cellini whose autobiography, in a translation published in 1822, was just then delighting the Parisian public. Yet even this was not enough for his most devoted admirers. Philippe Burty seriously claimed that Cellini's famous salt cellar was a poor thing – ill composed, overcharged with conceits, crowned by badly proportioned figures – in comparison with the masterpieces of Froment-Meurice.

He was born in Paris on 31 December 1802, the son of François Froment, a goldsmith who died young. His mother soon married another goldsmith, Pierre Meurice, from whom François-Désiré took the second barrel of his name. He began his career in his step-father's workshop which, as he later recalled, had been much occupied in supplying plate for Biennais and Odiot. In 1818 he left Meurice's atelier to complete his apprenticeship under a 'ciseleur'. He also studied painting and sculpture. Little is known of his activity during the next twenty years, though he is said to have been intimate with Jacques-Henri Fauconnier, who worked in the Renaissance style, and a German, Karl Wagner who revived the niello technique.

Anglomania was rife in Restoration Paris, and no English products seem to have been more generally admired than table silver. In some notes on *Orfèvrerie* written in 1852, Froment-Meurice declared that the many Englishmen who settled in Paris from about 1817 and brought their own plate with them 'completely overthrew the pure and classic style of French silver substituting for it the English Rococo, a degenerate version of the Louis XV style which still reigns supreme in London'. According to Froment-Meurice, Fauconnier was one of the few who tried to stem this English invasion by attempting a Renaissance revival – but he went bankrupt.

Taste had, however, begun to change by 1839 when Froment-Meurice made his artistic debut. This was probably due to the strongly nationalistic sentiments of the romantic writers who were later to lavish such praise on him. The works he showed at the 1839 exhibition won him a silver medal. According to Jules Janin his showroom was promptly thronged with *lions* and fashionable ladies who went to examine, if not always to buy, brooches, bracelets and scarf-pins. Five years later, at the 1844 exhibition, he was awarded a gold medal and ranked as the leading jeweller and goldsmith in France. The extent of his rapidly increasing

Massive silver bracelet made by Froment-Meurice in 1841. Two women are resting upon the skin of a lion. Musée des Arts Décoratifs, Paris.

success may be gauged from the number of assistants he employed: twenty-five in 1839, eighty in 1844, and one hundred and twenty in 1848.

The jury of the 1839 exhibition commended both the design and the execution of his works. He employed, they recorded, M. Richard as founder and Antoine Vechte as a 'ciseleur', but also did much himself. One of his exhibits was a Gothic bracelet with a relief of St Louis – destined to break any but the brawniest arm. He also showed a tea-set described as being 'in the sixteenth-century style with features that recall the oriental style'. Generally, however, he aimed at reviving the style of the Mannerist goldsmiths with much strapwork, foliage and figures, sometimes derived from large scale sixteenth-century sculpture, French or Italian.

Froment-Meurice's literary friends and patrons enjoyed the sensation of playing François I or Cosimo de' Medici to his Benvenuto Cellini. But the contrast between their high-flown phrases and the types of object he made is often comic. Balzac told him that his monkey encrusted cane-handle was 'of an unheard of perfection, and worthy of you'. Eugène Sue asked his 'dear Benvenuto' to make some little statuettes of children to hold menus on his dining table. And, he said, he would also like some salt cellars decorated with vine-leaves arranged with holders for tooth-picks, adding: 'C'est très vulgaire, mais très commode'.

Though writers were largely responsible for Froment-Meurice's fame, they were not his most generous clients. He was more lavishly

above left Design made by Froment-Meurice for the *surtout de table* of the Duc de Luynes.

above right The central part of the *surtout de table* of the Duc de Luynes, as executed by Froment-Meurice.

opposite Engraving of the dressing-table created by Froment-Meurice for the ladies of France to give the Duchess of Parma in 1849. From the catalogue of the 1851 Exhibition.

patronized by a large company of rich people – both *anciens* and *nouveaux* – for whom he made the elaborate confections illustrated in the art magazines of the day. For the Duc de Luynes – perhaps the most enthusiastic patron of goldsmiths of the time – he executed a vast *surtout de table*. As Orfèvre to the City of Paris, he made a large vase charged with symbolic decoration which was presented to the Paris water engineer Emery. Another of his ecstatically praised performances was a racing trophy made for a Russian patron in 1844 – a large shield richly embossed with scenes illustrating the history of the horse and with a statuette of Neptune driving his sea-horses in the centre. A contemporary account reveals who was responsible for the design and execution of each part.

As a wedding present for the ladies of France to give the Duchess of Parma in 1849, Froment-Meurice and many named assistants made a

JARVIS.

right Toilette de Venus, a statuette in gold and ivory made by Froment-Meurice.

below Engraving of the cane-handle created for Balzac by Froment-Meurice. The handle is covered with tiny figures of monkeys.

La Canne de Mr. de Balzac.

toilet table surmounted by a looking-glass, in all some three metres (10 feet) high, encrusted with figurative sculpture, enamel paintings, niello work – indeed, practically every type of decoration ever applied or misapplied to silver and gold. It was mainly in the Gothic style though scantily dressed putti introduced an eighteenth-century note. The niello plaques were said to be the largest ever made. It was one of the costliest fabrications of its period and – to judge from engravings – one of the least likely to appeal to us today. In addition to his secular work, Froment-Meurice made a fair amount of ecclesiastical plate. An enamelled gold and silver chalice was commissioned from him by the Abbé Combalot who gave it to Pope Pius IX. He also made a gold inkstand for presentation to Pius IX and a large ostensory (given by Queen Amélie) which he passed on to Cologne Cathedral.

right Engraving of the gold inkstand made by Froment-Meurice for presentation to Pope Pius IX.

Froment-Meurice made use of a very wide variety of materials. At the 1851 exhibition in London he showed, among many other things, 'a chased iron casket, the property of the Comte de Paris'. But he generally confined himself to a mixture of precious substances. He made much use of ivory, often in large pieces, as for a statuette of Leda with gold drapery and an oxidized silver swan. Anxious to establish himself as both jeweller and goldsmith he wrote in 1852 that 'to separate the profession of goldsmith from that of *bijoutier*, and that of *bijoutier* from that of jeweller has always seemed to me contradictory . . .'. He longed for a return to 'the time of the great goldsmiths of the past' when the art of the orfèvre comprehended work in precious metals, the mounting of stones, chasing, enamelling, nielloing and so on. But he was clear-sighted enough to see that although the artist-goldsmith could not hope to compete with industrial manufacturers in the production of useful household wares, he could not merely survive but flourish by concentrating on decorative objects.

Froment-Meurice died at the height of his fame in 1855. Obituary notices accorded him a final fanfare of unqualified praise. His studio was taken over by his son Émile, born in 1837, who continued to produce work in much the same style until late in the century when Art Nouveau came into fashion. Émile Froment-Meurice died in 1913.

Charles Christofle

(1805–63)

Charles Christofle received no poetical encomiums comparable with those showered on his contemporary F.-D. Froment-Meurice; yet there can be no doubt that he played a role of far greater importance in the history of the decorative arts. He was an industrialist, the founder of a firm which still produces a very large proportion of the table wares in daily use in France. Born in 1805, he was apprenticed to his brother-in-law Calmette who ran a jewellery workshop in Paris. In 1825 he became Calmette's partner and in 1831 succeeded to the direction of the business. At the exhibition of 1839 he received the first of the many medals he was to gather on such occasions. By this date he had, however, begun to turn his attention from trinkets to household plate and to new methods of production.

Several French firms were already making Sheffield plate, by the English process and also to English-inspired designs. But Charles Christofle soon realized that the future lay with electro-plate. In 1842 he bought for 150,000 francs the right to use the plating process patented in the preceding year by the chemist Ruolz. Discovering that Elkingtons' process, using the same chemicals to the same effect, had been patented a few months earlier he was obliged to pay them 500,000 francs. He had, however, obtained the monopoly of making electro-plate in France and his outlay was soon yielding handsome dividends. By 1847 his annual turnover had risen to more than 2,000,000 francs. His first products were designed mainly in the Louis XV and Louis XVI styles with plenty of relief decorations which could so much more easily and economically be silvered by electrolysis than by the old Sheffield process.

The second great turning point in Christofle's career came in 1852 when he took his nephew Henri Bouilhet into the firm. Born in 1830, Bouilhet had received a liberal education at the College Saint-Barbe and then at the École des Arts et Manufactures in Paris, where he won a diploma in engineering and chemistry in 1851. With this scientific training he was able to introduce several novel processes to the Christofle factory, devising a new type of machine for stamping out spoons and forks, and developing a galvanoplastic method of mass producing large scale architectural ornaments and statues in single pieces. But he was interested in art no less than science. Later he was to serve as vice-president of the Union Centrale des Arts Décoratifs responsible for the establishment of the Musée des Arts Décoratifs in Paris. And his last years were devoted to writing a history of *L'Orfèvrerie française aux XVIIIe et XIXe siècles* which, not unnaturally, gives great prominence to the house of Christofle.

In 1853 Napoleon III gave an accolade not only to Christofle but to electro-plate by commissioning a very large plated dinner service for the Tuileries. This was construed as an attempt to 'démocratiser le luxe'.

Fragments of the Pompeiian *surtout* made by Charles Christofle for Prince Joseph Charles, the cousin of Napoleon III. The *surtout* had a flat base encrusted with silver and gold; on which was placed a candelabrum column. This was surmounted by leopards, Bacchus and statues of Melpomene and Thalia. The *surtout* was dismembered and fragments of the leopards and Bacchus are all that remain. Musée Christofle.

right Dish from the electro-plated service made by Christofle for Napoleon III in 1853. Musée des Arts Décoratifs, Paris.

left Coffee set made by Charles Christofle in the 1830s. Musée Christofle.

Table-centre from the service made for Napoleon III. The greater part of the service was destroyed in 1871. Musée Nationale de la Château de Compiègne.

Each piece was in the Louis XVI style, so beloved by the Empress Eugénie, with the addition of Napoleonic symbols. It is said to have cost 618,708 francs – a large sum, but a fraction of what it would have been if executed in solid silver. Princess Pauline Metternich snobbishly remarked that it was 'amusing to eat off "Ruolz"', to which the Emperor replied that 'the silver of kings serves only to be melted down at some moment'. In the event it was not to answer the needs of the exchequer that this dinner service perished: the greater part was destroyed when the Tuileries was burnt down in 1871.

The Christofle factory was also patronized by Napoleon III's cousin, Prince Joseph-Charles, known as Plonplon, who had no desire to democratize anything. For the fantastic Pompeiian house in the Champs Elysées, Christofle made an appropriate table-centre incorporating statues with ivory flesh and silver-gilt drapery. The decorative details were all taken from casts of objects found at Pompeii.

But the factory was, of course, occupied mainly in producing electro-plated wares at reasonable prices for middle class clients. A catalogue

Jug in the Louis-Philippe style by
Christofle, 1830–40. Musée Christofle.

issued in about 1860 has fancy lithographs of a range of objects including
a Turkish style jug with embossed chasing, trays, tureens, tea-urns and so
on, mainly in the neo-Rococo manner which was highly fashionable in
France at that moment. The titles to the illustrations are printed in
French, English and Spanish which suggest the extent of the firm's
foreign trade.

On Charles Christofle's death in 1863 the direction of the firm then
passed to his twenty-five year old son, Paul, and Henri Bouilhet. Under
their direction it grew in size and prosperity. On Paul's death in 1907 it
was employing one thousand, five hundred workmen, mainly in the
factory at Saint-Denis. Branches were established in Karlsruhe, Vienna
and Brussels.

The various Christofle price lists point out that all their products
were available in solid silver as well as electro-plate. This was important

at a time when appearances counted for so much: wares easily identifiable as electro-plate (because the same patterns were unavailable in solid silver) would hardly have appealed to the middle class public. However, it is very significant that a price list of 1891 claimed that Christofle's 'orfèvrerie argentée' was used in administrative offices of the French Republic, on Atlantic liners, in the largest hotels and in 'princely and private houses' throughout the world. It had, the price list claimed, more or less replaced solid silver, 'and costs a fifth of the price, having a solidity and beauty in no way inferior to the best wares made in solid silver'. When new it cannot be visually distinguished from solid silver, though it is generally lighter in weight. At the 1900 Paris exhibition Christofle introduced a new type of plated ware called 'Gallia Metal' which was heavier and more sonorous when struck.

Although Bouilhet himself was obsessed with the need to create a new

Drawings of tea-urns made by the
factory of Christofle.
left In the style of Louis XVI.
right In the style of Louis XV.

decorative style, nearly all the objects made at the Christofle factory in
the nineteenth century were derived from Louis XV and Louis XVI
silver and occasionally Japanese metalwork. Outside designers, including
the sculptor Carrier-Belleuse, were occasionally employed for such
special works as table-centres and trophies. The limp flowers of Art
Nouveau made their first rather timid appearance on wares of the 1890s.
Most of the more expensive Gallia Metal objects in the 1904 catalogue
are conceived in the new style which had by then won widespread
popularity. There are butter-dishes adorned with chrysanthemums,
crumb-scoops with lank ears of corn in relief, and many articles decorated
with drowsy, heavy-headed poppies.

After World War I, Christofle began to employ more adventurous
designers. They produced much in the 1925 Art-Deco style. Table wares
made for the Atlantic liner *Normandie* in 1935 are of rather greater
interest, including some appealing spherical salt-cellars. Since World
War II the firm has much employed the distinguished Finnish designer,
Tapio Wirkkala. It still produces much of the best electro-plated
table wares.

Plate in the Japanese style, by the
Christofle factory. Museum für
angewandte Kunst, Vienna.

Henry Gooding Reed

(1810–1901)

H.G. Reed of Reed & Barton was the pioneer of electro-plating in the United States, and was thus the transatlantic opposite number of G.R. Elkington or Charles Christofle. He was born in 1810 in Taunton, Massachusetts, where his family had been established for some five generations. After working for a while as a book-keeper in his father's shop, he began his career as an apprentice in a factory founded in 1824 by Isaac Babbitt and William Crossman to produce the first Britannia metal wares made in America.

Britannia metal is an alloy similar in substance and appearance to pewter, though lighter in weight and whiter in tone (hence the alternative name 'white metal'). As Mr G.S. Gibb remarks in his excellent book *The Whitesmiths of Taunton*, it lent itself to industrial production more readily than pewter. 'Because Britannia metal could be rolled in the sheet and spun into thin-walled vessels over inexpensive wooden moulds, production costs were lower, and a much less expensive product could be placed on the market.' This alloy appears to have been discovered in England shortly after the middle of the eighteenth century when pewterers were beginning to suffer from competition by the makers of Sheffield plate and also by the recently modernized potteries of Staffordshire. Large-scale manufacture did not begin until about 1780 and it was not until 1804 that James Dixon in Sheffield established the factory that was to become the leading producer. From 1816 large quantities of Britannia wares were imported into America where several attempts were made to reproduce them.

When Reed began to work for Babbitt and Crossman the firm was employing only fifteen hands. But it had already built up a trade connection not only in Massachusetts and Rhode Island but further south in New York. In 1829, indeed, more than half of the factory's output was sold to New York retailers. It specialized in tea-table equipment and in 1829 sold 1,784 teapots at about 2 dollars apiece, 556 coffee-pots, 256 cream and sugar sets. The teapots were of the late eighteenth-century English urn-shaped pattern still being made in the Sheffield factories which, despite the costs of transatlantic shipping, were the company's most formidable rivals.

After a bad year the factory stopped production in the winter of 1834. Early next year Reed, who had been working as a spinner, Charles E. Barton, a solderer, and Benjamin Pratt, the sales agent, persuaded the chief shareholder, Horatio Leonard, to allow them to rent the concern. They began under the name of 'The Taunton Britannia Manufacturing Company', changed to 'Reed & Barton' in 1840. From that moment on the development of the concern is a simple industrial success story.

The firm's first products were copied from English wares. They were, indeed, unashamed plagiarisms. Writing to a Boston retailer they de-

Britannia metal tea-set made by Reed and Barton at Taunton. Massachusetts, c. 1837–47. Messrs Reed and Barton.

clared: 'You ask if we have seen the new Importers pattern Tea Ware. We have them all at our Mill and shall make the best and put them into the market much less than the English'. They kept abreast not only of English designs but also of new manufacturing techniques. As electro-plated wares gradually drove those of Britannia metal out of fashion, Reed & Barton began to specialize in the new medium.

By the 1850s when several American firms were producing wares in Britannia metal and electro-plate as good as those made by Reed & Barton and at similar prices, Reed seems to have appreciated that the key to future success lay with the designer as much as the technician. He also realized that the public was likely to assess metal wares by the quantity rather than the quality of applied ornaments. A drawing office was set up under an immigrant English die-sinker, Parkin, and Reed designed some of the wares himself. The new patterns were not conspicuously original, but they were derived rather than copied from English prototypes. In 1858 the firm began to take out patents for its designs.

Long after Reed & Barton had become one of the leading producers of electro-plate in America they began to make wares of solid silver. As we have seen, good silver wares had been made in America since the early colonial period. But the public for silver remained small even in the early nineteenth century and no efforts were made to industrialize production. It was not until after the discovery of the Comstock silver lode in 1859 and the introduction of new refining processes, which lowered the price of unwrought silver, that an increased supply seems to have

271

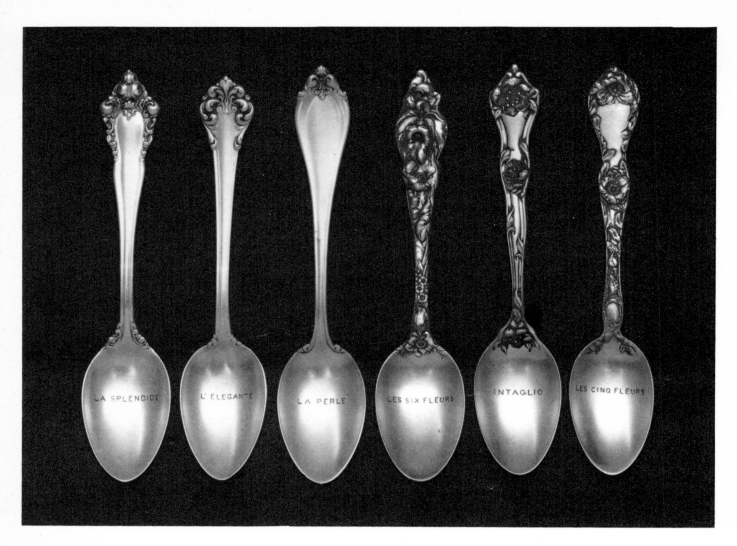

Spoons made by Reed and Barton in the 1890s; they could be supplied in electroplate or solid silver. Messrs Reed and Barton.

created a demand for silver table wares. Soon the Gorham Manufacturing Company was exploiting a new public for solid silver. Reed & Barton were never to abandon electro-plate, but from 1889 they manufactured increasing quantities of silver articles, especially objects suitable for wedding presents. In three years, from 1890 to 1892, they expanded their output of solid silver from the value of 66,055 to 312,005 dollars.

Their first solid silver products are restrained and seem reminiscent of the eighteenth century – answering no doubt, the new interest in Americana. But most of their electro-plated wares are very richly decorated with flowers and scrolls and figures of putti. For special occasions they created still more elaborate confections like the Progress Vase which won a first prize at the Centennial Exposition in Philadelphia in 1876 – a monstrous object one metre (40 inches) high with an urn between groups representing progress from barbarism to civilization.

For more than seventy years Reed was engaged in what he called 'just putting one dollar on top of another'. Though he is said to have regarded the drawing office as the 'heart' of the concern, his attitude to it was purely commercial. Under his control the company efficiently answered the demands of a public who wished to realize the American dream of affluence in glittering table wares. He died on 1 March 1901 when the direction of the firm passed to his son-in-law H. B. Dowse – an industrialist of the new era, educated in the Harvard Law School – who was to be succeeded in 1923 by his son-in-law Sinclair Weeks.

left Electro-plated tea-set made in the Reed and Barton Factory in 1875, probably to the design of H.G. Reed. Messrs Reed and Barton.

right Display wagon used to show the wares of the Reed and Barton factory in 1889. Messrs Reed and Barton.

Charles Lewis Tiffany

(1812–1902)

When Marcel Proust wanted to give a present to Gaston Calmette, editor of *Le Figaro*, he bought from Tiffany's a black moiré cigarette case with a monogram in brilliants. That Proust should have gone to Tiffany's is no less appropriate than that Balzac should have patronized Froment-Meurice. In grand *fin de siècle* society on both sides of the Atlantic, Tiffany was a by-word for luxury goods. It is nevertheless surprising to find that an American firm was able to establish itself successfully, indeed pre-eminently, in Paris, so long regarded as the capital of the decorative arts.

Charles Lewis Tiffany was a vendor rather than a maker of precious objects and the story of his career illuminates the increasingly important role of the retailer. He was born at Killingly, Connecticut, on 15 February 1812, of a family established in New England for five generations. His father, Comfort Tiffany, was a cotton manufacturer, and at the age of fifteen Charles Lewis left school to take charge of a little country store which sold his father's products. But in 1837 Charles Lewis decided to go and seek a larger fortune in New York. With a capital of 1,000 dollars, and in partnership with a school friend, John B. Young, he opened a fancy goods and stationery store at 259 Broadway, in half of a double-fronted house. It was hardly a propitious moment: the city was in the grip of a financial crisis and many well-established firms were slipping towards bankruptcy. Nevertheless, Tiffany & Young contrived to sell a stock consisting of various types of bric-à-brac, papier maché, umbrellas, walking sticks, writing cases and dressing cases, fans, pottery and stationery.

In 1841 Tiffany & Young enlarged their showrooms by renting the house next door. By this date they were selling Bohemian glass, French and Dresden porcelain, clocks, cutlery and Parisian jewellery as well as the simpler types of article with which they had begun. Business continued to improve and the firm, now styled Tiffany, Young & Ellis, moved to better premises at 271 Broadway. As Tiffany's biographer, G. F. Heydt was to remark: 'The political disturbances of 1848 in Paris afforded many opportunities for shrewd investments'. When the price of diamonds fell by about fifty per cent, Tiffany and his partners hastened to buy as many as they could afford. It was probably this act that enabled them to set up a small workshop for manufacturing jewellery. In 1850 they established a branch in the rue Richelieu, Paris, which not only provided them with an outlet in Europe but also added Parisian lustre to their reputation at home.

It was to Tiffany's that Jenny Lind went, on arriving for her first concert tour of America in 1850, to order a silver tankard for presentation to the captain of the ship that had brought her across the Atlantic. This memento was made by John C. Moore, a silversmith mainly engaged

Pitcher made by Tiffany & Co. in 1859 for presentation to Colonel A. Duryee of the 7th Regiment of the National Guard 'as a mark of high appreciation from his Fellow Citizens for his soldier-like qualities and the valuable services rendered by the Regiment . . .'. Museum of the City of New York.

in making objects for another firm of New York retailers. Put under contract to work exclusively for Tiffany, his and his son's small shop with a handful of assistants quickly became a factory occupying the best part of an entire block in Prince Street and employing some five hundred men. It was he who made a little silver chariot given by Tiffany to the famous midget General Tom Thumb on his marriage in 1863.

In 1853 Charles Lewis Tiffany obtained sole command of the firm, henceforth called Tiffany & Co. In 1854 he moved to a new building specially erected for him at 550 Broadway; after no more than six years this proved too small and he added the shop next door. To go so far north of Downtown seemed, at the time, surprising. But he had foreseen the way in which the city was to develop and soon found himself in the middle of the most fashionable shopping district – contributing not a little to its status. Significantly, he moved north again in 1870, to the junction of Union Square and 15th Street. Later the premises were moved to their present site on 5th Avenue and 57th Street.

At the Paris exhibition of 1867 Tiffany's display was given an award of merit. This was the first occasion on which such a prize had been given to an American firm for silver at a European exhibition. Cunningly, he had shown some of his simpler wares which stood out among the richly overwrought products of European makers and pleased the critics and press no less than the jury. These objects had presumably been made for him by John C. Moore. In the following year he had the firm incorporated as a manufacturing company and began making clocks, watches and silver wares. His trade was so considerable that he built what was then the largest watch factory in Switzerland, just outside Geneva. But, according to Heydt, 'the conditions surrounding European labour were ... wholly inapplicable to American methods', and he soon found it prudent to sell the building and turn his patents and patterns over to a Swiss company which supplied him. The establishment of a branch of Tiffany's in Argyll Street, London, in 1868 was more satisfactory (he later moved it to Argyll Place and then to Regent Street).

In 1883 William Chaffers described the Tiffany factory as 'the largest devoted solely to the manufacture of silver ware in America and probably in the world. A building of five stories in height, of which the top floor is used as a designing room, with a large library and a vast number of models, and the designers now employed have all been educated in the house'.

Having begun with jewellery and passed to silver, Tiffany now turned his attention to electro-plate. This is a somewhat surprising development for, as we have seen, the decrease in the cost of silver was eroding the market for electro-plate and firms like Reed & Barton in America were beginning to make sterling silver wares. But Tiffany's

Candelabrum made by Tiffany & Co. to the 'Chrysanthemum Pattern' patented in 1880. It forms part of a dinner service of some 165 pieces given as a wedding present in 1890. Museum of the City of New York.

above right Tureen made by Tiffany & Co. *c.* 1870. The firm specialized in the production of presentation plate. Museum of the City of New York.

below right Gold tea-set made by Tiffany & Co. and given as an eightieth birthday present to Samuel Sloan, for thirty years President of the Delaware, Lackawana and Western Company. Museum of the City of New York.

Tray made by Tiffany & Co. and presented to August Belmont in about 1904 on the completion of the New York City Subway; it is engraved with a map of the Subway. Museum of the City of New York.

opposite The Adams gold vase made by Tiffany & Co. to the design of Paulding Earnham, 1893–5, for presentation to Edward Dean Adams, Chairman of the American Cotton Oil Company. It is made of solid gold, studded with pearls and semi-precious stones. Metropolitan Museum, New York.

venture was, once again, successful. His small plating shop grew in size and in 1892 he built an extensive electro-plate factory at Forest Hill, a suburb of Newark, New Jersey.

Awards were made to Tiffany at nearly all the big exhibitions. By 1893 he could boast of official appointments to no less than twenty-three royal patrons, including Queen Victoria, the Czar of Russia, the Shah of Persia and the Khedive of Egypt.

Conforming to the taste of his times, Tiffany's products are in the usual range of historical and exotic styles. The richest pieces were those made for official presentations. In 1873, for example, he was commissioned to provide table decorations each consisting of a centre-piece, two jardinières and two candelabra to be given to the arbitrators of the 'Alabama' claims (by which heavy damages were won from England). A silver centre-piece was made in 1887 for presentation to Gladstone in recognition of his efforts to secure home rule for Ireland. And, of course, thousands of smaller objects were made for presentation to lesser men – presidents of companies, civic officials – not to mention the still greater number made to be given away at weddings and at Christmas. Tiffany maintained consistently high standards of craftsmanship not only for these articles but also for ordinary household wares.

In his latter days he marketed some of the daring Art Nouveau glass lamps and vases made under the direction of his more famous son, Louis Comfort Tiffany, who succeeded him as head of the firm in 1902. Where the father had been a keen businessman with some artistic sense, the son was an aesthete with an exceptionally sharp eye for business. He became a prominent member of the mondaine millionaire world, and this, no doubt, shed added lustre on the house of Tiffany in the eyes of clients like Marcel Proust.

Lucien Falize

(1838–97)

Dish made by Germain Bapst and Lucien Falize in 1889. Musée des Arts Décoratifs, Paris.

Engraving of the toilette created by the Maison Bapst et Falize for Princess Laetitia Bonaparte on her marriage to Prince Amedeo of Savoy in 1888. Bibliothèque Nationale.

On the base of a gold cup made for the Union Centrale des Arts Décoratifs in Paris and intended as a demonstration of the excellence of late nineteenth-century French craftsmanship, Lucien Falize had himself depicted in enamel. The little plaque shows him dressed in sixteenth-century costume, seated at a table and inspecting a beaker brought to him by a craftsman who stands at his side. By him lie a bunch of flowers and a book, symbolic of the cults of nature and erudition which he held to be the foundations of his craft. He knew more about old gold and silver than most museum officials of the time, and was as much a scholar and writer as a goldsmith.

His father, Alexis Falize, was born at Liège in 1811, orphaned when young, went to Paris and applied himself to making 'art jewellery'. He built up a flourishing concern which Lucien was to take over. Lucien was born in 1837 and trained by Alexis. Under the direction of Barbet de Jouy he began studying examples of goldsmiths' work in the Louvre and conceived a desire to revive the technique of basse taille or translucent enamel painting. But it was not until after fifteen years of study and experiment that he was able to exhibit the first examples of his work in 1878. A contemporary claimed that he initiated a 'veritable renaissance of the art of enamel'.

In 1880, when Alexis Falize retired, Lucien went into partnership with Germain Bapst, descendant of at least three generations of silversmiths and himself a notable historian of French silver. The Maison Bapst et Falize specialized in producing jewellery, enamels and what were called *pièces d'art*. As Falize himself remarked, 'what we made least of was table silver; and we had recourse for hammered work to craftsmen elsewhere, like the chasers we employed'. They did, however, make table-centres and Falize explained his views on them. 'For the table heavy and solemn architecture with figures in hackneyed poses or making disquieting pyramids must be avoided. It is necessary to strive for a picturesque effect: if the human figure appears among the flowers, fruits, crystals and lamps it ought to partake of witty and gay fantasy, as if familiar spirits had been embodied to descend in the midst of the chatter of the meal to animate the occasion'.

The works to which Falize attached most importance were showpieces which were described at length in the art magazines. The earliest of note – executed before Bapst joined the concern – was the Urania clock decorated with low reliefs of Gaston de Béarn, Marguerite de Navarre, Marguerite de Foix and Anne de Bretagne. In 1888 they were commissioned to make a toilet table and service to be given to Princess Laetitia Bonaparte on her marriage to Prince Amedeo of Savoy. Appropriately it was executed in the style of Juste-Aurèle Meissonnier and is one of the more exuberant examples of Rococo revival work of this period. Next

left Enamelled gold cup by Lucien Falize completed in 1896 for the Union Centrale des Arts Décoratifs in Paris. Musée des Arts Décoratifs.

year they produced a massive ivory and gold bust of *Gaul* – an attempt to rival the chryselephantine sculpture of ancient Greece – which was acquired for the Musée du Luxembourg. So careful were they to record every craftsman who had been engaged on this piece that one critic suggested that the elephant who provided the ivory ought also to have been named. The enamelled gold 'hanap' or cup executed in the Renaissance style, on commission from the Union Centrale des Arts Décoratifs for the Musée des Arts Décoratifs, was the last work of importance executed before Lucien Falize's untimely death in 1897. In both design and craftsmanship it is one of the most competent essays in an historical style produced by any nineteenth-century goldsmith. It was, however, made some years after the more enterprising had abandoned all such revivalism and gone in quest of an Art Nouveau.

above Detail from the enamelled cup. Musée des Arts Décoratifs, Paris.

right Detail from the base of the enamelled cup by Lucien Falize, showing Falize in sixteenth-century costume, inspecting a beaker made by one of his craftsmen. Musée des Arts Décoratifs, Paris.

Peter Carl Fabergé

(1846–1920)

For many people today the works of Fabergé are alone enough to justify the Russian Revolution. Some of his products are among the most hideous objects ever made out of materials that are in themselves not only precious but beautiful. But his workshops also made *objets de luxe* of rare delicacy and technical refinement. Designed for a clientèle which included many of the richest and most powerful, if few of the most intelligent, patrons in Czarist Russia and the rest of Europe, these glittering trifles reflect both the splendours and *misères* of the *belle époque*. And, of course, all are coloured by the veil of sentiment that hangs over every doomed society – whether of Pompeii, the Paris of Louis XVI or the St Petersburg of Nicolas II.

The history of Fabergé's reputation is revealing. Although widely employed by the rich and great, he attracted surprisingly little critical attention in his lifetime. Accounts of his Easter eggs were published in the magazine *Mir Iskusstva* run by Benois and Diaghilev between 1899 and 1904. But little notice was taken of him in the art periodicals of the West. Reviewers hardly mentioned his contributions to the Munich Sezession Exhibition of 1899 and the Paris Exposition Universelle of 1900 (though he served on the jury and thus won the Légion d'Honneur). Henry Havard, in the *Revue de l'Art* remarked that Fabergé was showing in 1900 'very rich jewels belonging to two Emperors of Russia and various charming objects, notably an Easter egg supported on violets, and a basket of lilies of the valley of rare and delicate taste'; but he reserved his encomiums for the products of Lalique, André Falize and Tiffany.

It was not until after the Revolution that Fabergé began to achieve fame in intellectual circles. To some extent this was encouraged by the vogue for the *ballets russes* as well as nostalgia for the Czarist period encouraged by the White Russians. But the change in his critical fortunes may also be ascribed to the fact that in his life he had always played safe stylistically. Working mainly in well-loved and well-worn historical styles, his designers adopted Art Nouveau – which was not very popular among the richest and greatest of patrons – rather late and without evident enthusiasm. This is probably the reason why his works were so little noticed by writers on the decorative arts of his own day. But in the 1920s, when this style had come to be regarded as a joke both poor and old, Fabergé's immunity from it proved a positive advantage.

Though born and brought up in Russia, Fabergé was essentially West European in his attitudes. The origins of his family are obscure but he is said to have been descended from Huguenots. His father, Gustav, was born at Pernau on the gulf of Riga, went to St Petersburg, served an apprenticeship in a firm of jewellers and in 1842 set up on his own in the fashionable Morskaya Bolshaya Street. He married a wife of Danish or Swedish extraction, the mother of Peter Carl who was born on 30 May

above Imperial Russian Easter Egg by Peter Carl Fabergé made for Czar Nicholas II to present to his mother the Dowager Empress Marie Feodorovna in 1897. The egg consists of eight hinged oval plaques with paintings on ivory by Zehngraf of the various institutions of which the Dowager Empress was patroness. Virginia Museum of Fine Arts.

below Imperial Russian Easter Egg by Fabergé, made for the Czar Nicholas II to present to the Czarina Alexandra Feodorovna in 1912. The egg is of lapis lazuli mounted in gold and set with diamonds: the surprise which it contains is a miniature portrait of the Czarevitch Alexey in an eagle-shaped frame set with diamonds. Virginia Museum of Fine Arts.

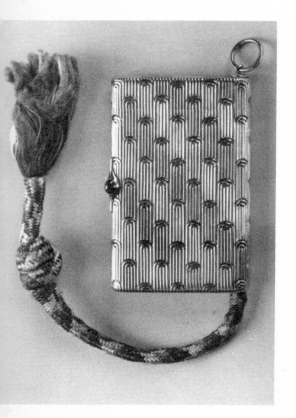

Cigarette case of red and yellow gold, made in Fabergé's St Petersburg factory under the workmaster A. Fredrik Hollming, 1912–15. Musée des Arts Décoratifs, Paris.

opposite Six Russian Imperial Easter Eggs dating from the beginning of the twentieth century. They are all of gold, decorated with precious stones and enamels. Virginia Museum of Fine Arts.

1846. Gustav retired from business and settled in Dresden in 1860 leaving a manager in charge of the shop and his eldest son at the bourgeois Gymnasium Sviataia Anna, but taking his younger son, Agathon, with him. Peter Carl, or Carl as he was generally known, was carefully educated to take over the jewellery business. He learned the art of the goldsmith from Peter Heskias Pendin in St Petersburg, he attended a business school in Paris, was set to work for a firm of jewellers in Frankfurt and visited England and Italy.

In 1870 he returned to St Petersburg and took control of the shop which he moved to better premises. It soon became the leading firm of jewellers in the city and received the Imperial appointment in 1881. Up to this time Fabergé seems to have made little but jewellery. In this same year, however, he began to make the series of Easter eggs which Alexander III gave to his Empress and Nicolas II gave to his mother and his Empress annually. In 1882 he was joined by his younger brother Agathon who is said to have encouraged him to produce more 'works of fantasy'. As Agathon had been brought up in Dresden it seems likely that he had been inspired by the works of Dinglinger.

The subsequent history of the firm is a simple commercial success story – the establishment of a branch in Moscow in 1887, larger premises in St Petersburg in 1890, branches in Odessa, Kiev and finally London – until the 1914 War, and the explosion of the Revolution in 1917. Carl Fabergé escaped from Russia in September 1918 and travelled by way of Riga (attacked by the Bolsheviks), Berlin (with revolution breaking out), Frankfurt and Wiesbaden to Lausanne where he died on 24 September 1920. Most of the large stock which he had left behind in Russia was slowly sold off to tourists from the West.

Apart from the Easter eggs, perhaps his most important works were those made for the Romanovs to give to their many royal relations in other parts of Europe, for they diffused his fame beyond Russia. Marie Fedorovna, wife of Alexander III, was the sister of Queen Alexandra of England who was so delighted by the Fabergé objects sent her as birthday presents that she began to buy and collect them on her own account. Edward VII himself seems to have warmed to these costly trifles and commissioned Fabergé to send an artist from St Petersburg to Sandringham to make models of his livestock – dogs, horses, cattle, even a pig – from which hardstone carvings were made. Nearly all members of Edwardian society soon became infected with a passion for Fabergé. Leopold de Rothschild bought cigarette cases and other objects by the dozen – all enamelled in his dark blue and yellow racing colours.

Henry Charles Bainbridge who managed the London branch from 1906 has left an appealing account of Carl Fabergé. 'He rarely if ever wore black but favoured well-cut tweeds with the coat of tails, the

whole finished off with just a slight show of clean linen', he wrote. 'There was an air of the country gentleman about him.' Though probably as endearing as Bainbridge suggests, he can hardly have been as feckless and unbusinesslike. To control a staff of more than five hundred craftsmen and to prosper, calls for more than average powers of organization and business acumen.

There were drawing offices and workshops in both St Petersburg and Moscow. Each workshop was headed by a workmaster, and those in St Petersburg applied their own marks to products which also carried the firm's stamp. What part did Fabergé himself play in this large organization? Bainbridge refers to him reverently as 'the Craftsman', but it is unlikely that he did more than direct the artistic and commercial policy of the firm and can have designed only the most important pieces.

Much of his success can be attributed to his exploitation of the cults of craftsmanship and uniqueness. Designs for specially commissioned works were, of course, used only once. But few of the other patterns – except perhaps for cigarette cases and such less expensive items – seem to have been repeated very often. Thus, the client who bought an object to give away could be reasonably sure that the recipient would not already have one exactly like it. People were, moreover, enabled to make collections of Fabergé objects – just as they made collections of eighteenth-century porcelain or silver – but without the risk of being either overcharged or deceived by fakes. He gave the rich all the fun of collecting without any of the hazards.

The Imperial Easter eggs are as ingenious in design as in craftsmanship. Each has an ornamented shell which may be opened to reveal a 'surprise'. Very much smaller and simpler Easter eggs were made for less important clients – the most appealing being those crowned with the helmets of Imperial guardsmen. Other decorative objects included figures of grinning *muzhiks* and the 'picturesque' poor of Russia, all carved out of hard stones and often mounted in gold. The most attractive of these works of fantasy are perhaps the sprays of flowers with gold stalks and jewelled petals standing in rock-crystal vases. Useful products included dinner services and tea services, relatively few of which appear to have been exported from Russia.

Most of the ornamental motifs on his Easter eggs and table silver appear to have been derived from Louis XV and Louis XVI objects of which there were so many fine examples in the Imperial collections. He was most successful when least obviously under the spell of eighteenth-century works, as in the design of cigarette cases with simple enamelled or engraved ornaments and no more than a few rose-diamond or sapphire chips on the thumbpiece. Reflecting the *douceur de vivre* of both the ancien régime in France and the last days of Czarist Russia, these objects have a double sentimental appeal.

Charles Robert Ashbee

(1863–1942)

left Altar cross, designed by C.R. Ashbee and made by the Guild of Handicraft at Chipping Campden. It was presented to Lichfield Cathedral by Miss Sophia Lonsdale in 1907. The cross is of silver, partly enamelled and set with moonstones and pearl clusters.

right Design by C.R. Ashbee for an electric lamp for the Grand Duke of Hesse. The lamp was to be made in purple glass and silver, set with amethysts.

'The Arts and Crafts movement began with the object of making useful things, of making them well and of making them beautiful, goodness and beauty were to the leaders of the movement synonymous terms.' So wrote C.R. Ashbee, himself one of the leaders, in 1908. It is against the background of these high-minded ideals that the silver made by the Guild of Handicrafts to his designs must be seen. Seen, but not too severely judged. In everything he attempted his aim exceeded his grasp. And he is of much greater interest and importance for his ideas than for his works.

Charles Robert Ashbee, born at Isleworth on 17 May 1863, came from a prosperous family with Continental connections and was given a good upper-middle-class education at Wellington College and King's College, Cambridge. Either at school or at Cambridge he was fired by the writings of John Ruskin and William Morris – both aesthetic and political. At Cambridge he certainly found many friends with similar ideals, notably Goldsworthy Lowes Dickinson (whose biography was written by E.M. Forster). Another Kingsman, Roger Fry, joined his group of friends a little later.

Leaving Cambridge in 1886, Ashbee was articled to the architect G.F. Bodley (a friend of Morris) and worked in the office with Ninian Comper, 'the gentle and pious Comper' whose 'only interest is saints and a couple of clergymen: his speciality drawing angels'. But he lived and taught at Toynbee Hall, the East End 'Settlement' where he became ever more closely involved with Socialism and popular education and tried 'to get to know the people'.

The Guild and School of Handicraft was established by Ashbee at Toynbee Hall in 1888 and contributed metalwork (embossed copper and brass) to the first show of the Arts and Crafts Exhibition Society later that year. In 1891 Ashbee moved it to a fine eighteenth-century building, Essex House, in Mile End, London. Its products included metalwork, woodwork, leather-work and, later, books printed with the type and on the presses of the Kelmscott Press which he acquired after Morris's death in 1896. In 1902 he moved the whole concern – numbering one hundred and fifty men, women and children – to Chipping Campden in Gloucestershire. But new difficulties in marketing its products could not be overcome and it was wound up in 1907. Next year an American, Joseph Fels, put up money as a kind of mortgage to continue the scheme and Ashbee devised a system by which the Guildsmen should divide their time between smallholdings and the workshop. The 1914 War put an end to the brave experiment.

Apart from books printed on the Essex House Press, the most interesting of the Guild's products were the silver wares designed by Ashbee. Taking his cue from Ruskin, he reacted sharply against the silver pro-

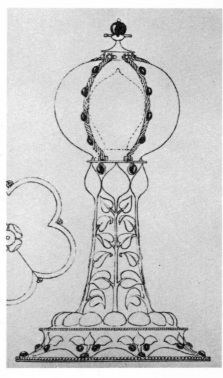

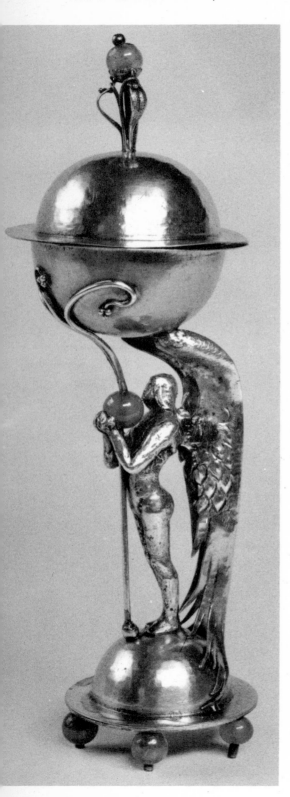

Salt cellar made by the
Guild and School of Handicraft
under C. R. Ashbee, 1899.
Victoria and Albert Museum, London.

duced by the trade – 'heavy, usually debased reproductions of the work of the eighteenth century – the last degraded leavings of Lamerie and Adam' or 'tawdry stampings backed in plaster of Paris, or pitch, the unspeakable rubbish of fancy goods'. He thus regarded trade workshop experience as detrimental for his metalworkers; and only one of the original Guildsmen, John Pearson, had received any training as a silversmith. His own knowledge seems to have been derived mainly from Benvenuto Cellini's *Treatise* of which he published an English translation in 1899. But by working together – the notion of teamwork was something of an obsession with Ashbee – the Guild built up a stock of experience which enabled its members to perform complicated feats of embossing and enamelling.

The repertory of products was wide, ranging from tiny salt cellars to bowls, embossed trays, covered cups and electric light fittings. They made trophies, including a challenge mace given to the Chipping Campden Sports Club 'to be competed for by girls who race in the annual swimming sports for a silken smock'. The most elaborate works were a lamp made for the Grand Duke of Hesse with a globe of purple glass on a silver stem set with some fifty amethysts, and an altar cross commissioned by Miss Sophia Lonsdale for Lichfield Cathedral in 1907.

Most of these pieces of silver – with long looped handles, excessively attenuated or very stocky plant motifs, studded with obsidians, carbuncles, chrysophrases, cornelians or amazons cut *en cabochon* – would now be classified as Art Nouveau. But that was not what Ashbee thought. He refers acidly to an Italian patron who 'wanted something more in the manner of "L'Art Nouveau" which I was unable to give him.' Later he said 'we were troubled by a creature calling itself "L'Art Nouveau". One particular form of it crept in from Belgium, another through *The Studio*.' In fact, no artist of that date who strove to free himself from the tyranny of historical revivalism could avoid Art Nouveau motifs – with the notable exception of Christopher Dresser who, as we have seen, provided designs not for soulful lovers of the crafts but for industrial concerns like Dixons and Elkingtons.

As the Guild slowly faltered and died, Ashbee seems to have lost his faith in the mystique of craftsmanship. He was never as hostile to the machine as Ruskin and Morris – 'we do not reject the machine, we welcome it, but we desire to see it mastered' he wrote in 1901 – and by 1908 he was referring to their 'intellectual Ludditism'. In 1911 he declared that 'modern civilization rests on machinery, and no system for the endowment or the teaching of the arts can be sound that does not recognize this'. He was unable to put the lesson he had learned into practice. But he had made a significant break with Victorian traditions in silver, and a younger generation was to profit from his example.

above Pair of salts, only 5 cms. (2 ins)
high and set with semi-precious stones.
Made by the Guild of Handicraft,
probably to the design of C. R. Ashbee,
1900. Collection of C. Jerdein.

centre Dish set with a cabachon, made
by the Guild of Handicraft, probably
to Ashbee's design, 1900, Victoria and
Albert Museum, London.

left Tray designed by C. R. Ashbee and
made by the Guild of Handicraft,
London 1896.

Georg Jensen

(1866–1935)

above Belt buckle made of silver set
with opals, 1904. Kunstindustrimuseum,
Copenhagen.

Trained as a silversmith in the tradition handed down from master to
apprentice through the centuries, Georg Jensen established in Copenhagen first a workshop then a factory making wares which maintained
all the standards Ashbee was struggling to revive in England. He appears
to have cherished no mystique of craftsmanship and no desire to revolutionize society. Nor was he troubled by any of the technical problems
which perplexed the leaders of the Arts and Crafts Movement. Hence,
perhaps, the success of his silver wares which were to attain world-wide
popularity. Combining modernism in design with traditionalism in
quality, they have an air of untroubled self-assurance.

He was born on 31 August 1866 in the village of Raadvad in Denmark,
the son of a cooper. After serving his goldsmith's apprenticeship, partly
under Holm in Svartgade, Copenhagen, he became a journeyman in
1884. He also attended the technical school and the Academy of Art. In
the later 1890s he came into contact with Mogens Ballin, one of the most
interesting men in Copenhagen at the time, who had been trained as a
painter in Paris, where he was a friend of Gauguin, and set up in Copenhagen a pewter and silver workshop inspired by the German Benedictine
monastery at Beuron. Jensen is said to have spent some time in Ballin's
workshop, which was founded in 1899.

In 1900 Jensen won a travelling scholarship which enabled him to visit
France and Italy. On his return to Denmark he and a painter friend,
Joachim Petersen, began a small porcelain factory in a back-yard in
Nørrebrogade. This was not successful and he turned his attention to
jewellery, with better results. For financial as much as artistic reasons he
made use of silver rather than gold, and semi-precious stones rather than
diamonds, emeralds or rubies. He also began to produce such silver
vessels as coffee-pots and cream jugs. In 1905 he showed jewellery in an
exhibition in The Hague. Next year the learned historian of porcelain,
Emil Hannover, bought pieces of his jewellery for the Kunstindustrimuseum, Copenhagen, of which he was director.

In 1907 Jensen began his long and very fruitful collaboration with the
painter Johan Rohde. Rohde was interested in all the more recent
developments in painting. A tour made in 1892 had brought him into
contact with the works of van Gogh in Holland, Rops and Rijsselberghe
in Belgium, and of Gauguin, Lautrec and the Nabis in Paris. Shortly after
returning to Copenhagen the following year he organized an exhibition
of fifty works by Gauguin and thirty by van Gogh. He was not very
distinguished as a painter, but his intellectual temperament and his understanding of the modern movement in the figurative arts made him the
ideal collaborator for the more craftsmanlike Jensen. Together they succeeded in translating the forms of post-Impressionist painting into terms
of silver without resorting to the facile imitation of motifs.

left Silver fruit-cup by Georg Jensen,
1914, the first of his pieces to be
acquired by the Musée des Arts
Décoratifs in Paris.

295

left Cocktail shaker by Georg Jensen.
The cocktail shaker was one of the
few entirely new types of silver vessel
invented in the twentieth century.
Jensen & Co., Copenhagen.

right Fruit bowl by Georg Jensen in the
Art-Deco Style of the Paris 1925
Exhibition. Busch–Reisinger Museum,
Harvard University.

Art Nouveau jewellery, like that made by Jensen, owed and still owes
much of its appeal to its honesty. It could never be mistaken for paste.
And this counted for much at a time when the less successful *demi-
mondaines* were loading their bosoms with parures and their arms with
bracelets of glass cunningly cut to glitter like diamonds. The new
jewellery also proclaimed that its wearer valued materials for their
intrinsic beauty and the craft with which they were wrought rather than
their commercial value. Jensen may not have been consciously aware of
this. But it is significant that he made a similar approach to silver wares.
For he not only abandoned the imitations of historical styles and most of
the fussy decorations popular with lesser Art Nouveau designers, but
gave his products an almost matt hammered finish which provides an
unmistakably hand-made look and distinguishes them from the very
sleek and glossy silver made in most factories at the time.

Even if Jensen was not initially aware of the commercial potentialities
of his style of silver wares, he had enough business acumen to exploit
them. He achieved international acclaim, and thus a wider market than

that of Copenhagen, by winning a gold medal at the Brussels International Exhibition in 1910. Three years later he exhibited in Paris for the first time at the *Salon d'automne* and a piece of his silver was acquired by the Musée des Arts Décoratifs next year. In 1912 he moved to a larger workshop and in 1916 made his concern into a limited company. He took over another factory building in 1919. An attempt to establish an art workshop in Paris in 1926 proved unsuccessful. But the Copenhagen factory continued to flourish and by 1929 he was employing some two hundred and fifty men. His designers included the sculptor Gundar Albertus and the architect Harald Nielsen.

In 1917 Jensen made a cup for the Master Butchers' Guild of Copenhagen, designed by the architect Anton Rosen with a frieze modelled by Jean Gauguin and carved in ivory. This has been described as his masterpiece. But, in fact, his fame rests not on such presentation pieces as on ordinary table wares – elegant, well-poised bowls, teapots and

Knife, fork and spoon by Georg Jensen, made in the 1920s. Jensen was later to make flat-ware of greater austerity. Jensen & Co., Copenhagen.

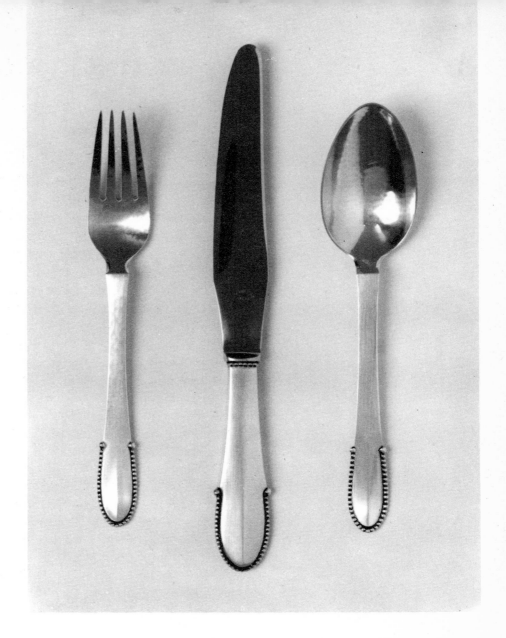

coffee-pots and especially solid-handled flatware. His knives have shorter blades, his spoons rounder bowls, and his forks shorter and more widely spaced prongs than had been usual. Very soon they were being imitated throughout the world. In the 1920s he flirted with the Art Deco style, the style of the Paris 1925 Exhibition, which he used most appropriately for cocktail shakers and cigarette boxes. Some of these pieces have a hammered surface, but the majority have the famous 'Jensen surface' – a satiny finish produced by annealing the piece, immersing it in sulphuric acid and then buffing it very lightly so that some of the oxidization remained.

Georg Jensen died on 2 October 1935, a few months after his friend and collaborator Johan Rohde. His son, Søren Georg Jensen, born in 1917, subsequently became chief designer of the firm, which has branches all over the world, notably in New York and London, and which still retains untarnished its reputation for good, solid sensible silverware. It also continues to produce silver jewellery.

Joseph Maria Olbrich

(1867–1908)

Joseph Maria Olbrich was neither a silversmith nor an industrialist but an architect who occasionally turned his attention to the design of metalwork (including silver), glass, furniture, ceramics and even, in his last years, motor cars. He is one of a small number of highly gifted designers – most of them architects by training – who helped to change the appearance of the decorative arts throughout the Western world.

After four years at the Staatsgewerbeschule – technical college – in Vienna he went to the Akademie der bildenden Künste where, from 1890 to 1893, he studied architecture under Baron Carl von Hasenauer. In July 1893 he began to work as a draughtsman in the office of Otto Wagner, an architect, who had begun in a staunchly academic manner, but was already beginning to introduce Art Nouveau decorative elements into his work, notably the street railway stations which anticipate the more famous Metro stations by Hector Guimard in Paris. As winner of the Rome prize, Olbrich travelled through Italy to North Africa in the winter of 1893–4, then returned to Wagner's office. He visited Germany, France and England in 1895.

Throughout the nineteenth century the more thoughtful people involved in architecture and the decorative arts – including Karl Friedrich Schinkel in Germany and Christopher Dresser in England – had been obsessed by the problem of creating a nineteenth-century style. Various historical and exotic styles were tried, both independently and mixed, without much success. It was not until the 1880s that, partly by a return to the more abstract ornaments of Rococo designers and partly by a new attention to natural forms, the lankly curving, swirling and sweeping forms of Art Nouveau – *Jugendstil*, the style of youth as it came to be called in Germany – were evolved. Olbrich began by adopting these motifs not only for the Secession building, but also for the exterior and interior decoration of a few houses he designed while in Vienna and, more notably, for the saloon of a pleasure boat devised in 1899 for the display of the products of various Viennese manufacturers at the Paris Exhibition of the following year. In the same manner he provided decorations for the Secession magazine *Ver Sacrum*.

In 1899 the young Ernst Ludwig, Grand Duke of Hesse, invited Olbrich to join a colony of artists he was establishing at Darmstadt. Olbrich designed the Ernst Ludwig Haus which was to serve as the communal studio, and most of the houses for the artists, including one for himself. He was given the title of Professor and spent the remaining years of his life in Darmstadt.

Work for the artists' houses involved him more closely in the design of both useful and decorative household objects. He made numerous drawings for door-handles, for lamps, for furniture and metalwork. The designs for metalwork seem at first to have been strongly influenced

Tea caddy in silver with amethysts made to Olbrich's design for the Darmstadt artists' colony in 1901. Hessisches Landesmuseum.

by the works of Charles Rennie Mackintosh and his fellow designers and craftsmen constituting the Glasgow School, which were frequently illustrated in the internationally read *The Studio*, and were exhibited in Venice in 1899 and Vienna in 1900. As an alternative to the soft and fluid forms of Belgian and French Art Nouveau, these artists had evolved a style which retained no trace of Rococo ornament and thus seemed purer and more distinctively modern. A two-branch candlestick and a tea-caddy, both made to Olbrich's designs for the Darmstadt artists' colony in 1901, might easily be mistaken for the work of Mackintosh. But in

301

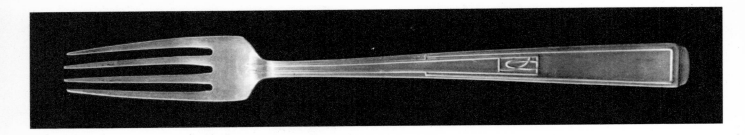

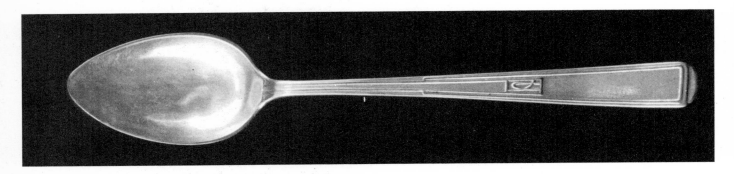

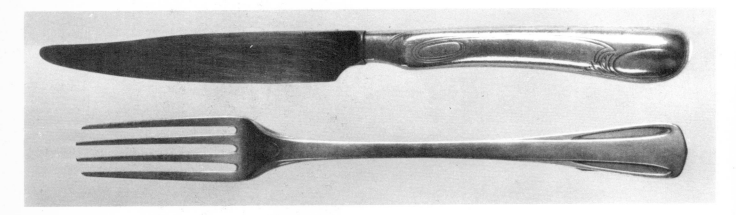

above Fork and spoon by Olbrich. Collection of Lotte Rauff.

below Knife and fork. Hessisches Landesmuseum, Darmstadt.

opposite Candlestick, made to the design of J.M. Olbrich by P. Bruckmann and Söhne of Heilbronn, of silver set with an amethyst, *c.* 1901. Hessisches Landesmuseum, Darmstadt.

designs for useful wares – notably a set of cutlery made by Charles Christofle – Olbrich abandoned the exaggerated proportions which were an expression of modernity for its own sake, the besetting sin of the Glasgow School. He also limited decorations to those which could be easily and successfully produced mechanically. He did not abandon ornament, but such late works as his silver table lamp of 1906 rely for their effect on clear-cut form rather than surface detail. This lamp was also one of the first successful solutions to the problem presented by the introduction of electricity to the designer of furnishings. And it may well have influenced the revolutionary street lamps designed for AEG, one of the big German electrical combines, by Peter Behrens, a member of the Darmstadt colony soon to emerge as the leading industrial designer in Germany. Olbrich's work also exerted some influence through his friend Josef Hoffman on the craft products, especially silver, of the Wiener Werkstätte, the association of artists and craftsmen in Austria.

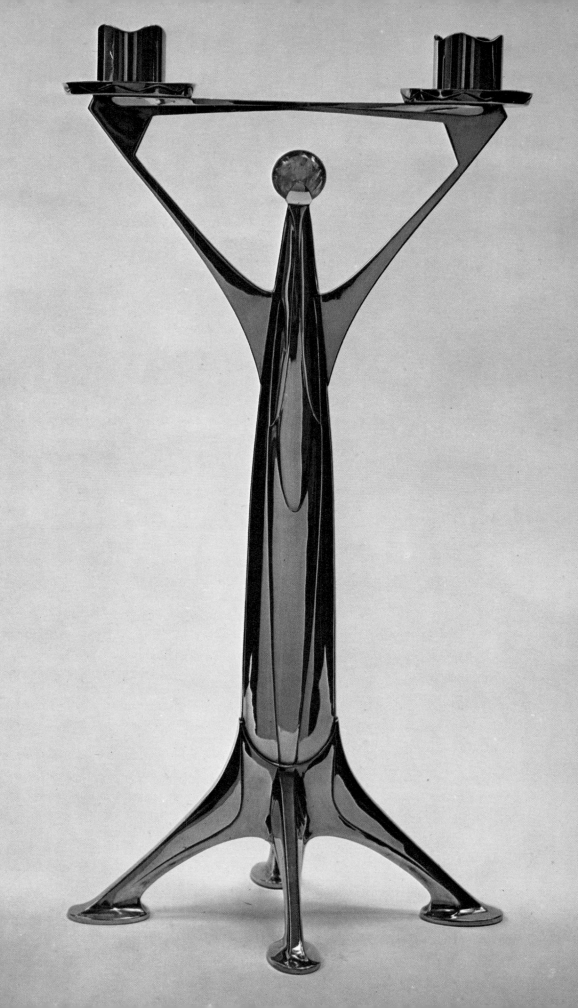

Jean Puiforçat

(1897–1945)

Some of the finest pieces of Louis XV and Louis XVI silver now in the Louvre once formed part of a very large collection of old French plate assembled between World War I and World War II by Jean Puiforçat, a prominent Parisian silversmith. Among connoisseurs of silver he is remembered mainly as a collector. His own works are much less well known than the objects he collected. And it might easily be supposed that he was a backward-looking antiquarian craftsman out of touch with the twentieth century. But this could hardly be further from the truth. Although he reacted against industrialization and maintained an Arts and Crafts faith in the aesthetics of the hand-made, he was in other respects almost insistently 'modern'. He was, indeed, the best of the several silversmiths working in the Art Deco style of the Paris 1925 Exhibition.

He was born in Paris on 5 August 1897, the son of a prosperous silversmith. After the war he studied for a while under the fashionable sculptor, Louis Lejeune, who later recalled him as 'ce solide garçon sportif, vigoureux et en même temps doux et attachant'. *Sportif* he certainly was – a tennis champion, member of the French national rugby-football team and of the Olympic ice-hockey team. One can think of no other silversmith or collector of silver so distinguished on the sports field. His only notable work of sculpture is a statue of a football-player.

Those inclined to assume that athletes are philistines may expect Puiforçat's attitude to his craft and trade to have been distinctly down to earth. But he never fails to surprise. For in the 1930s he developed a philosophical – one should perhaps say mystical – attitude to the designing and making of silver.

I began by designing *de chic* until the day when, as a result of working on antiques, I came to realise that they had some mysterious quality which escaped me ... I plunged back into mathematics, going beyond my first and insufficient studies and fell on Plato. The way was open. From him I learned of the arithmetic, harmonic and geometric mean and of the five famous Platonic bodies ...

The Golden number, that is the solution.
The Golden number without which no ancient worked ....

It is interesting to recall that he was developing these notions at the very moment when Le Corbusier was working out his Modulor.

He began to work as an independent silversmith in 1922. A coffee-pot of that year, bought by the Musée des Arts Décoratifs in Paris, as soon as it was made, is presumably an example of what he later came to regard as his merely 'chic' style. In his later works he continued to combine silver with semi-precious materials – handles of jade, ivory or rare woods – but strove after purer forms, especially the sphere, the drum and the cone, avoiding all but the very simplest moulded or incised decorations.

In 1925 he was, of course, involved in the great Exposition des Arts Décoratifs in Paris and contributed silver objects to Ruhlmann's *Hôtel du Collectionneur*, which most visitors declared to be the chief attraction of the whole massive show (while Le Corbusier's more forward looking *Maison de l'Esprit Nouveau* was almost totally ignored). Next year he became one of 'Les Cinq' who exhibited at the Galerie Barbazanges. The other members of this group were the furniture designers Pierre Chareau and Pierre Legrain, the jeweller Raymond Templier and the architect-interior decorators André Domin and Marcel Genevrière, who worked under the name of Dominique and designed the Houbigant scent factory of Neuilly. Puiforçat's own house was designed by Dominique. In 1928 he joined the Union des Artistes Modernes (U.A.M.) which, under the leadership of René Herbst, seceded from the Société des Artistes Décorateurs (the organization responsible for the 1925 exhibition). Taking 'le beau dans l'utile' – beauty in the useful – as its motto, the U.A.M. began a reaction against the Art Deco style. Its members included Charlotte Perriand, who had assisted Le Corbusier in the design of his tubular steel furniture.

Coffee pot in silver with lapis-lazuli handle and decoration, made by Jean Puiforçat in 1922. Bought by the Musée des Arts Décoratifs in Paris in the year that it was made.

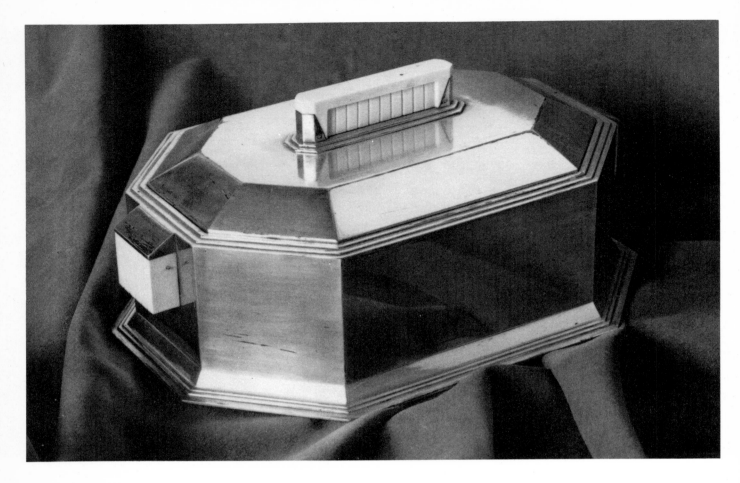

Soup tureen by Jean Puiforçat. Musée de peinture et sculpture, Grenoble.

Though he may have believed in 'beauty in utility' as a doctrine – it has a good Platonic basis – Puiforçat can hardly be described as a functionalist. Working for a prosperous clientèle, he produced silver objects which were as obviously expensive as they were simple. He was, in fact, a master of costly simplicity. His best pieces have a clean and appropriately, for him, athletic elegance. Sometimes he verged on the jazz modern or Odeon style as in an ashtray composed of a cone and sphere (which he presumably thought purely Platonic). Occasionally the influence of 'L'art nègre' is apparent.

Because of its simplicity of form and smoothness of finish, Puiforçat's silver was often compared with machinery. Nothing made him more angry. As early as 1925 he declared: 'although France has produced great scientists, the Machine is not French – it is not French in spirit'. Some years later he remarked that 'to say I am inspired by aircraft or wireless is ridiculous. Engineers working with figures have no chance to find simple and pure forms'. There was, he thought, a vital difference 'in the soul' between the artist and the engineer – 'As I always say, numbers in the service of the heart'. One of his most elaborate geometrical drawings, of 1934, is inscribed: 'Tracé Harmonique. Figure de départ $R\sqrt{2}$'. It was the design for a golf trophy.

left Sugar caster by Jean Puiforçat.

below Knife, fork and spoon in silver executed in the workshop of Puiforçat in 1943. The handle of each implement is decorated by the seven stars, the symbol of the office of marshal, and by 'le francisque', the personal emblem of Marshal Pétain. Musée des Arts Décoratifs, Paris.

Wilhelm Wagenfeld

(Born 1900)

By the end of the nineteenth century the silversmith had been absorbed into the industrial system – as skilled labour. The industrial designer – rarely a silversmith by training – began to play the most important part in the production of domestic metalwork, whether it was made of silver, electro-plate or any other substance. Neither the Art Nouveau cult, which stressed artistic individuality, nor the English Arts and Crafts movement had succeeded in restoring the silversmith to his ancient position as the most highly respected of all craftsmen. Few leading industrial designers of today confine their attention to any one medium or type of article. Tapio Wirkkala, for example, who has provided some excellent silver designs for Christofle is also (and is better known as) a designer of glass, porcelain and wooden objects.

One of the most distinguished of living industrial designers, Wilhelm Wagenfeld, did however begin his career as a silversmith. He was born on 15 April 1900 in Bremen and worked in a local silverware factory while attending classes at the state school for arts and crafts. After a period in the state drawing academy at Hanau, and qualifying as a journeyman silversmith and chaser, he went to the Weimar Bauhaus, first as an assistant then as an instructor.

From 1922 the technical supervisor of the Bauhaus metal workshop was Christian Dell, but the painter and theorist Johannes Itten (who originated the famous *Vorkurs* or preliminary course which all Bauhaus students underwent) seems to have been mainly responsible for it until 1923 when Laszlo Moholy-Nagy took control, remaining in charge until 1925 in Weimar and 1928 in Dessau. The most interesting products of the workshop were those of Marianne Brandt, born at Chemnitz in 1893, and thus seven years older than Wagenfeld. Experimenting in the use of Platonic forms – like Puiforçat in Paris but with strikingly different results – she produced pieces which are more successful as small-scale purist sculptures than as useful articles. A teapot with a perfectly spherical body, straight spout and a solid ebony disc for a handle was among her first efforts. She then passed to teapots with hemispherical bodies, one with a handle arching above the top in a graceful semicircle, others with handles made of semicircular pieces of wood tacked to the side. Wagenfeld worked in a similar style, making a columnar tea-caddy, a handsome if very simple coffee-pot, a gravy-boat with two spouts – for fat and skim – and a complete tea and coffee service. He was less doctrinaire than Marianne Brandt and his vessels are a good deal more efficient. They were made of nickel-silver, the alloy used as a base for most electro-plated wares.

The challenge presented by electric-light fittings was taken up at the Bauhaus and answered with better effect than that presented by such traditional objects as teapots. One of the most successful was, however,

Electric lamp of glass and chromium-plated metal by Wilhelm Wagenfeld and K. J. Jucker, and ashtrays by Marianne Brandt, all made in the Bauhaus workshops at Weimar, 1923–4. Museum of Modern Art, New York.

above Nickel-silver tea-set by Wilhelm Wagenfeld, made at the Bauhaus, Weimar. Schlossmuseum, Weimar.

below Nickel-silver tea cannister made by Wilhelm Wagenfeld in the metal workshop of the Bauhaus at Weimar, 1924. Schlossmuseum, Weimar.

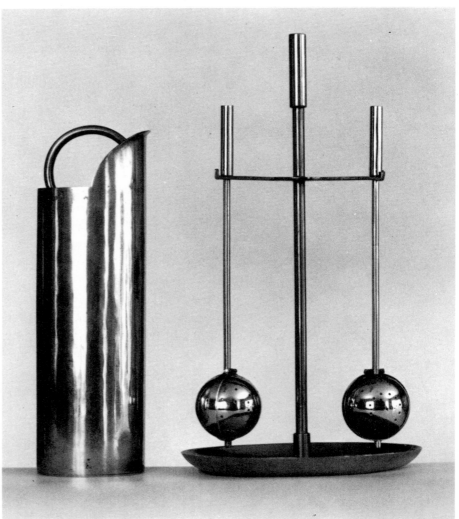

Nickel-silver tea-pot by Marianne Brandt, 1924. Museum of Modern Art, New York.

among the first to be made, a table lamp of chromium-plated metal and glass made by K.J. Jucker in collaboration with Wagenfeld. It has an easy unostentatious simplicity without any of the Bauhaus quirks.

Wagenfeld was later to say that the objects made at the Bauhaus were really craft products which, through the use of geometrically clear shapes, were given the appearance of industrial production.

It is characteristic of that moment [he wrote] that Moholy-Nagy who watched me at Jenaer [Glasfabrik] while I changed my earlier cylindrical milk jugs into drop-shaped ones, said to me 'Wagenfeld, how can you betray the Bauhaus like this? We have always fought for simple basic shapes, cylinder, cube, cone, and now you are making a soft form which is dead against all we have been after.'

In fact, such objects as Marianne Brandt's teapots were composed not merely of simple basic shapes, but of so many different parts that they were wholly unsuitable for mechanized production. But if the Bauhaus was built on craft-guild ideas which owe much to Ruskin, Morris and possibly Ashbee, and on aesthetic notions with a still more ancient history, it did help to encourage rational simplicity in design.

After leaving the Bauhaus, Wagenfeld was mainly occupied in the design of glass and ceramic wares. Perhaps his best work was a simple, practical and elegant tea service in heat-resistant glass, designed for the Jenaer glass factory in 1932, still in production. But he also designed some good sets of cutlery with short fork prongs and knife blades and circular spoon bowls, possibly influenced by Jensen. He taught at the Berliner Kunsthochschule from 1931 to 1934 when he became chief designer to the Furstenburg porcelain factory. Since 1949 he has worked in Stuttgart, where he established the Werkstatt Wagenfeld in 1954. Recently he has been experimenting in plastics and designed the dining trays, with their plates, cups and cutlery, for Lufthansa aircraft – the best of their kind.

311

Bibliography

This bibliography is not comprehensive.
I have listed only the works that I found
most useful in writing this book.
To save repetition I have used
the following abbreviations:

Bulgari C.G. Bulgari:
Argentari Gemmari e Orafi d'Italia,
Rome, 1958

Rosenberg M. Rosenberg:
Der Goldschmiede Merkzeichen,
Frankfurt-am-Main, 1922–8

Thieme-Becker U. Thieme and F. Becker:
Allgemeines Lexikon der bildenden Künstler,
Leipzig, 1907–50

VUOLVINUS

G. de Francovich in *Römisches Jahrbuch
für Kunstgeschichte*, VI (1942–4),
pp. 182–228 (with a summary of earlier
theories about Vuolvinus); G.B. Tatum
in *The Art Bulletin*, XXVI (1944),
pp. 25–47; V.H. Elbern: *Der
Karolingische Goldaltar von Mailand*,
Bonn, 1952

NICOLAS OF VERDUN

The most up-to-date general account is
by Otto Demus in *Encyclopaedia of
World Art*, vol. IX, pp. 917–22, with
good bibliography; see also
E. Panofsky: *Renaissances and
Renascences*, Stockholm, 1960;
E. Castelnuovo: *Nicolaus di Verdun*,
Milan, 1966

UGOLINO DI VIERI

G. della Valle: *Storia del Duomo di
Orvieto*, Rome, 1791, pp. 111, 230–4,
277; I. Machetti in *La Diana*, IV (1929),
pp. 17–43; E. Carli: *Il Duomo di
Orvieto*, Rome, 1965, pp. 123–32,
138–42; Paolo Dal Poggetto: *Ugolino di
Vieri: Gli smalti di Orvieto*, Florence,
1965

LEONARDO DI SER GIOVANNI

P. Franceschini: *Il dossale d'argento
del tempio di San Giovanni in Firenze*,
Florence, 1894; P. Bacci: *Documenti
toscani per la storia dell'arte*, Florence,
1910, vol. I, pp. 143 ff.; E. Steingräber
in *The Connoisseur*, CXXXVIII (1956),
pp. 148–54 with bibliography

ANTONIO DEL POLLAJUOLO

G. Poggi: *Catalogo del Museo dell'Opera
del Duomo*, Florence, 1904;
M. Cruttwell: *Antonio Pollaiuolo*,
London, 1907; A. Sabatini: *Antonio e
Piero del Pollaiuolo*, Florence, 1944;
L. Becherucci and G. Brunetti; *Il
Museo dell'Opera del Duomo a Firenze*.
Vol. II, Florence, 1970

SEBASTIAN LINDENAST

For Neudörfer's account, which is
probably based on reports of people

BIBLIOGRAPHY

who had known Lindenast, see
G.K. Lochner: *Des J. Neudörfer …
Nachrichten von Künstlern und
Werkleuten daselbst*, Vienna, 1875,
pp. 37–48; W. Fries in *Anzeiger des
Germanisches Nationalmuseum*, 1933,
pp. 74–83; H. Kohlhausen: *Nürnberger
Goldschmiedkunst des Mittelalters und der
Dürerzeit*, Berlin, 1968

ENRIQUE DE ARFE

F.J. Sanchez Canton: *Los Arfes*, Madrid,
1920; Charles Oman: *The Golden Age of
Hispanic Silver 1400–1665*, London,
1968

LUDWIG KRUG

G.K.W. Lochner: *Des J. Neudörfer …
Nachrichten von Künstlern und Werkleuten
daselbst*, Vienna, 1875, p. 124; O. von
Falke in *Pantheon*, IX (1933), pp. 184–94;
Charles Oman: *Medieval Silver Nefs*,
London, 1963; H. Kohlhausen:
*Nürnberger Goldschmiedkunst des
Mittelalters und der Dürerzeit*, Berlin,
1968, pp. 357 ff.

BENVENUTO CELLINI

Cellini's *Vita* was first published in
1728, translated into English in 1771,
German 1791 and French 1822. The
standard edition of the text is that by
Orazio Bacci, Florence, 1901, but there
are many others including one in
paperback. The best English translation
is that by J.A. Symonds republished
with introduction and notes by John
Pope-Hennessy, London, 1949.
Eugène Plon: *Benvenuto Cellini*, Paris,
1883 (with appendices published
separately) is still the standard
monograph including many documents
and illustrations of a large number of
objects which had previously been
ascribed to Cellini. E. Camesasca: *Tutta
l'opera del Cellini*, Milan, 1955, is a
useful up-to-date survey. For Cellini
and Mannerist theory see John
Shearman: *Mannerism*,
Harmondsworth, 1967. The famous
Rospigliosi cup in the Metropolitan
Museum, New York, was
persuasively attributed to Jacopo
Bilivert by Y. Hackenbroch in *The
Connoisseur*, CLXXII (1969), pp. 175–9

WENZEL JAMNITZER

M. Rosenberg: *Jamnitzer*,
Frankfurt-am-Main, 1920; M.
Frankenburger in Thieme-Becker,
XVIII, pp. 366–73 (with bibliography to
1925); E. Kris in *Jahrbuch der
Kunsthistorischen Sammlungen in Wien*,
n.s. I (1926), pp. 137–208 ('Der Stil
"Rustique"'); J. Hayward in *The
Connoisseur*, CLXIV (1967), pp. 148–54;
J.D. Farmer: *The Virtuoso Craftsman*,
Worcester, Mass., 1969; M.M. Prechtl:
*Jamnitzer, Lencker, Stoer: Drei
Nürnberger Konstruktivisten des 16
Jahrunderts*, Nurnberg, 1969

ANTONIO GENTILI

G. Baglione: *Le vite de' pittori, sculptori
et architetti …*, Rome, 1642, p. 109;
A. Bertolotti: *Artisti Lombardi a Roma*,
Rome, 1881, II, pp. 120–61 (for lawsuit
with Teodoro della Porta); E. Kris in
Dedalo, IX (1928–9), pp. 97–111;
C.L. Avery in *Metropolitan Museum
Bulletin*, V (1946–7), p. 252; Bulgari, I,
pp. 509–10. A drawing for the base of
the cross in St Peter's is in the Cooper
Union Museum, New York, see
*Chronicle of the Museum for the Arts of
Decoration of the Cooper Union*, II (1952),
p. 97

HANS PETZOLT

O. von Falke in *Jahrbuch der preuszischen
Kunstsammlungen*, XL (1919), pp. 72–92;
Rosenberg, III, p. 123; E. Böhm: *Hans
Petzolt*, Munich 1939; J.F. Hayward in
The Connoisseur, CLXV (1967),
pp. 162–7; J.D. Farmer: *The Virtuoso
Craftsman*, Worcester, Mass., 1969,
pp. 134–6

GASPARE MOLA

Thieme-Becker, XXV, pp. 27–8; Baudi
de Vesme in *Atti della Società Pietmontese
di Archeologia e Belle Arti*, XIV (1932),
pp. 818–9; Bulgari, II, p. 160

PAULUS VAN VIANEN

Thieme-Becker, XXXIV, pp. 320–1
(with bibliography to 1926); J.W.
Frederiks: *Dutch Silver*, The Hague,
1952–61, I, pp. 59–96, IV, pp. 37–41.

For works by a member of the van
Vianen family (probably Paulus) in the
collection of Charles I, see *Walpole
Society*, XXXVII (1958–60), p. 76

CLAUDE BALLIN

Mercure de France, May 1726; April
1745; May 1754; P. Mantz in *Gazette
des Beaux Arts*, X (1860), pp. 138–9;
J. Guiffrey: *Inventaire générale du
mobilier de la couronne sous Louis XIV*,
Paris, 1885, I passim; C. Hernmarck in
Gazette des Beaux Arts 6th s., XLI (1953),
pp. 103–8; R.A. Weigart and
C. Hernmarck: *Les Relations artistiques
entre la France et la Suède 1693–1718*,
Stockholm, 1964; Y. Bottineau and
O. Lefuel: *Les Grands Orfèvres*, Paris,
1965

CLAES FRANSEN BAERDT

J.W. Frederiks: *Dutch Silver*, The
Hague, 1952–61, I, pp. 287–90, IV,
pp. 87–91

GIOVANNI GIARDINI

Thieme-Becker, XIII, pp. 590–1;
L. Montalto: *Un Mecenate in Roma
barocca*, Florence, 1955; Bulgari, I,
p. 529; G. Grignoni: *Giovanni Giardini*,
Rocca San Cassiano, 1963; A.M. Clark
in *Minneapolis Institute of Arts Bulletin*,
LIII (1964), pp. 27–8; *Analecta
Reginensia*, Stockholm, 1966, I,
pp. 48–58, 138–49

ANTHONY NELME

C.J. Jackson: *History of English Plate*,
London, 1911; J.F. Hayward:
Huguenot Silver in England 1688–1727,
London, 1959

JOHN CONEY

Herman Frederick Clarke: *John Coney
Silversmith*, Boston, Mass., 1932;
H.J. Gourley III: *The New England
Silversmith* (Exhibition Catalogue),
Providence, Rhode Island, 1965

JOHANN ZECKEL

Thieme-Becker, XXXVI, p. 424 (with
full bibliography); *Augsburger Barock*
(Exhibition Catalogue), Augsburg,
1968

DAVID WILLAUME

Proceedings of the Huguenot Society of London, XIV (1929–33), pp. 496–554; XLV (1965), pp. 4–14; J.F. Hayward: *Huguenot Silver in England 1688–1727*, London, 1959. The account presented to Lady Irwin is in the archive of the Leeds Public Library: I am grateful to Mr Christopher Gilbert for drawing my attention to it. A copy of D. Willaume's will is at Somerset House, proved 22 January 1741 O.S.

JOHANN MELCHIOR DINGLINGER

Johann Georg Keyssler: *Travels through Germany, Bohemia* ..., London, 1757, IV, pp. 102, 124–5; Erna von Watzdorf: *Johann Melchior Dinglinger*, Berlin, 1962

THOMAS GERMAIN

G. Bapst: *Études sur l'orfèvrerie française du XVIIIe siècle*, Paris, 1867; A. de Montaiglon and J. Guiffrey: *Correspondance des Directeurs de l'Académie de France à Rome*, Paris 1907–13, I, pp. 205, 251, 405, II, pp. 192, 270, IX, pp. 254, 257, 272, 310; T. and A. Crombie in *The Connoisseur*, CXXXIV (1954), pp. 259–65

PAUL DE LAMERIE

P.A.S. Phillips: *Paul de Lamerie*, London, 1935; J.F. Hayward: *Huguenot Silver in England 1688–1727*, London, 1959; F. Selvig in *The Minneapolis Institute of Arts Bulletin*, LI (1962), pp. 72–7; J. McNab Dennis in *Metropolitan Museum Bulletin*, XXVI (1967–8), pp. 174–9

JUSTE-AURÈLE MEISSONNIER

Contemporary sources cited in text; F. Kimball: *The Creation of the Rococo*, Philadelphia, 1943; Baudi de Vesme: *Schede Vesme: L'Arte in Piemonte del XVI al XVIII secolo*, Turin, 1966, II, pp. 675–8

PHILIP SYNG

H.F. Jayne and S.W. Woodhouse in *Art in America*, IX (1921), pp. 248–59; K.A. Kellock in *Dictionary of American Biography*, New York, XVIII, p. 261; J.H. Pleasants and H. Sill: *Maryland Silversmiths 1715–1830*, Baltimore 1930, pp. 72–4 (for Philip Syng I); P.P. Prime and H.P. McIlhenny: *Exhibition of Philadelphia Silver*, Philadelphia, 1956; ed. L.W. Labaree: *The Papers of Benjamin Franklin*, New Haven, 1960 ff. (see index)

CHRISTIAN PRECHT

Gustaf Munthe: *Konsthantverkaren Christian Precht*, Stockholm 1957

JACQUES ROETTIERS

Contemporary sources cited in text. V. Advielle in *Réunion des Sociétés des Beaux-Arts des départements*, XII (1888); Thieme-Becker, XXVIII, pp. 507–8 (with bibliography to 1932); C. le Corbellier in *Metropolitan Museum Bulletin* NS, XXVII (1968–9)

VINCENZO BELLI

G.C. Claretta: *I Reali di Savoia*, Turin, 1893, pp. 140–1; Bulgari, I, pp. 124–9

THOMAS HEMING

Thieme-Becker, XVI, p. 367; A.G. Grimwade in *The Connoisseur*, CXXXVII (1956), pp. 175–8; Charles Oman: *English Church Plate, 597–1830*, London, 1957; E. Zahle in *Det danske Kunstindustrimuseum Virkomhed*, 1954–9, pp. 14–34; H.D.W. Sitwell in *The Archaeological Journal*, CXVII (1960), pp. 131–55

LUIGI VALADIER

I. Ciampi: *Vita di Giuseppe Valadier*, Rome, 1870; G. Sforza in *Archivio Storico Italiano* 4th series LX (1887), pp. 415, 426, 427; R. Righetti in *L'Urbe*, V (1940) November pp. 2–16; Bulgari, II, p. 494

WILLIAM FARIS

J.H. Pleasants and H. Sill: *Maryland Silversmiths 1715–1830*, Baltimore, 1930; Lockwood Barr in *Maryland Historical Magazine*, XXXVI (1941), pp. 420–39, XXXVII (1942), pp. 423–32

MATTHEW BOULTON

H.W. Dickinson: *Matthew Boulton*, Cambridge, 1937; E. Robinson in *The Economic History Review*, 2nd series, XVI (1963), pp. 39–60; R. Rowe: *Adam Silver 1765–1795*, London, 1965

ROBERT-JOSEPH AUGUSTE

Thieme-Becker, II, p. 249 (with bibliography); Y. Bottineau and O. Lefuel: *Les Grands Orfèvres*, Paris, 1965; *Le Danemark* (Exhibition Catalogue, Musée du Louvre), Paris, 1965, pp. 75–6; F.J.B. Watson: *The Wrightsman Collection: I Furniture*, New York, 1966, II, pp. 562–3

PAUL REVERE

E.H. Goss: *The Life of Colonel Paul Revere*, Boston, Mass., 1891; Esther Forbes: *Paul Revere & the World he lived in*, Boston, Mass., 1942; F. Selvig in *The Minneapolis Institute of Arts Bulletin*, III (1963), pp. 136–40; H.J. Gourley: *The New England Silversmith*, Providence, Rhode Island, 1965 (Exhibition Catalogue) nos. 154–73

MARTIN-GUILLAUME BIENNAIS

P. Burty: *F.D. Froment-Meurice*, Paris, 1883; S. Grandjean: *L'Orfèvrerie du XIXe siècle en Europe*, Paris, 1962; S. Grandjean in *Archives de l'art français* N.P., XXIV (1969), pp. 57–63

PAUL STORR

N.M. Penzer: *Paul Storr, the last of the Goldsmiths*, London 1954. A transcript of the memoirs of G. Fox is in the library of the Victoria and Albert Museum, London

ROBERT GARRARD

A.G. Grimwade in *The Proceedings of the Society of Silver Collectors*, 1961 (an invaluable account of the firm begun by Wickes and Wakelin); P. Wardle: *Victorian Silver and Silver Plate*, London, 1963. I am grateful to Mrs Shirley Bury for information about the will of Robert Garrard I and the date of the death of Robert Garrard II

BIBLIOGRAPHY

GEORGE RICHARDS ELKINGTON

Contemporary sources cited in text; P. Wardle: *Victorian Silver and Silver Plate*, London, 1963. I am grateful to Mrs Shirley Bury for allowing me to consult the Elkington registers in the Department of Metalwork at the Victoria and Albert Museum, London

FRANÇOIS-DÉSIRÉ FROMENT-MEURICE

P. Burty: *F.-D. Froment-Meurice argentier de la Ville de Paris 1802–1855*, Paris 1883; H. Bouilhet: *L'Orfèvrerie Francaise aux XVIIIe et XLXe siècles*, Paris, 1910, II, p. 232 ff.; F. Dumont in *Connaissance des Arts*, November 1956, pp. 42–5

CHARLES CHRISTOFLE

E. Bouilhet and others: *Paul Christofle 1838–1907*; H. Bouilhet: *L'Orfèvrerie Francaise aux XVIIIe et XIXe siècles*, Paris, 1910, passim; V. Champier: *La vie et l'oeuvre de Henri Bouilhet, 1830–1910*, Paris, n.d.

HENRY GOODING REED

George Sweet Gibb: *The Whitesmiths of Taunton: A History of Reed and Barton 1824–1943*, Cambridge, Mass., 1946

CHARLES LEWIS TIFFANY

W. Chaffers: *Gilda Aurifabrorum ...*, London, 1883, p. 222; G.F. Heydt: *Charles L. Tiffany and the House of Tiffany & Co.*, New York, 1893; M. Amaya in *Apollo*, LXXXI (1965), pp. 102–9

LUCIEN FALIZE

L. Falize: *Exposition Universelle Internationale de 1889 à Paris. Rapports du Jury International, classe 24 Orfèvrerie*, Paris, 1891; O. Massin: *Lucien Falize, Orfèvre Joaillier ...*, Paris, 1897; *Gazette des Beaux Arts* (1897), part II, p. 343

PETER CARL FABERGÉ

H.C. Bainbridge: *Peter Carl Fabergé*, London, 1949; A.K. Snowman: *The Art of Carl Fabergé*, London, 1953; M.C. Ross: *The Art of Karl Fabergé and his Contemporaries*, Norman, Oklahoma, 1965; J. McNab Dennis in *Metropolitan Museum Bulletin* NSXXII (1965), pp. 229–42

CHARLES ROBERT ASHBEE

Sources cited in text; Ashbee's unpublished memoirs in the library of the Victoria and Albert Museum, London; Shirley Bury in *Victoria and Albert Museum Bulletin*, III (1967), pp. 18–25

GEORG JENSEN

I.M. Olsen: *Sølvsmeden Georg Jensen*, Copenhagen, 1937; Walter Schwartz: *Georg Jensen*, Copenhagen, 1958

JOSEPH MARIA OLBRICH

The main source for Olbrich's architectural work is the series of portfolios of illustrations published by Wasmuth, Berlin, 1901–14; Thieme-Becker, XXV, pp. 588–9 (with good bibliography of contemporary references); N. Pevsner: *Pioneers of Modern Design* (revised edition), Harmondsworth, 1960; *Joseph M. Olbrich* catalogue of exhibition, Darmstadt, Vienna, Munich, 1967

JEAN PUIFORÇAT

R. Herbst and others: *Jean Puiforçat Orfèvre et Sculpteur*, Paris, 1951; *Les Années 25* catalogue of exhibition, Musée des Arts Décoratifs, Paris, 1966

WILHELM WAGENFELD

A. Drexler and G. Daniel: *Introduction to Twentieth-Century Design*, New York, 1959; R. Banham: *Theory and Practice in the First Machine Age*, London, 1960; W. Schedig: *Crafts of the Weimar Bauhaus*, London, 1967; G. Naylor: *The Bauhaus*, London, 1968; H.M. Wingler: *The Bauhaus*, Cambridge, Mass., 1969

Index

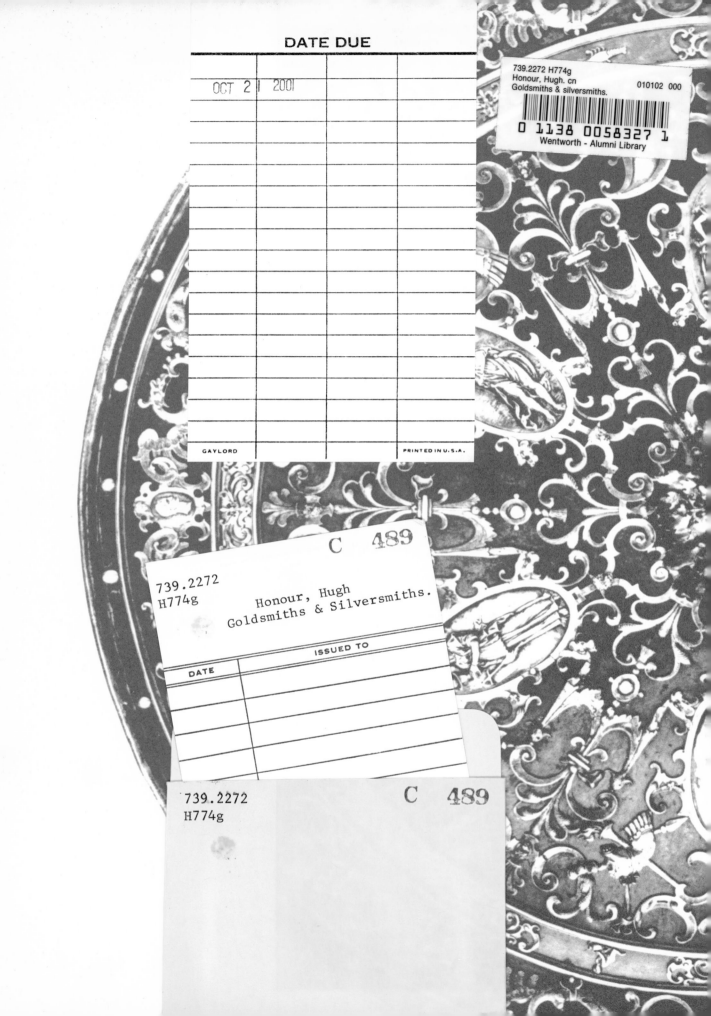